MANGA
FOR SUCCESS

RESILIENCE, CONFIDENCE, & POSITIVE THINKING

AUTHOR
KOJI KUZE

SCENARIO CREATION
YOKO MATSUO

ARTWORK
KOROMO ASATO

WILEY

Published by John Wiley & Sons, Inc., Hoboken, New Jersey.

Published simultaneously in Canada.

Library of Congress Cataloging-in-Publication Data is Available:
ISBN 9781394176106 (Paperback)
ISBN 9781394176113 (ePub)
ISBN 9781394176120 (ePDF)

Cover Design: JMA Management Center Inc.
Cover Images: JMA Management Center Inc.
© ShEd Artworks/Shutterstock

Contents

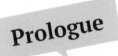

Prologue

Resilience Is . . .

Part 1

Controlling Negative Emotions

Part 2

Taming Negative Assumptions

Part 3

Get Social Support

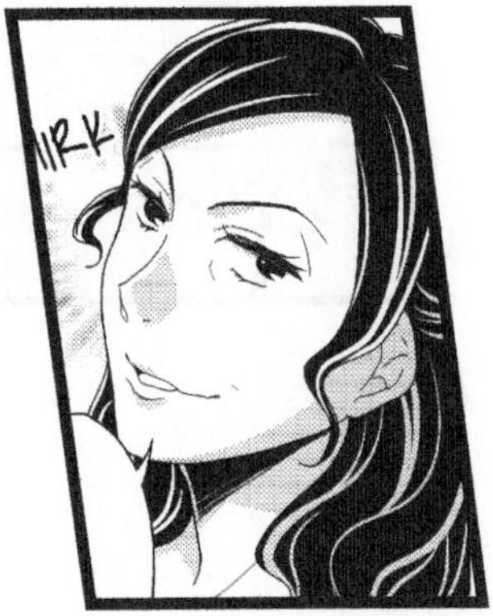
IIRK

Part 4

Restoring Your Self-Confidence

1. Why Are You Unable to Feel Confident?

2. The Psychological Resources to Heighten Self-Confidence

3. **How to Raise Your Self-Efficacy**

Part 5

Putting Your Strengths to Good Use at Work

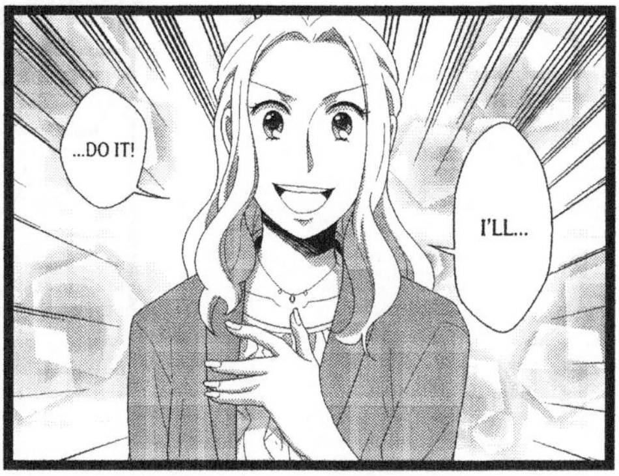

I'LL...
...DO IT!

Wheat Flour

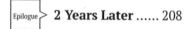

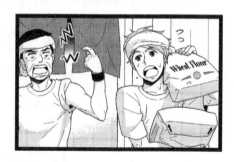

Preface

Do you know the term *resilience*? Resilience, in this stress-filled modern society, is used to describe the ability to recover mentally or psychologically.

Companies and schools overseas have been teaching how to increase resilience. Even within Japan, television shows have covered it. Resilience has garnered some attention as a precautionary measure for mental health and as a psychological strength to take on challenges without fearing failure.

In this book, I will be breaking down the basics of resilience. Specifically, I will be presenting techniques on how to make your heart stronger.

A sturdy and tough heart means a muscular heart. However, this doesn't mean it's a heart that's frozen solid or stubborn. It's a heart that has the ability to adapt. Such a heart can tolerate stress, have the elasticity to not feel hurt from upsetting things others say, and have the flexibility to respond to sudden problems.

That kind of heart will not feel down for long; it is able to recover quickly. By strengthening your heart, you are able to build resilience. Not fearing failure or taking on challenges, persevering, and not giving up until the end are also traits of a heart with high resilience.

Resilience will become the base of your success at work and life. It may even be more important than your IQ, academic background, skills, and experience in business. In an era full of stress and changes, only those who are able to prioritize caring for not only their physical health but also their mental health are able to thrive at work. And only those who are tenacious are able to succeed.

You may wonder how I became interested in resilience. Years ago, I found myself in a toxic work relationship that I struggled to manage. I was dragged into an unforeseen issue and desperately worked to solve it. However, I was unable to make much progress and lost all hope.

Being unable to meet the expectations of my superiors and those around me, I agonized all by myself, and almost lost my motivation. Feeling a sense of urgency, I searched in anguish to find a solution to retrieve my original self. And that's where I encountered resilience.

Resilience is something we all originally have; it is the source of our psychological well-being. We may find our resilience weakened over time, but we are able to regenerate it with focused effort.

I was personally able to take back my weakened resilience and as a result was able to use my adversity as nourishment for my self-growth.

The change I noticed right away was that my efficiency at work more than doubled. It really made me think about how much time I had wasted over useless worries.

I am now able to accept my failures. Even if I fail, I now have the confidence to stand right back up again. I have been able to try things I thought were impossible, not give up, and do what I really want to do.

Thank you to everyone who has taken this book into their hands. I hope it becomes the spark for you to take a step forward and to secure a chance for better opportunities at work and in life.

Koji Kuze

Prologue

Resilience Is . . .

RIGHT?
GLARE
THAT'S FOR ME TO DECIDE.
PLEASE DO IT AS YOU WERE INSTRUCTED TO.
MUNCH
IT'S SO GOOD!

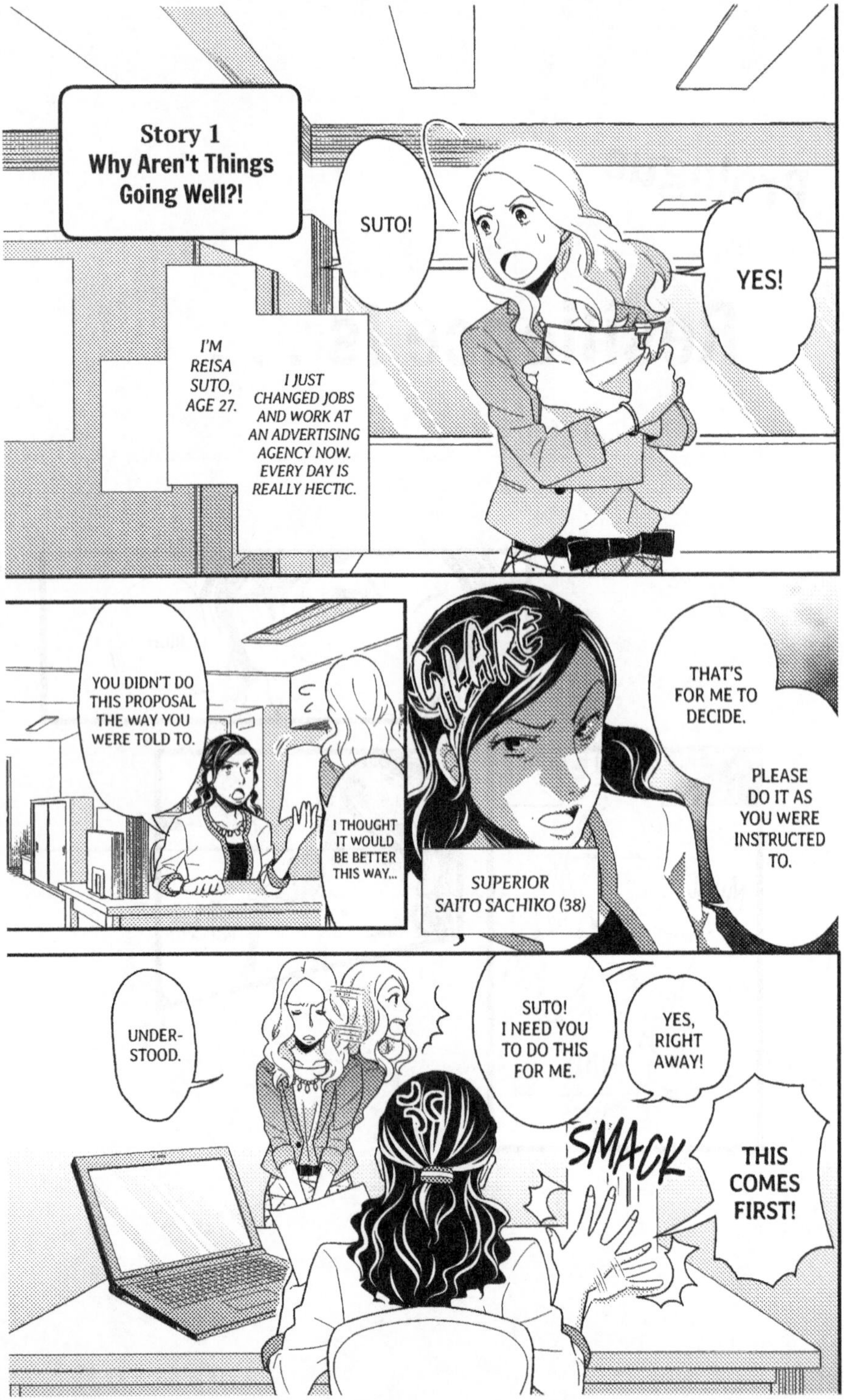
Story 1
Why Aren't Things Going Well?!
SUTO!
YES!
I'M REISA SUTO, AGE 27.
I JUST CHANGED JOBS AND WORK AT AN ADVERTISING AGENCY NOW. EVERY DAY IS REALLY HECTIC.
YOU DIDN'T DO THIS PROPOSAL THE WAY YOU WERE TOLD TO.
I THOUGHT IT WOULD BE BETTER THIS WAY...
GLARE
THAT'S FOR ME TO DECIDE.
PLEASE DO IT AS YOU WERE INSTRUCTED TO.
SUPERIOR SAITO SACHIKO (38)
UNDER-STOOD.
SUTO! I NEED YOU TO DO THIS FOR ME.
YES, RIGHT AWAY!
SMACK
THIS COMES FIRST!

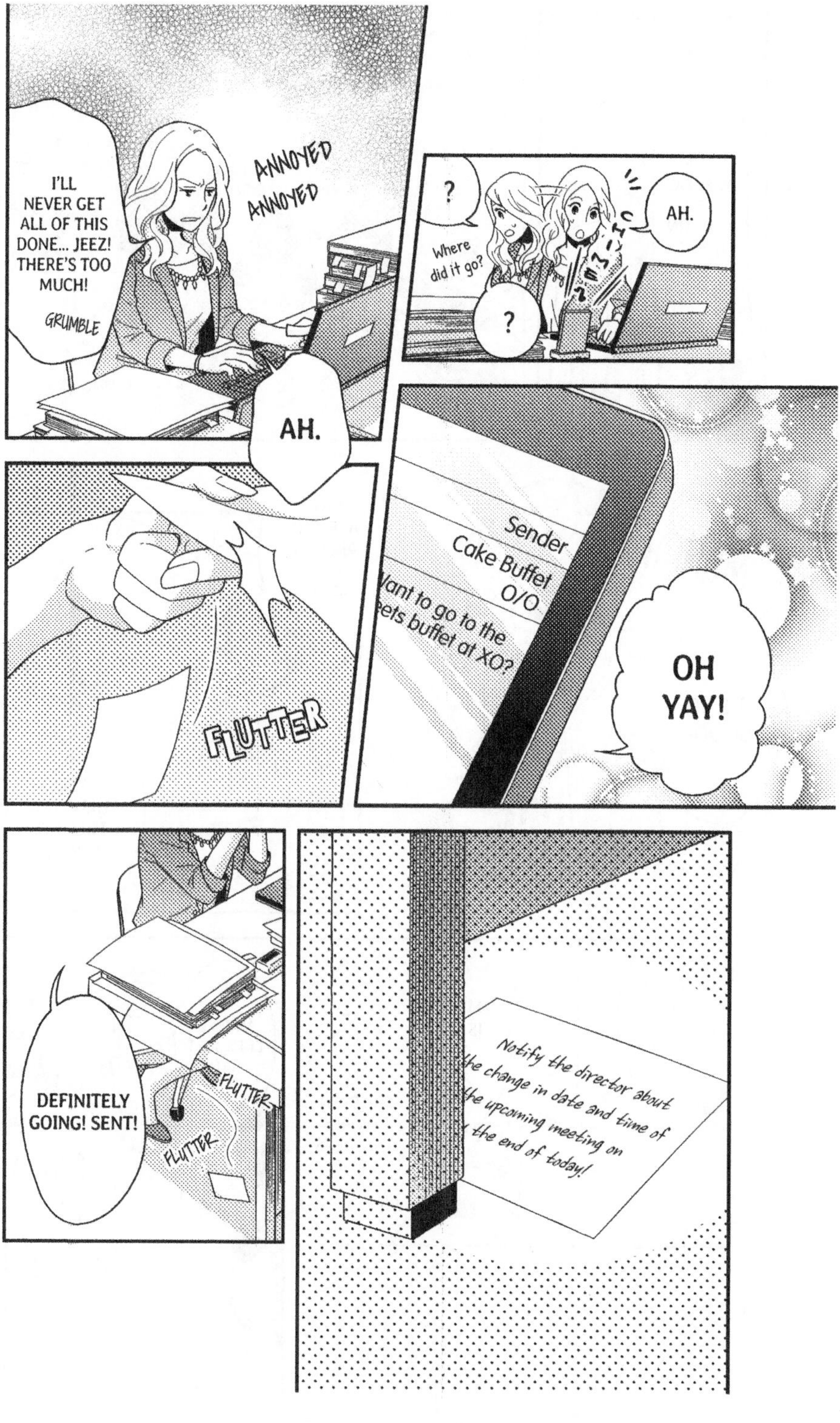
I'LL NEVER GET ALL OF THIS DONE... JEEZ! THERE'S TOO MUCH!
GRUMBLE
ANNOYED
ANNOYED
?
Where did it go?
?
AH.
AH.
FLUTTER
Sender
Cake Buffet
O/O
Want to go to the
eets buffet at XO?
OH YAY!
DEFINITELY GOING! SENT!
FLUTTER
FLUTTER
Notify the director about
he change in date and time of
he upcoming meeting on
the end of today!

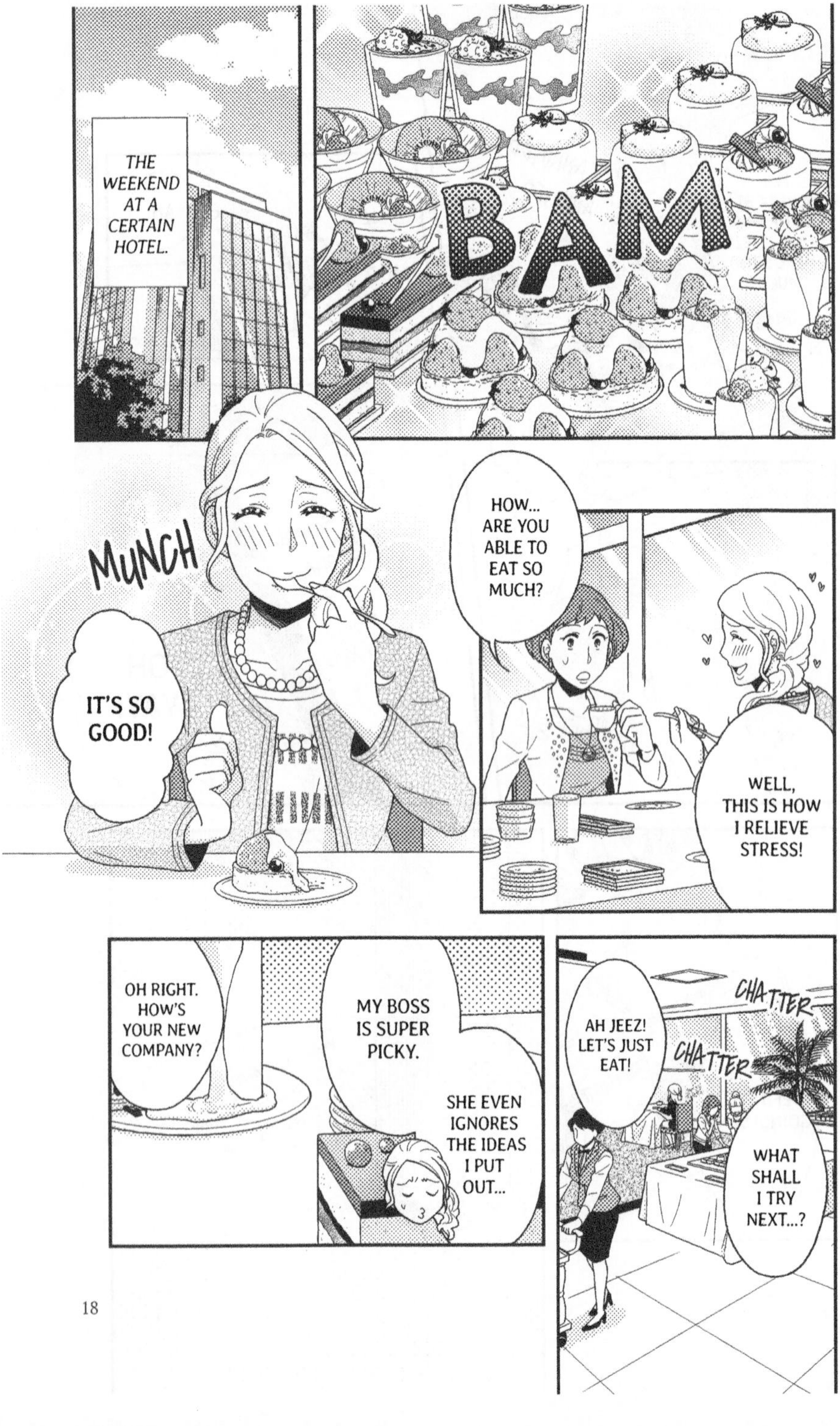
THE WEEKEND AT A CERTAIN HOTEL.
BAM
MUNCH
IT'S SO GOOD!
HOW... ARE YOU ABLE TO EAT SO MUCH?
WELL, THIS IS HOW I RELIEVE STRESS!
OH RIGHT. HOW'S YOUR NEW COMPANY?
MY BOSS IS SUPER PICKY.
SHE EVEN IGNORES THE IDEAS I PUT OUT...
AH JEEZ! LET'S JUST EAT!
CHATTER
CHATTER
WHAT SHALL I TRY NEXT...?

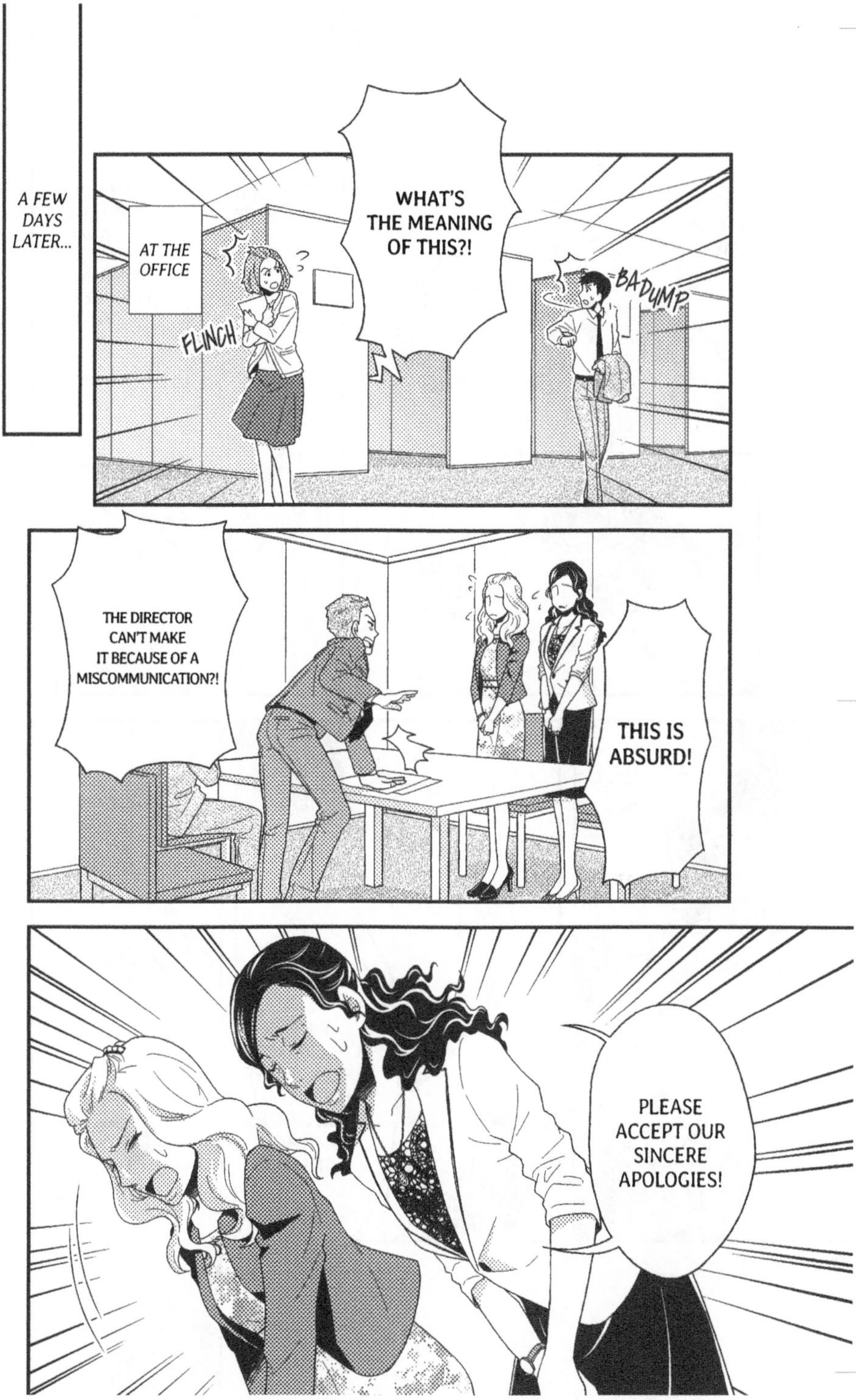
A FEW DAYS LATER...
AT THE OFFICE
FLINCH
WHAT'S THE MEANING OF THIS?!
BADUMP
THE DIRECTOR CAN'T MAKE IT BECAUSE OF A MISCOMMUNICATION?!
THIS IS ABSURD!
PLEASE ACCEPT OUR SINCERE APOLOGIES!

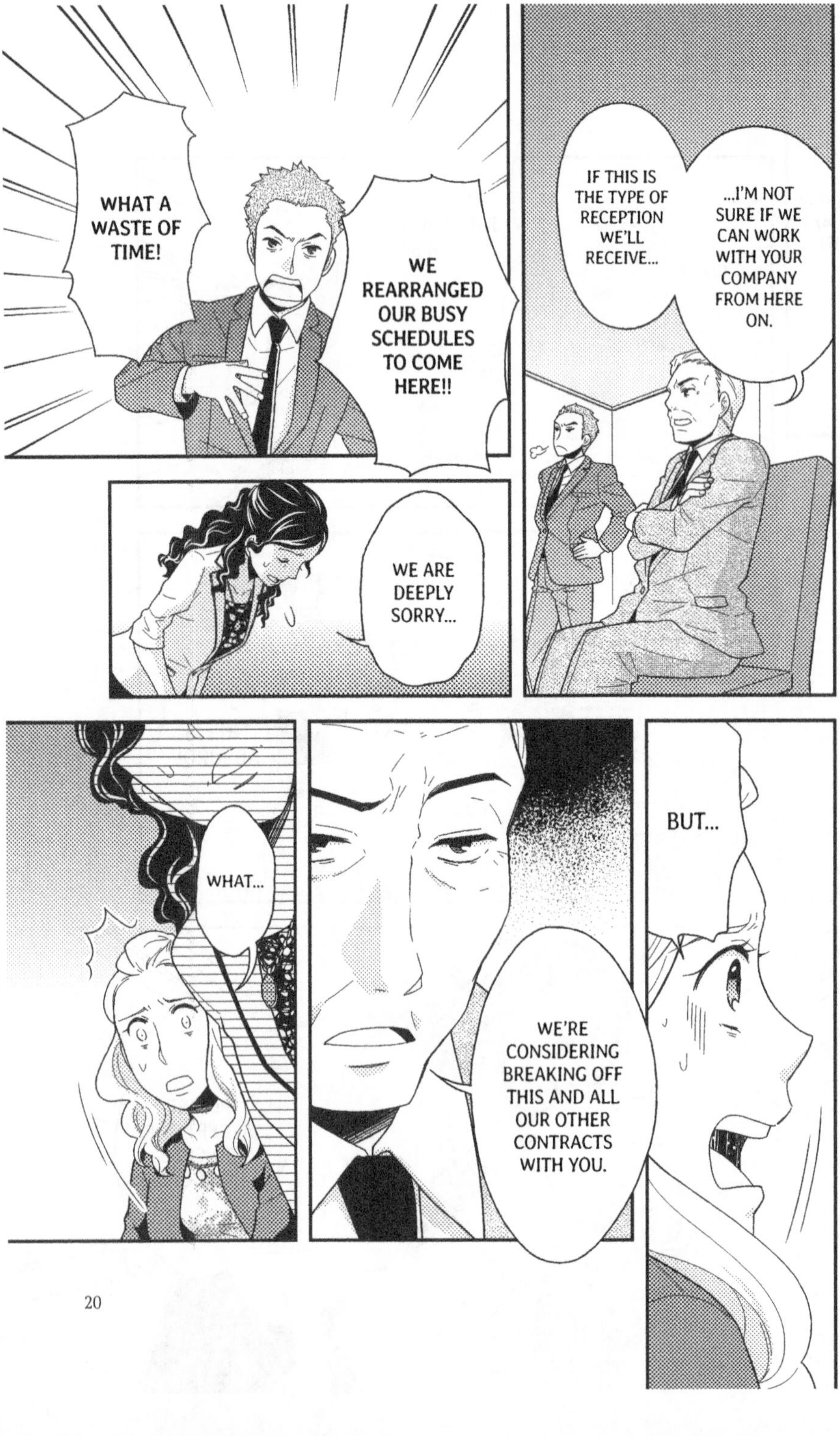
WHAT A WASTE OF TIME!
WE REARRANGED OUR BUSY SCHEDULES TO COME HERE!!
IF THIS IS THE TYPE OF RECEPTION WE'LL RECEIVE...
...I'M NOT SURE IF WE CAN WORK WITH YOUR COMPANY FROM HERE ON.
WE ARE DEEPLY SORRY...
WHAT...
WE'RE CONSIDERING BREAKING OFF THIS AND ALL OUR OTHER CONTRACTS WITH YOU.
BUT...

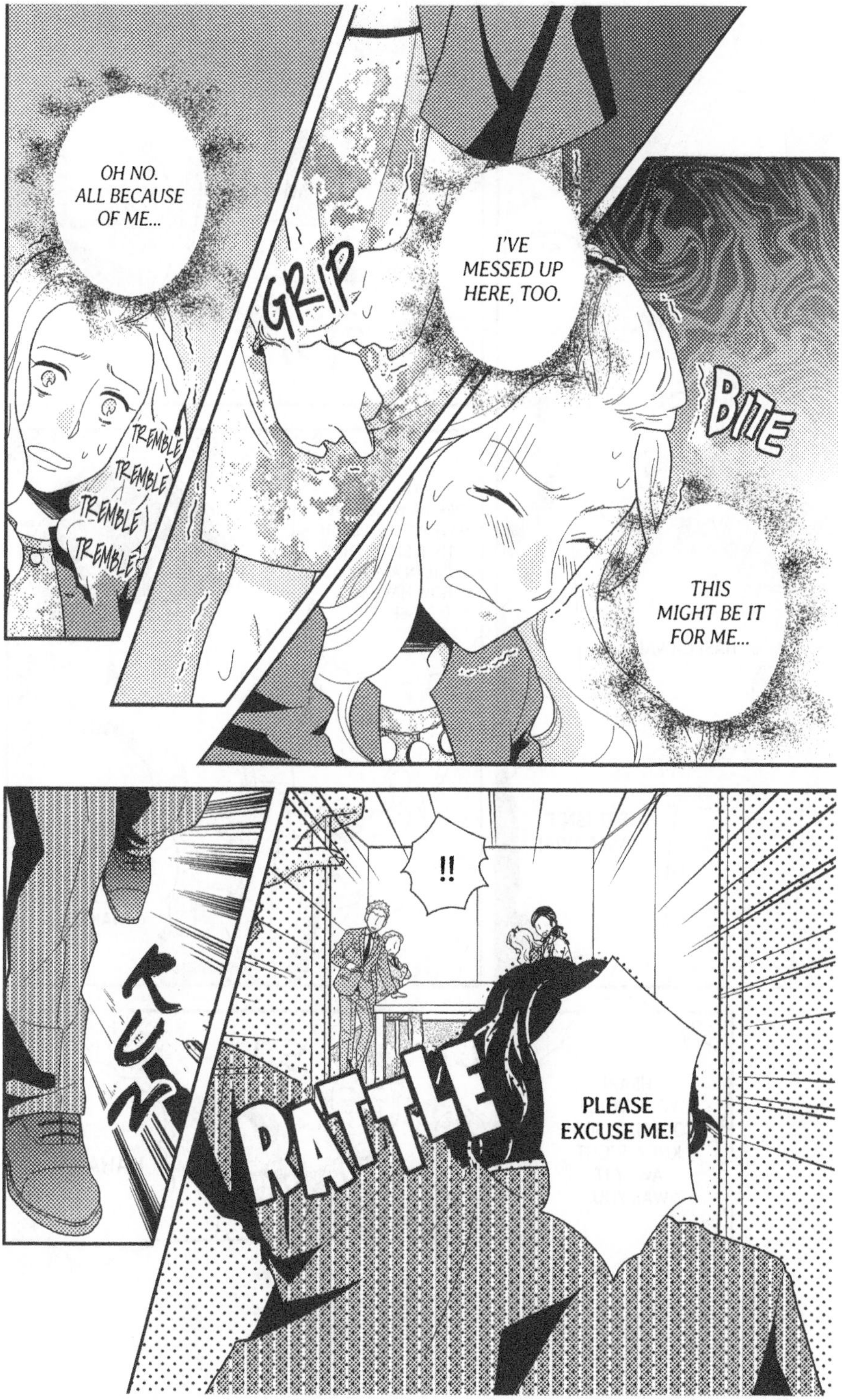
OH NO. ALL BECAUSE OF ME...
TREMBLE TREMBLE TREMBLE TREMBLE
GRIP
I'VE MESSED UP HERE, TOO.
BITE
THIS MIGHT BE IT FOR ME...
!!
RUN
RATTLE
PLEASE EXCUSE ME!

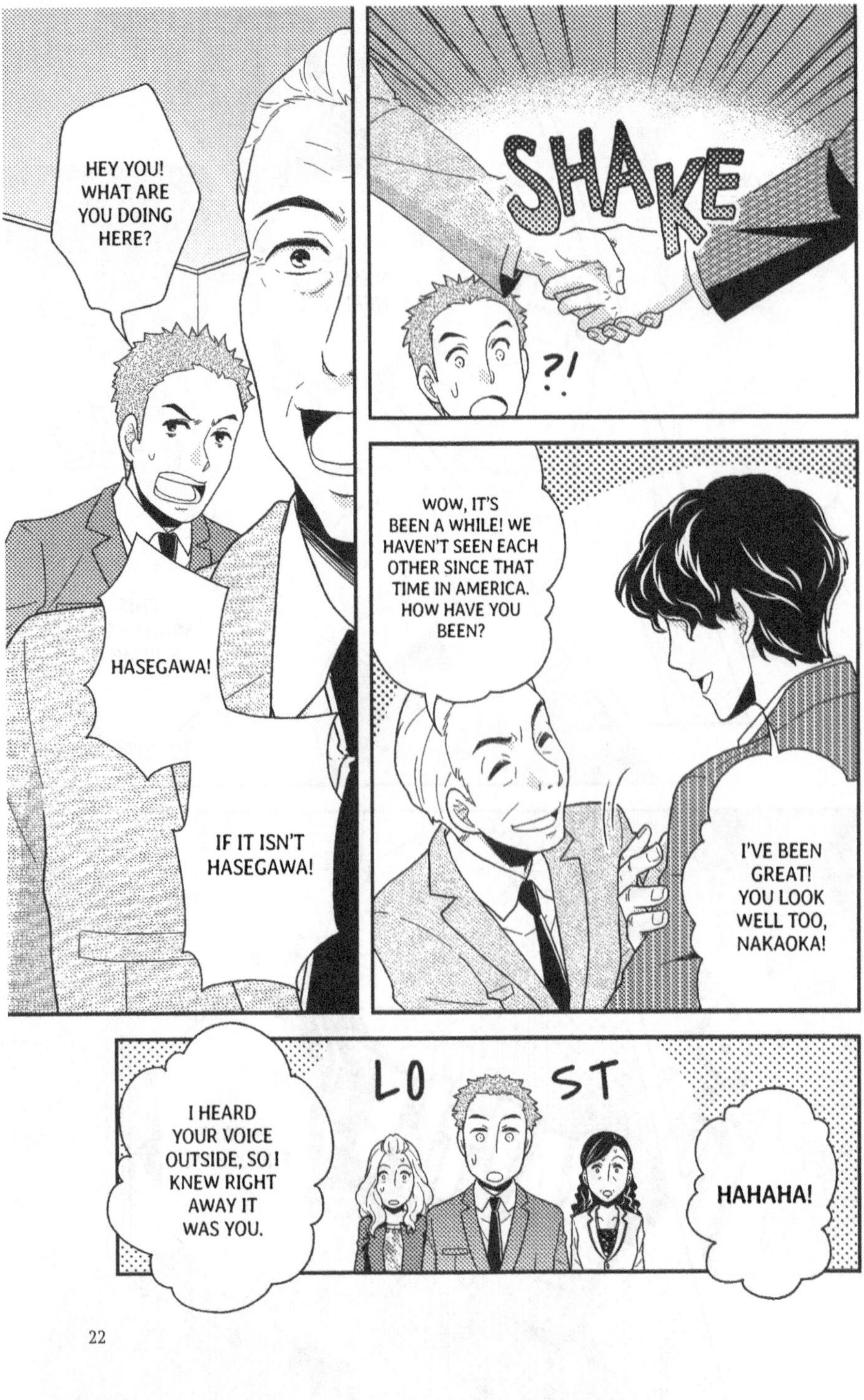
SHAKE
?!
HEY YOU! WHAT ARE YOU DOING HERE?
HASEGAWA!
IF IT ISN'T HASEGAWA!
WOW, IT'S BEEN A WHILE! WE HAVEN'T SEEN EACH OTHER SINCE THAT TIME IN AMERICA. HOW HAVE YOU BEEN?
I'VE BEEN GREAT! YOU LOOK WELL TOO, NAKAOKA!
HAHAHA!
I HEARD YOUR VOICE OUTSIDE, SO I KNEW RIGHT AWAY IT WAS YOU.
LO ST

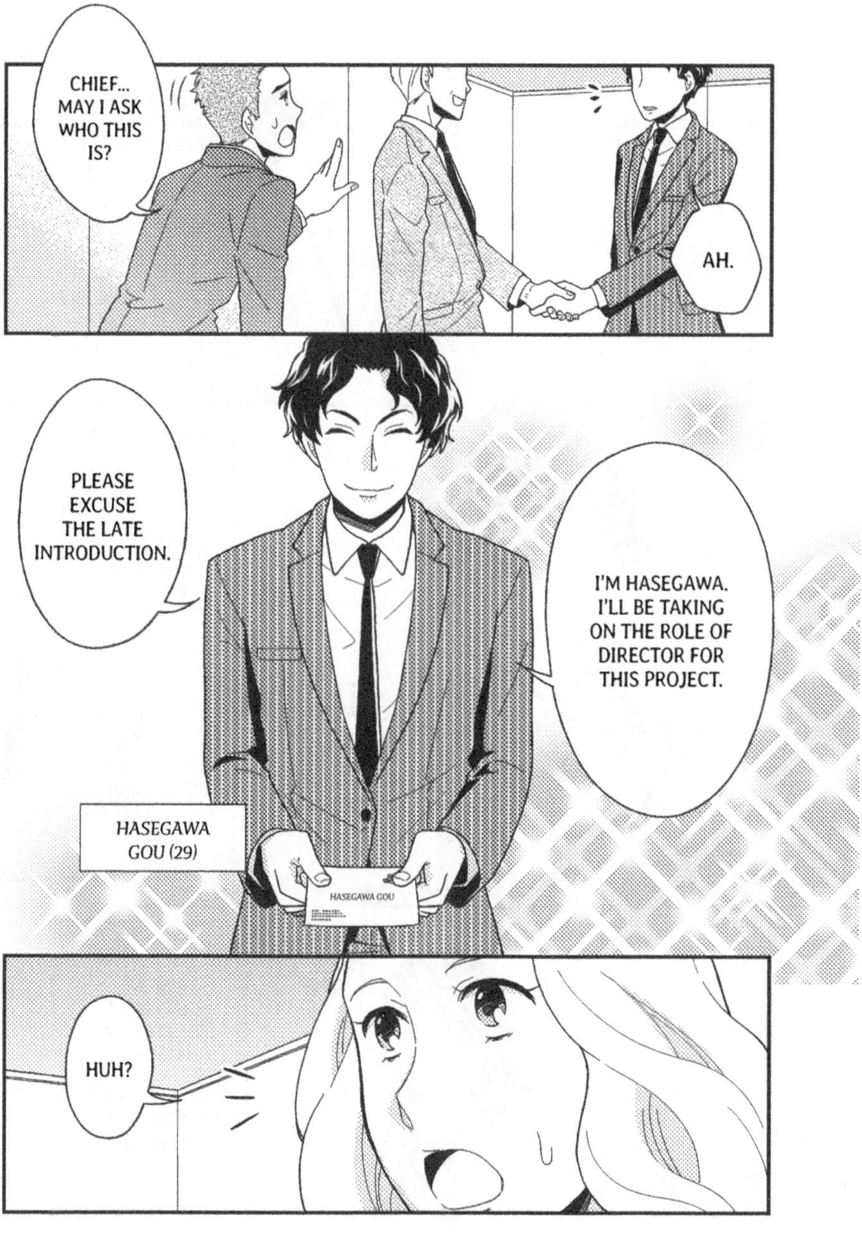
CHIEF... MAY I ASK WHO THIS IS?
AH.
PLEASE EXCUSE THE LATE INTRODUCTION.
I'M HASEGAWA. I'LL BE TAKING ON THE ROLE OF DIRECTOR FOR THIS PROJECT.
HASEGAWA GOU (29)
HASEGAWA GOU
HUH?

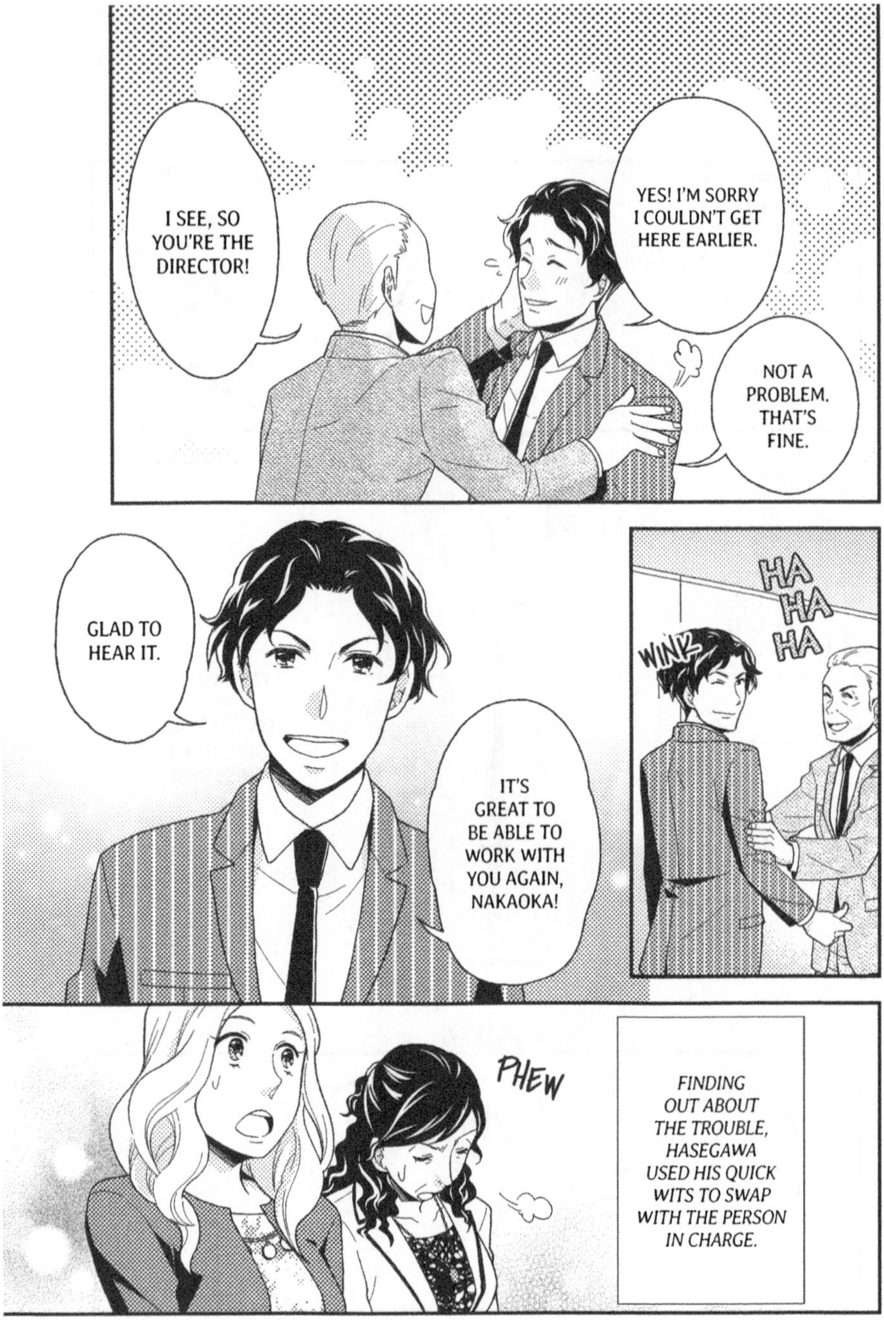
I SEE, SO YOU'RE THE DIRECTOR!
YES! I'M SORRY I COULDN'T GET HERE EARLIER.
NOT A PROBLEM. THAT'S FINE.
GLAD TO HEAR IT.
IT'S GREAT TO BE ABLE TO WORK WITH YOU AGAIN, NAKAOKA!
WINK
HA HA HA
PHEW
FINDING OUT ABOUT THE TROUBLE, HASEGAWA USED HIS QUICK WITS TO SWAP WITH THE PERSON IN CHARGE.

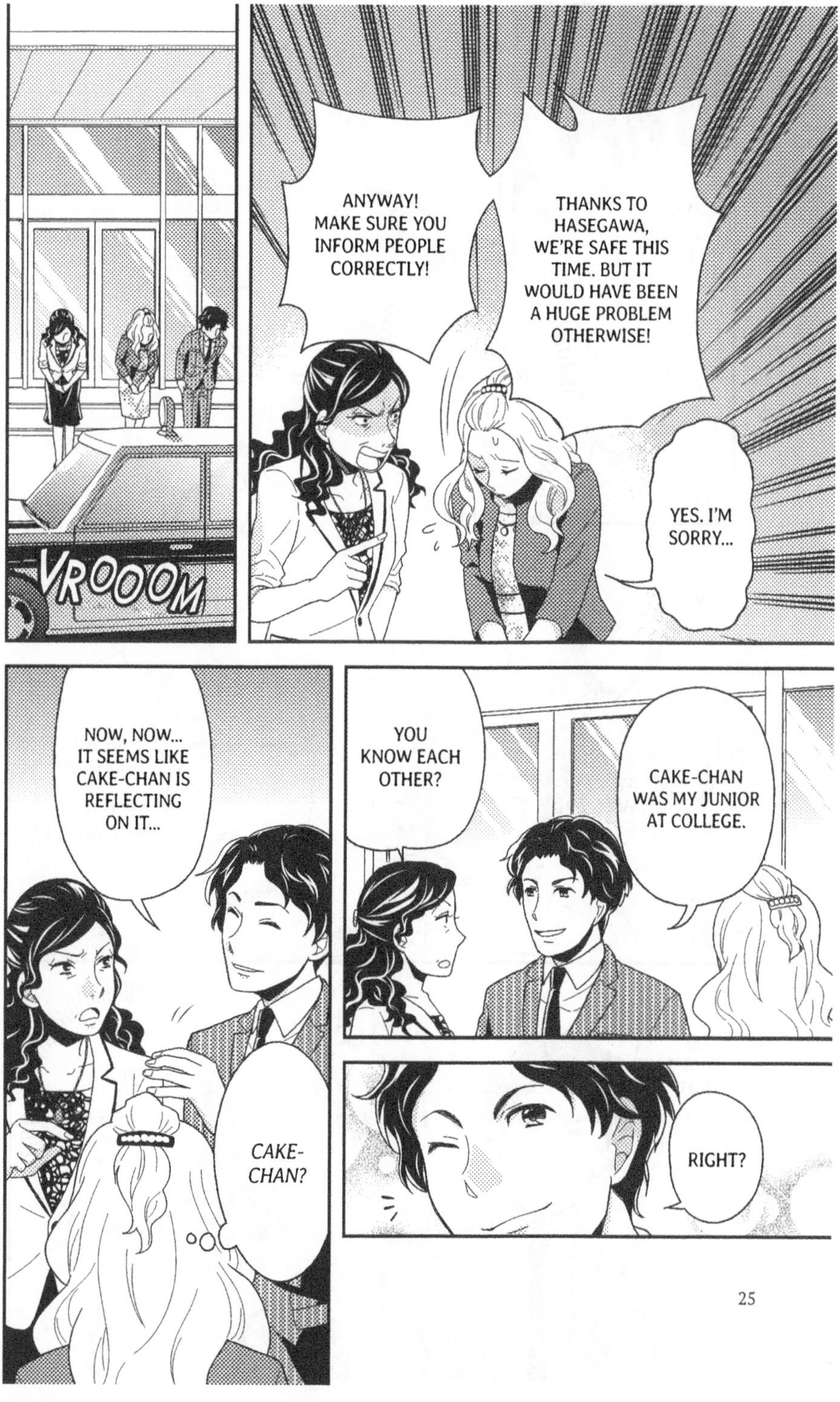
VROOOM
THANKS TO HASEGAWA, WE'RE SAFE THIS TIME. BUT IT WOULD HAVE BEEN A HUGE PROBLEM OTHERWISE!
ANYWAY! MAKE SURE YOU INFORM PEOPLE CORRECTLY!
YES. I'M SORRY...
CAKE-CHAN WAS MY JUNIOR AT COLLEGE.
YOU KNOW EACH OTHER?
NOW, NOW... IT SEEMS LIKE CAKE-CHAN IS REFLECTING ON IT...
RIGHT?
CAKE-CHAN?

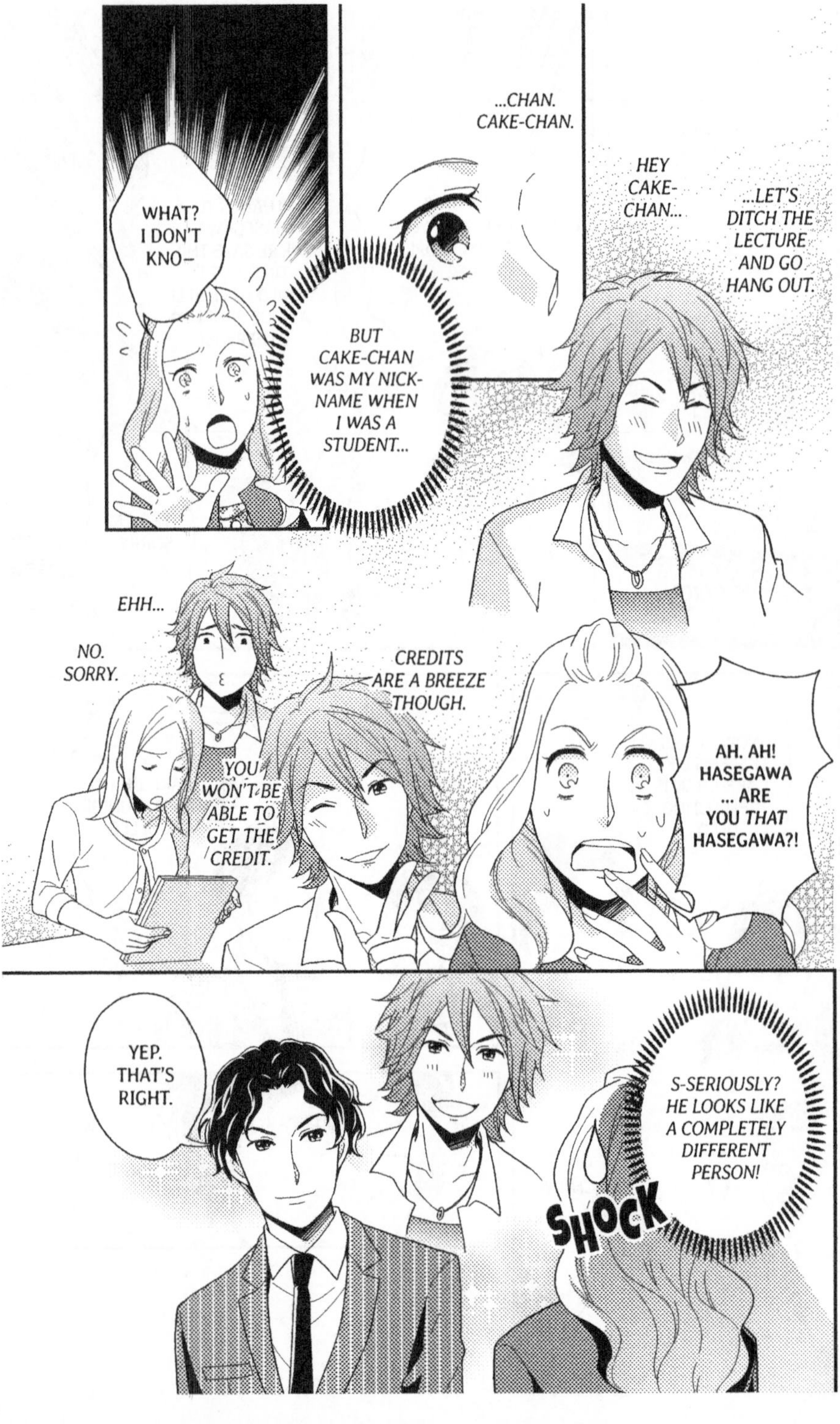
WHAT? I DON'T KNO—
...CHAN. CAKE-CHAN.
BUT CAKE-CHAN WAS MY NICK-NAME WHEN I WAS A STUDENT...
HEY CAKE-CHAN...
...LET'S DITCH THE LECTURE AND GO HANG OUT.
EHH...
NO. SORRY.
CREDITS ARE A BREEZE THOUGH.
YOU WON'T BE ABLE TO GET THE CREDIT.
AH. AH! HASEGAWA ... ARE YOU *THAT* HASEGAWA?!
YEP. THAT'S RIGHT.
SHOCK
S-SERIOUSLY? HE LOOKS LIKE A COMPLETELY DIFFERENT PERSON!

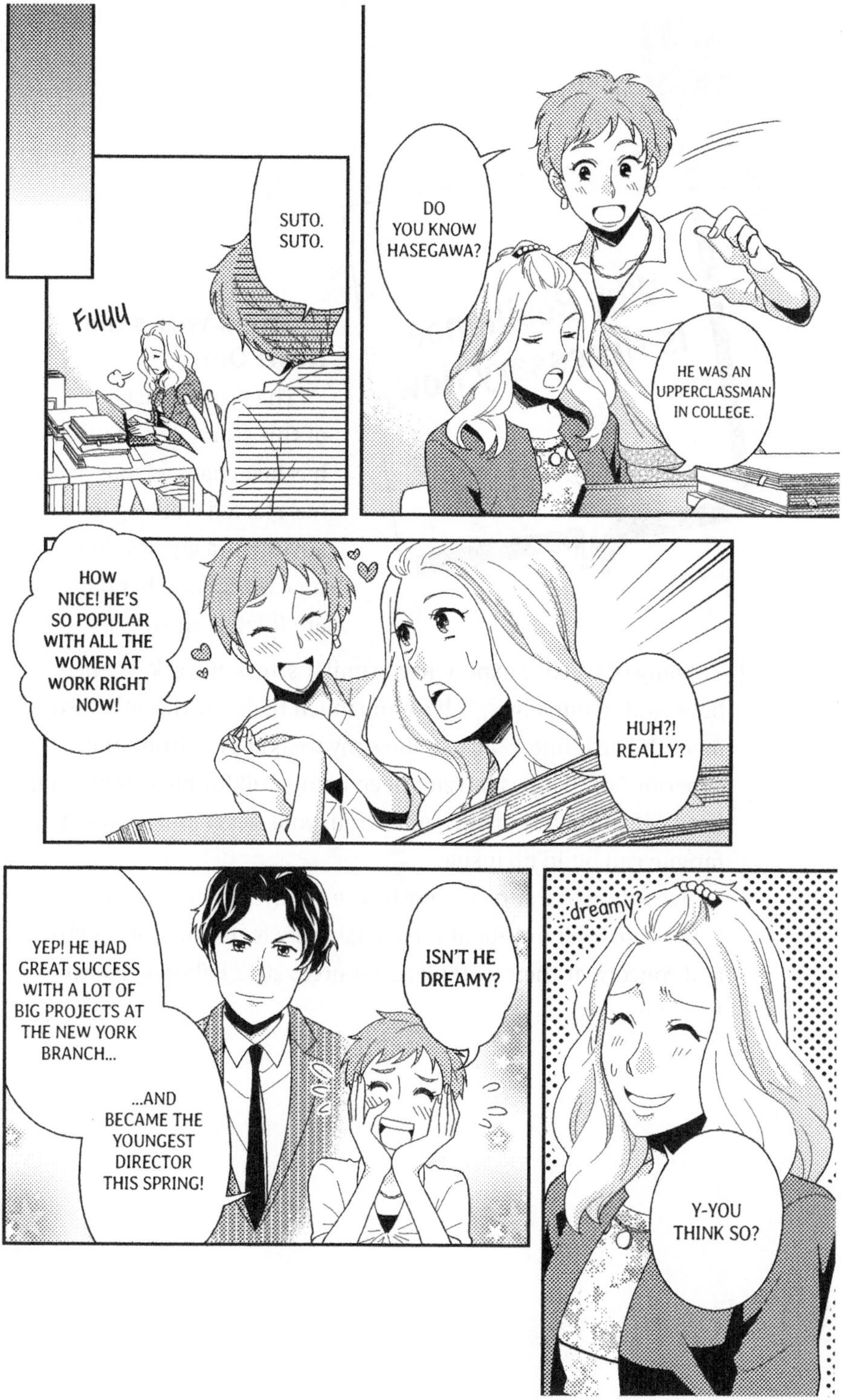
SUTO. SUTO.
FUUU
DO YOU KNOW HASEGAWA?
HE WAS AN UPPERCLASSMAN IN COLLEGE.
HOW NICE! HE'S SO POPULAR WITH ALL THE WOMEN AT WORK RIGHT NOW!
HUH?! REALLY?
YEP! HE HAD GREAT SUCCESS WITH A LOT OF BIG PROJECTS AT THE NEW YORK BRANCH...
...AND BECAME THE YOUNGEST DIRECTOR THIS SPRING!
ISN'T HE DREAMY?
...dreamy?
Y-YOU THINK SO?

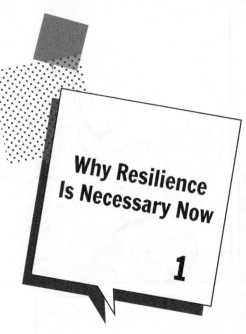

Why Resilience Is Necessary Now

1

⇨ Stress Wears the Heart Out

The protagonist of this story, Reisa Suto, has just changed jobs and has started working for an advertising agency. In her new workplace, her days are filled with stress.

Many of us have experienced similar stress at work. We may have said to ourselves, "I have too much to do for this job. I won't meet the deadline," "I can't show my weakness in front of my superior," or "Things haven't been going well for me recently. I'm tired." If you shut out such cries from your heart and try too hard, fatigue can build up inside.

According to a survey done by the Japanese Ministry of Health, Labor, and Welfare, about 60% of laborers feel some sort of stress and concern at their workplace. (Source: 2012 Laborer Health Investigation.)

Three main drivers account for workplace stress:

- Problems from interpersonal relationships
- Quality of work issues
- Workload concerns

A typical example of the first one, problems from interpersonal relationships, is the relationship with your superior. Reisa was also unable to get used to her superior's commanding attitude and started to feel irritated. If this relationship worsens, there's a chance that it will turn into harassment.

Various hierarchical relationships can also become a source of stress. Some examples include having cold coworkers, being unrecognized by superiors, and being unable to handle subordinates well.

Next, regarding quality of work issues, any nerve-wracking task can become a source of stress. For example, an advertising

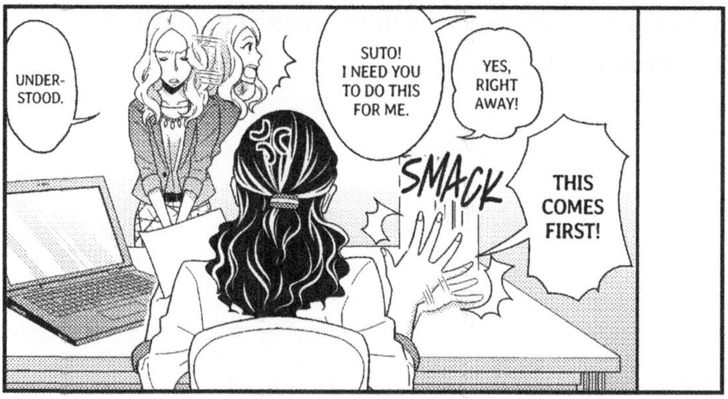
THIS COMES FIRST!
SMACK
YES, RIGHT AWAY!
SUTO! I NEED YOU TO DO THIS FOR ME.
UNDER-STOOD.

The protagonist, Reisa, had also been accumulating stress due to work she was not used to doing after changing jobs and to her interpersonal relationship with her superior.

agency, like the one where this story takes place, is a workplace that does not allow for mistakes or delays. In addition, jobs that involve money, that involve the lives of people, or that have time pressures are all jobs that can easily cause mental tension.

Finally, workload concerns are most applicable to jobs that have long hours, especially jobs that involve a lot of travel. People who have these jobs struggle with work-life balance as they are unable to spend a lot of time with their families.

⇨ Career Turning Points Are Dangers to the Heart

You may lose motivation in your life from time to time after feeling the stress and pressure from doing work. For example, a lot of stress is experienced by individuals starting a new job, as Reisa experienced in her job. Mid-career hires are often expected to become an immediate asset to the company, so they start to feel anxious. If they fail at such a time, they may lose motivation. Transferring to a new department or relocating can also be factors for adding to stress.

Overseas assignments can be some of the most stressful work experiences for individuals. In addition to the local language and culture that they may not be used to, if they fail to connect with local coworkers, they may end up becoming isolated, resulting in them returning to their home country early as an expat failure.

Even when a new opportunity carries with it a promotion, the situation can be experienced as an ordeal. Women may feel especially isolated in new leadership roles where there may not be many, if any, role models and mentors for them.

Career turning points are invariably stressful, and the heart can become tired and weakened, resulting in people being unable to move forward. Career turning points can be experienced by anyone. Consequently, each and every one of us is at risk of feeling stressed and losing motivation at one time or another. Because it is not always possible to escape the sources of stress, it is ideal to develop the skills necessary to live alongside this stress and pressure.

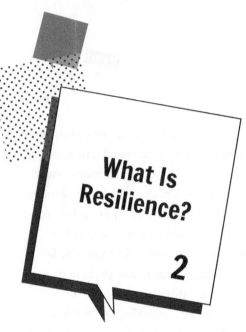

What Is Resilience?

2

⇨ **Resilience Is . . .**

We have been looking at the risks of the heart weakening due to stress and pressure in our daily lives. We need the power to overcome this weakening, regardless of the situation. Why? If you lose motivation and give up in the middle of your career, you won't be able to feel satisfaction from your job or from fulfilling your purpose in life.

This is where **resilience** comes in. Resilience is **the emotional and mental strength needed to deal with any adversity, problem, or stressful situation you may face.** It is **the strength to pick yourself back up.**

For almost 40 years, there has been ongoing research in the training of resilience, mostly centered around global corporations. Over 2000 schools in the United States have also introduced resilience in the classroom to teach children about mental strength.

The work started globally has also reached Japan, where there has been an increase in companies and schools training employees' and students' resilience. Local media have fostered interest in this topic, leading to the advances seen today.

⇨ Three Traits of Someone with High Resilience

Someone who has high resilience has the following traits:

• Recoverability

Recoverabilty is the ability to quickly return to a previous state of well-being after encountering hardship.

• Flexibility

Flexibility is the emotional capability of being able to handle any unexpected shock or stress. Flexible people are able to protect themselves without leaving a scar no matter what criticisms or unpleasant things are directed at them.

• Adaptability

Adaptability is the ability to accept a situation that may be stressful and logically handle it. Adaptable people do not resist unexpected changes.

⇨ **Resilience Is a Psychological Resource Everyone Has**

Despite the features that resilience has, it's actually not something special. It's something we all have inside of ourselves. The mental flexibility to recover and deflect stress is a psychological resource we all originally had. However, experiences such as stress and failure can lead to the exhaustion of resilience. Just like how your muscles weaken if you don't exercise, if your resilience weakens, you may not be able to show your strength when you need it. This is why it's important to raise the so-called heart's muscle at an early stage and to train it on a regular basis.

For the long 60 or more years that you may spend working, it will be vital for you to take care of your mental health alongside your physical health. Strengthening resilience is an important part of that care.

Resilience is . . .

Resilience is the emotional and mental strength needed to deal with any adversity, problem, or stressful situation you may face.

High resilience
Stress
Low resilience

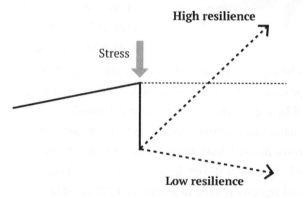

Three Traits of Someone with High Resilience
1. Recoverability 2. Flexibility 3. Adaptability

Strengthening Resilience

3

⇨ **Three Steps to Strengthen Resilience**

Research has demonstrated that it is possible for anyone to acquire the strength needed to recover from adversity or stress. The method used to acquire this strength is called **resilience training**.

In this book, we introduce the way to get the heart's muscle into shape based on SPARK Resilience Training, which was developed by the psychologist Dr. Ilona Boniwell.

I have used this method myself. I have made large mistakes at work, have hit rock bottom to the point that I could not pick myself up, and still somehow managed to get back on my feet and regain my motivation and ambition to continue with my work.

Through my experience with resilience training, I have personally gained confidence that although there will be times when I will make mistakes, I will be able to recover from them every time. This confidence has enabled me to take on the challenge of trying new jobs without hesitation.

The experience of picking yourself up from adversity is composed of three steps: (1) make sure your depression hits rock bottom, (2) plan for a smooth recovery, and (3) turn the experience into a lesson.

Step 1: Make sure your depression hits rock bottom.

Whenever you face hardship or failure, you are likely to become mentally tired and therefore more likely to become depressed. Negative emotions such as anxiety, melancholy, and guilt are the source of such depression. The first step in resilience training is to recognize when you have hit rock bottom. At that point, you will need to cut off all emotions related to the adversity in order to move forward.

Step 2: Plan for a smooth recovery.

The next step is to recover your psychological state to how it originally was. You will need the power to overcome obstacles and move forward. You can obtain this by training your heart.

Step 3: Turn the experience into a lesson.

The final step, after overcoming your hardships, is to reflect on your past adversities and consider how you might respond differently the next time around.

Remember to take time for your heart to heal and take action only when you have the emotional capacity to do so.

⇨ Challenges Become Nourishment for Resilience

In addition to repeating the three steps to train resilience, you can take a shortcut to build resilience quickly: you can actively take on a highly challenging job. For example, Reisa's upperclassman from college, Hasegawa, became mentally strong and reliable due to his experience overseas.

Overcoming difficulties related to job transfers, relocations, new projects, and reorganizations within companies can all lead to valuable experiences in strengthening resilience.

On page 40 is a list of the experiences that will help a person become a leader in an organization. Resilience is important to all of them.

The Three Steps to Strengthening Resilience

③
Ambition / Motivation
+
−
①
②

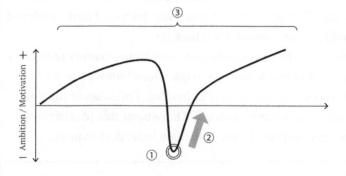

1. Make sure your depression hits rock bottom.
2. Plan for a smooth recovery.
3. Turn the experience into a lesson.

During my first relocation overseas, I almost had a nervous breakdown as I had not yet developed resilience. I was blessed with the chance to learn about resilience from Dr. Ilona Boniwell directly. I followed the three steps, put the training to practice, repeated it, and got stronger.

Of course even now, there are times when I make mistakes or have trouble with personal relationships. However, I no longer constantly feel down about these issues because I have developed the ability to pick myself right back up.

I now have the confidence to recover from adversity regardless of what happens and am able to take steps forward toward experiences that are new and unfamiliar. I'm different from my past conservative and timid self. I have been able to take on new challenges, and now I can do what my heart desires most.

The Eight Experiences That Make a Leader

1. Early work experience
2. Experience being taught by superiors
3. Experience of personnel change
4. Work experience from projects
5. Experience of being in a managerial position
6. Experience working overseas
7. Experience of starting up a project
8. Experience going through difficulties

(Source: Supporting "Subordinates with Good Prospects" by Tomohiko Taniguchi, PRESIDENT Inc.)

From the bottom of my heart, I would like everyone to strengthen their resilience through this book.

⇨ Resilience Becomes Stronger Through Practice

This book lays out what you will need to train your resilience:

• Parts 1 and 2 will teach you the vital method of controlling negative emotions when you hit rock bottom.
• Parts 3 and 4 will show you how to get social support and restore self-confidence in order to recover from adversity.
• Part 5 will highlight the importance of putting your newfound strength to good use in the workplace.

The three steps are all simple enough to be put into practice immediately. However, as someone who has gone through this experience, I can tell you that the heart's muscle will not be sufficiently trained with just the knowledge obtained through this book.

Just as it is with the muscles in the rest of your body, the heart gets stronger through practice. If you think something will be useful, please incorporate it into your work or personal life right away.

Part 1

Controlling Negative Emotions

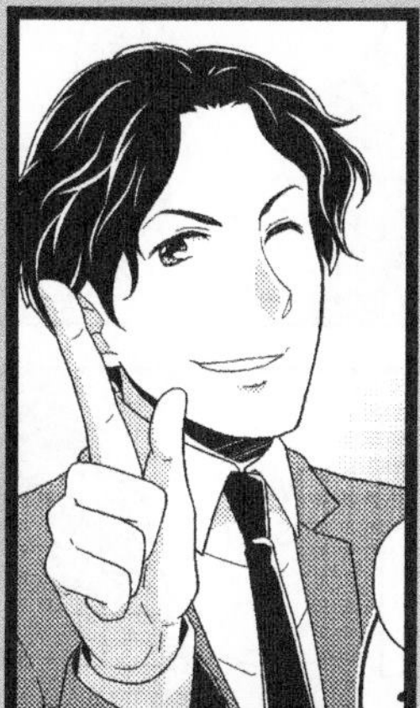

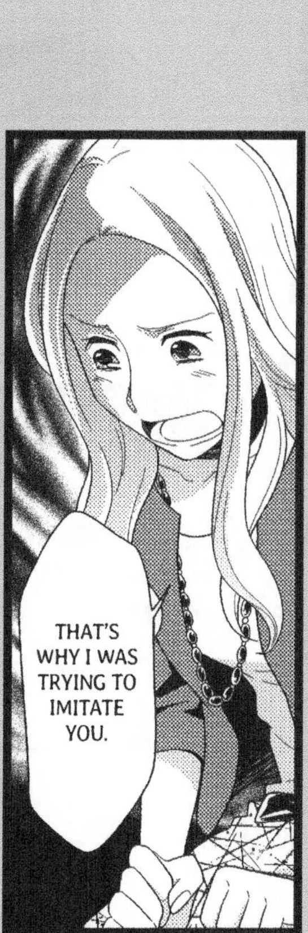
THAT'S WHY I WAS TRYING TO IMITATE YOU.

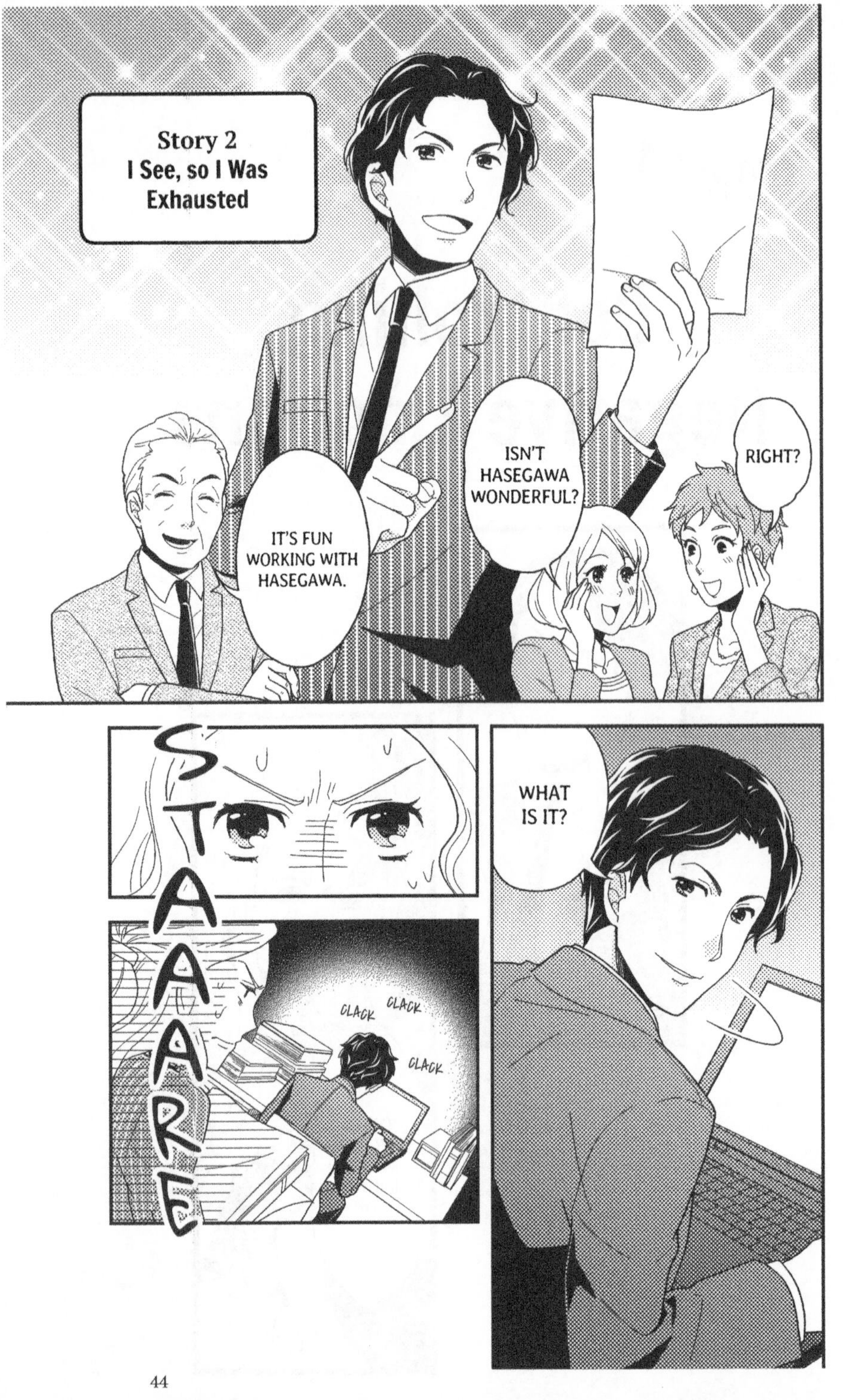
Story 2
I See, so I Was Exhausted
IT'S FUN WORKING WITH HASEGAWA.
ISN'T HASEGAWA WONDERFUL?
RIGHT?
STAAARE
CLACK
CLACK
CLACK
WHAT IS IT?

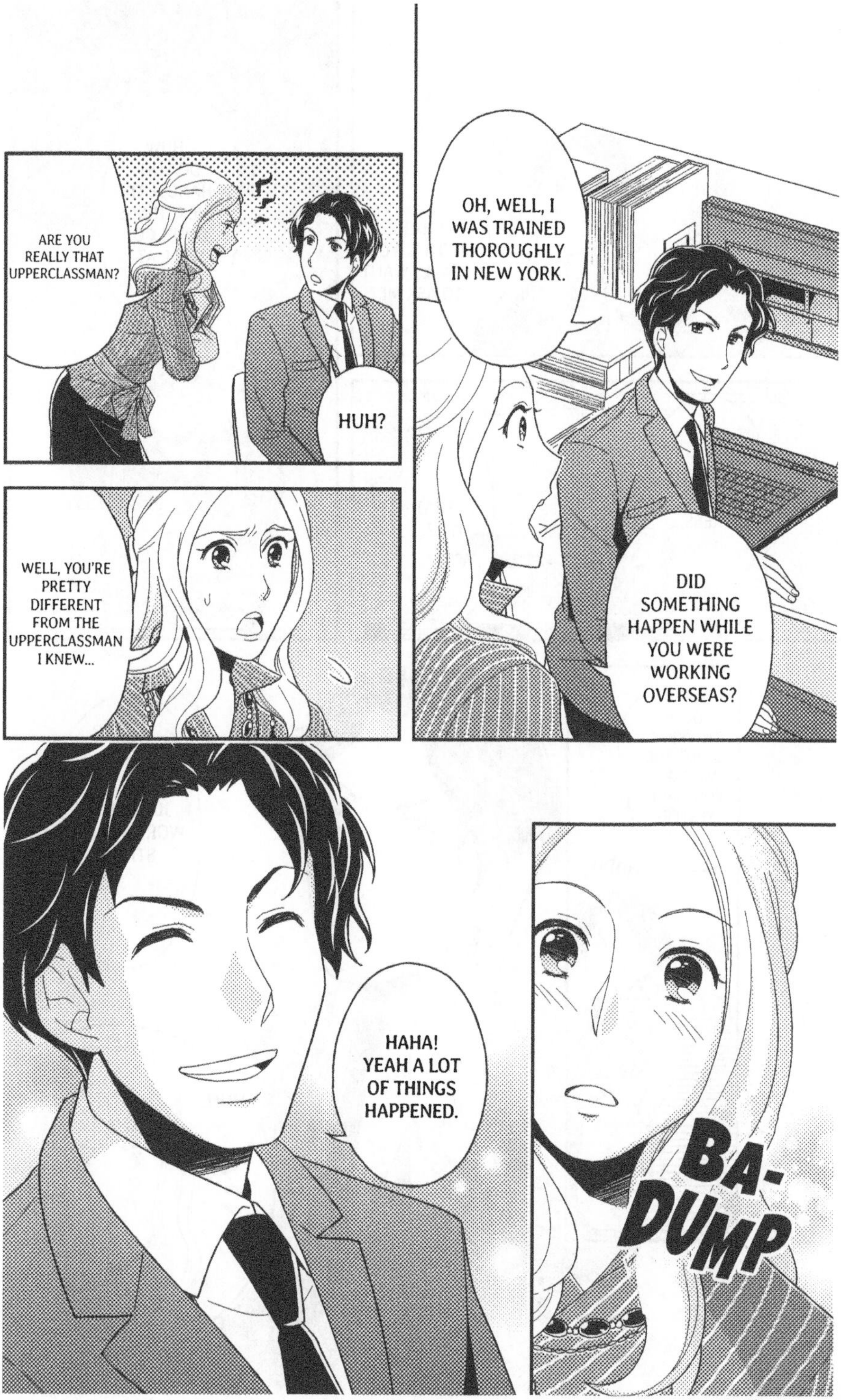
ARE YOU REALLY THAT UPPERCLASSMAN?
HUH?
WELL, YOU'RE PRETTY DIFFERENT FROM THE UPPERCLASSMAN I KNEW...
OH, WELL, I WAS TRAINED THOROUGHLY IN NEW YORK.
DID SOMETHING HAPPEN WHILE YOU WERE WORKING OVERSEAS?
HAHA! YEAH A LOT OF THINGS HAPPENED.
BA-DUMP

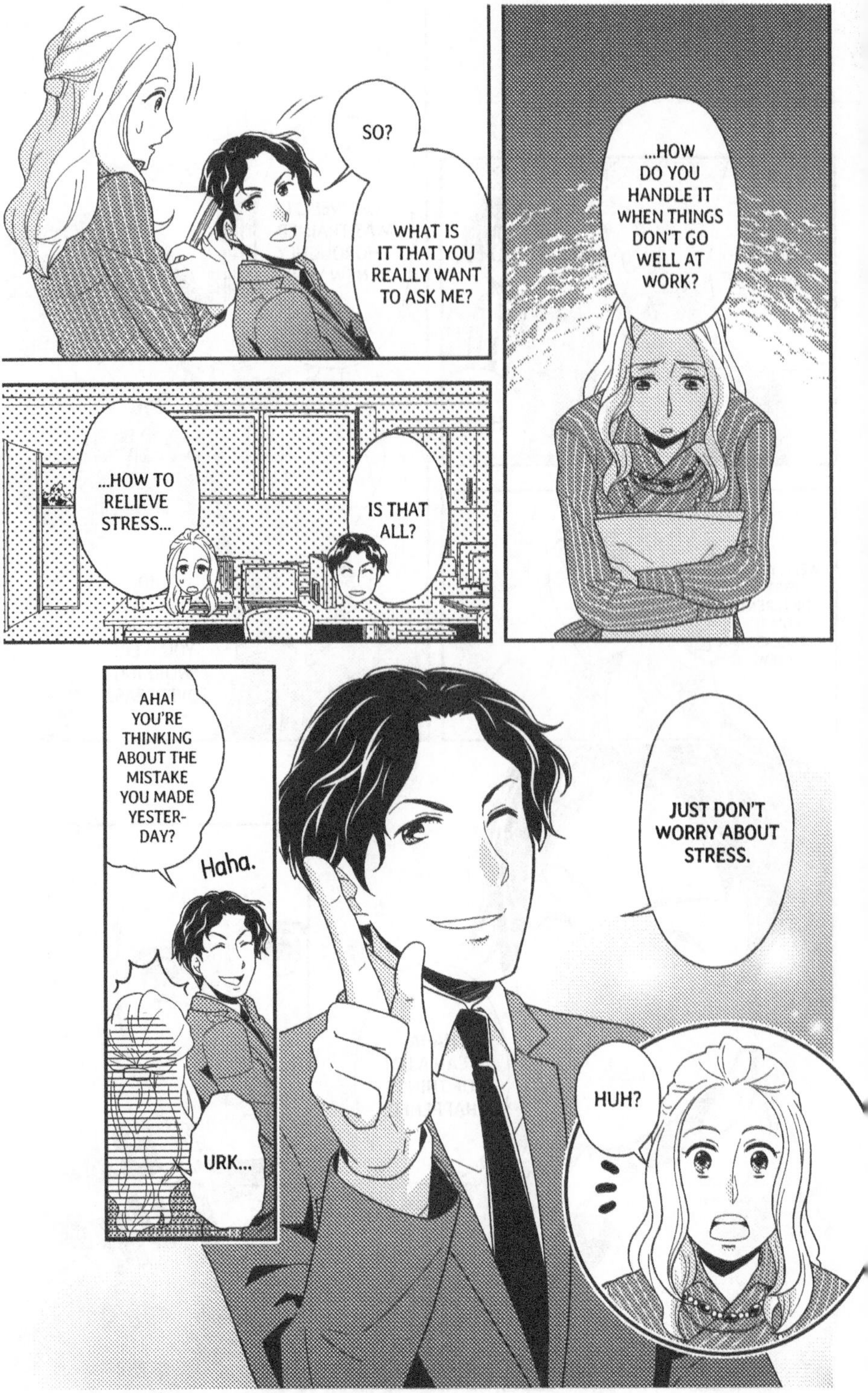
SO?
WHAT IS IT THAT YOU REALLY WANT TO ASK ME?
...HOW DO YOU HANDLE IT WHEN THINGS DON'T GO WELL AT WORK?
...HOW TO RELIEVE STRESS...
IS THAT ALL?
AHA! YOU'RE THINKING ABOUT THE MISTAKE YOU MADE YESTER-DAY?
Haha.
URK...
JUST DON'T WORRY ABOUT STRESS.
HUH?

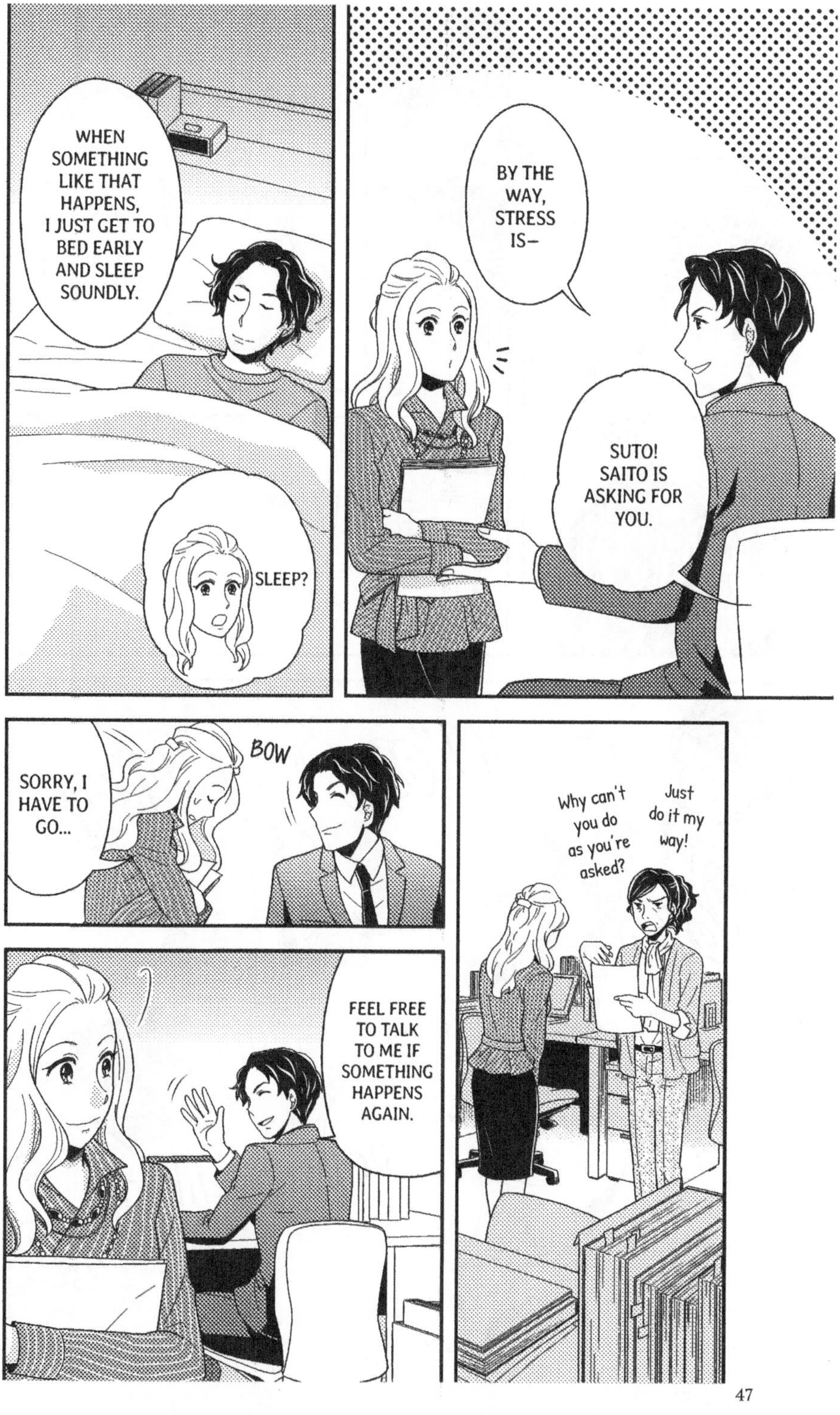
WHEN SOMETHING LIKE THAT HAPPENS, I JUST GET TO BED EARLY AND SLEEP SOUNDLY.
SLEEP?
BY THE WAY, STRESS IS—
SUTO! SAITO IS ASKING FOR YOU.
SORRY, I HAVE TO GO...
BOW
FEEL FREE TO TALK TO ME IF SOMETHING HAPPENS AGAIN.
Why can't you do as you're asked?
Just do it my way!

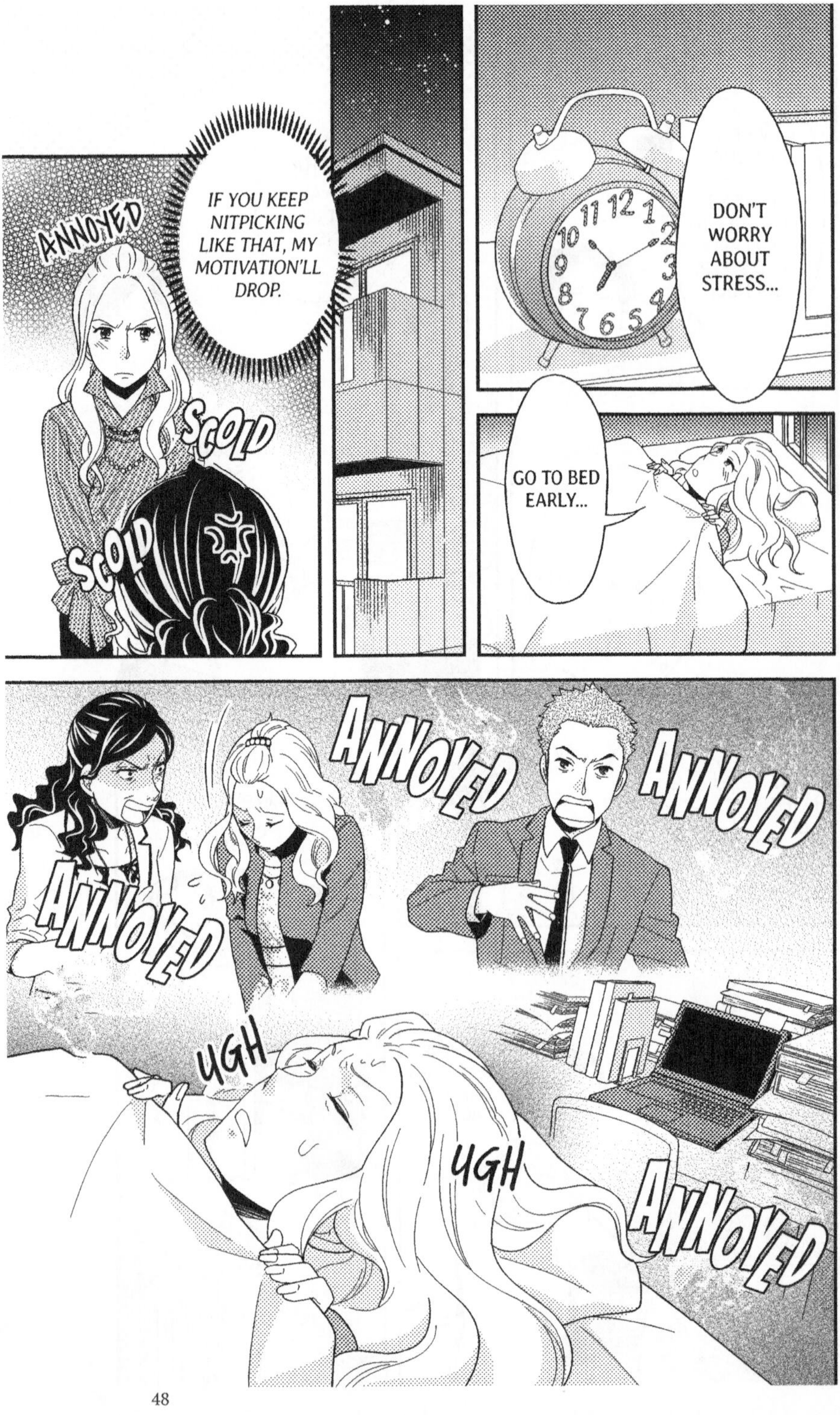
DON'T WORRY ABOUT STRESS...
GO TO BED EARLY...
IF YOU KEEP NITPICKING LIKE THAT, MY MOTIVATION'LL DROP.
ANNOYED
SCOLD
SCOLD
ANNOYED
ANNOYED
ANNOYED
UGH
UGH
ANNOYED

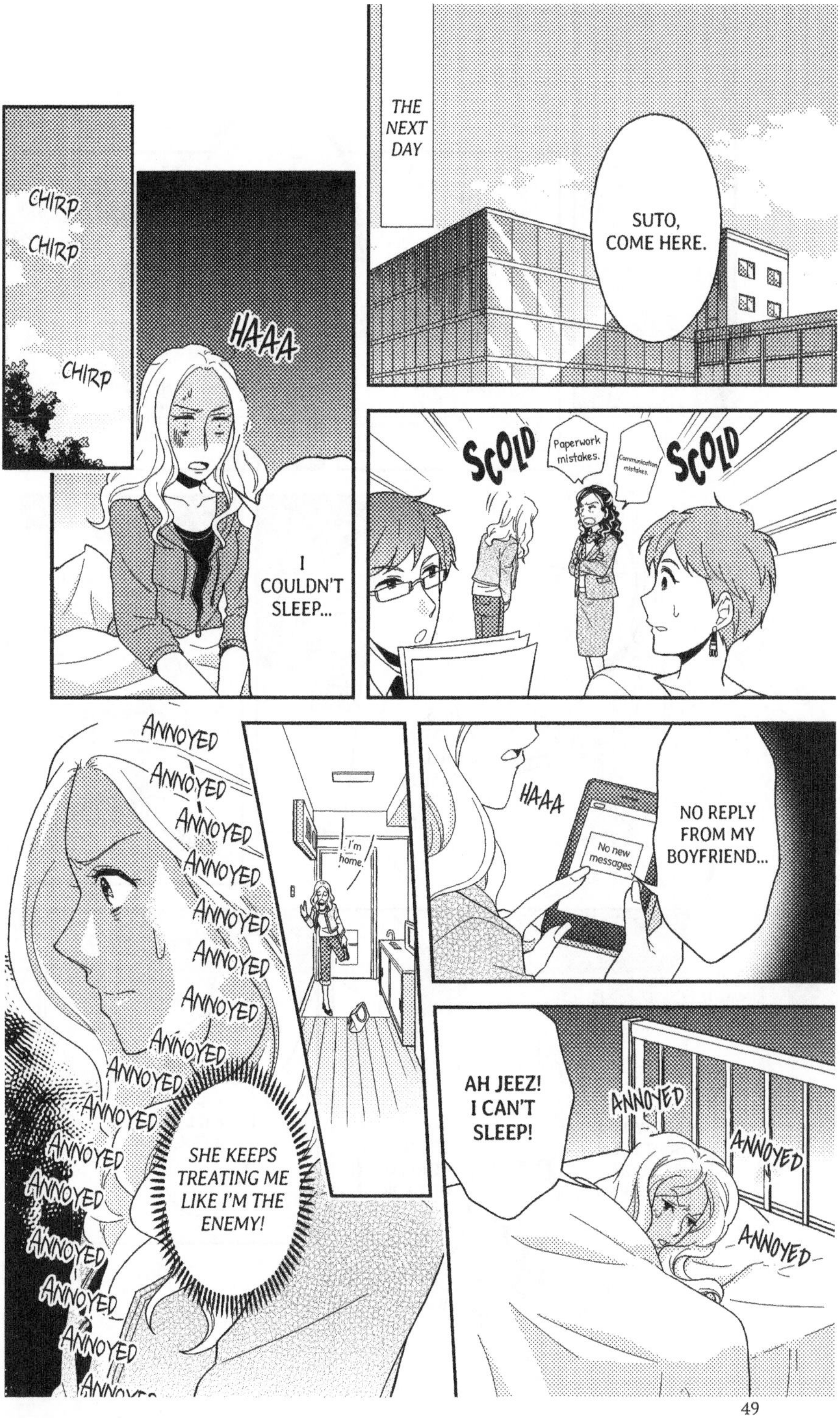
THE NEXT DAY
SUTO, COME HERE.
SCOLD
Paperwork mistakes.
Communication mistakes.
SCOLD
HAAA
I COULDN'T SLEEP...
CHIRP
CHIRP
CHIRP
NO REPLY FROM MY BOYFRIEND...
HAAA
No new messages
AH JEEZ! I CAN'T SLEEP!
ANNOYED
ANNOYED
ANNOYED
I'm home.
ANNOYED
ANNOYED
ANNOYED
ANNOYED
ANNOYED
ANNOYED
ANNOYED
ANNOYED
ANNOYED
ANNOYED
ANNOYED
ANNOYED
ANNOYED
ANNOYED
ANNOYED
SHE KEEPS TREATING ME LIKE I'M THE ENEMY!

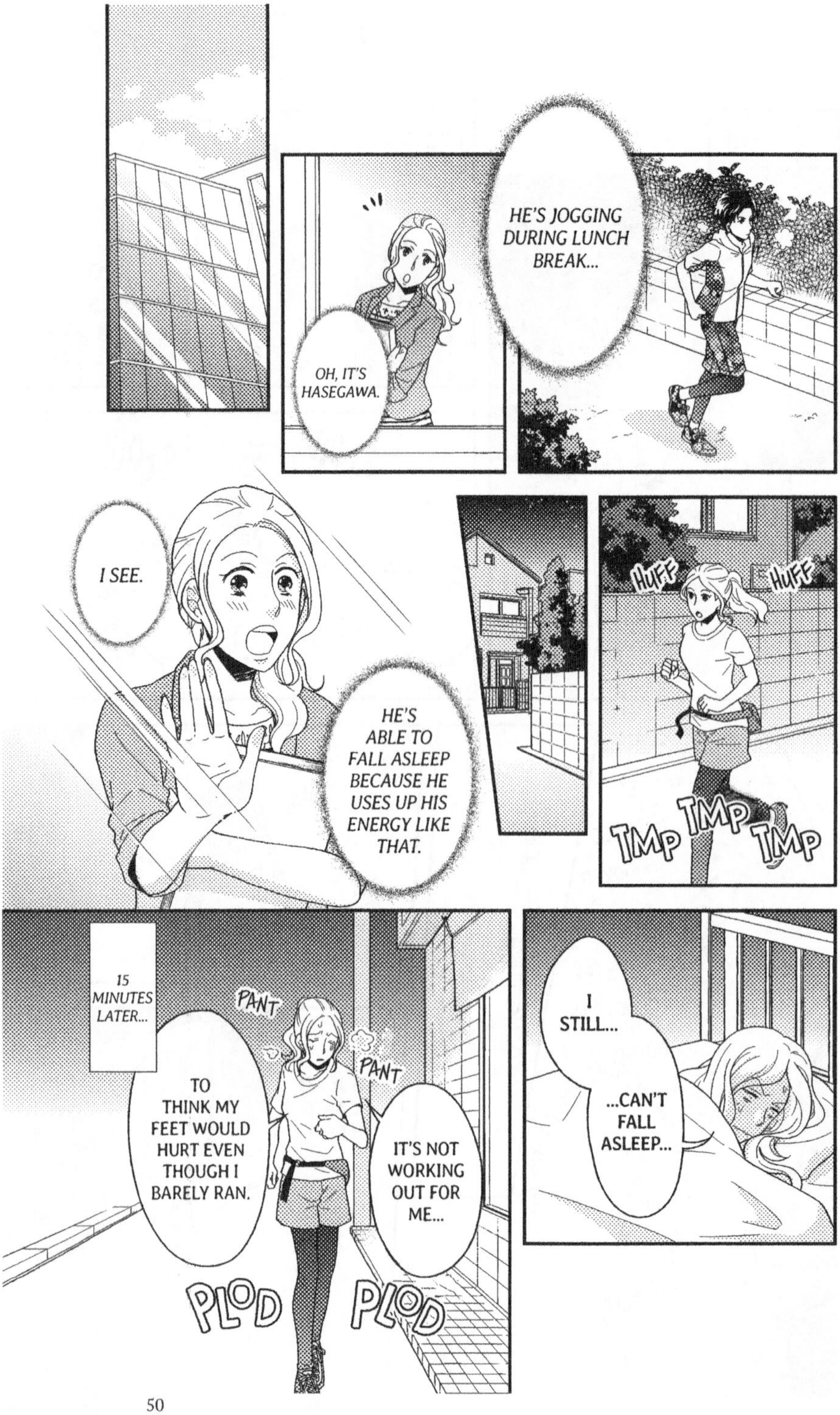
OH, IT'S HASEGAWA.
HE'S JOGGING DURING LUNCH BREAK...
I SEE.
HE'S ABLE TO FALL ASLEEP BECAUSE HE USES UP HIS ENERGY LIKE THAT.
HUFF
HUFF
TMP TMP TMP
15 MINUTES LATER...
PANT
PANT
TO THINK MY FEET WOULD HURT EVEN THOUGH I BARELY RAN.
IT'S NOT WORKING OUT FOR ME...
PLOD PLOD
I STILL...
...CAN'T FALL ASLEEP...

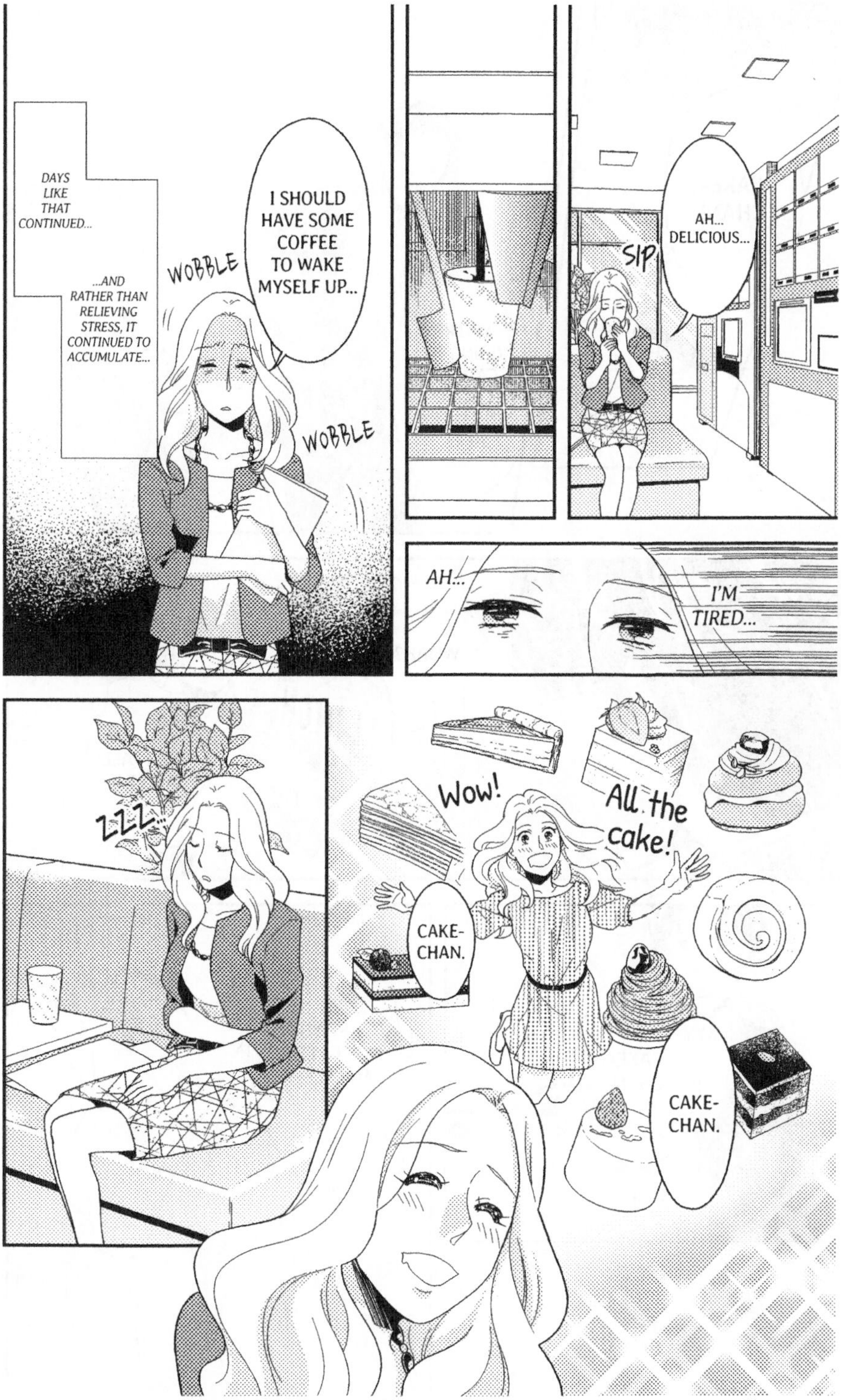

DAYS LIKE THAT CONTINUED...
...AND RATHER THAN RELIEVING STRESS, IT CONTINUED TO ACCUMULATE...
WOBBLE
I SHOULD HAVE SOME COFFEE TO WAKE MYSELF UP...
WOBBLE
SIP
AH... DELICIOUS...
AH...
I'M TIRED...
ZZZ...
Wow!
All the cake!
CAKE-CHAN.
CAKE-CHAN.

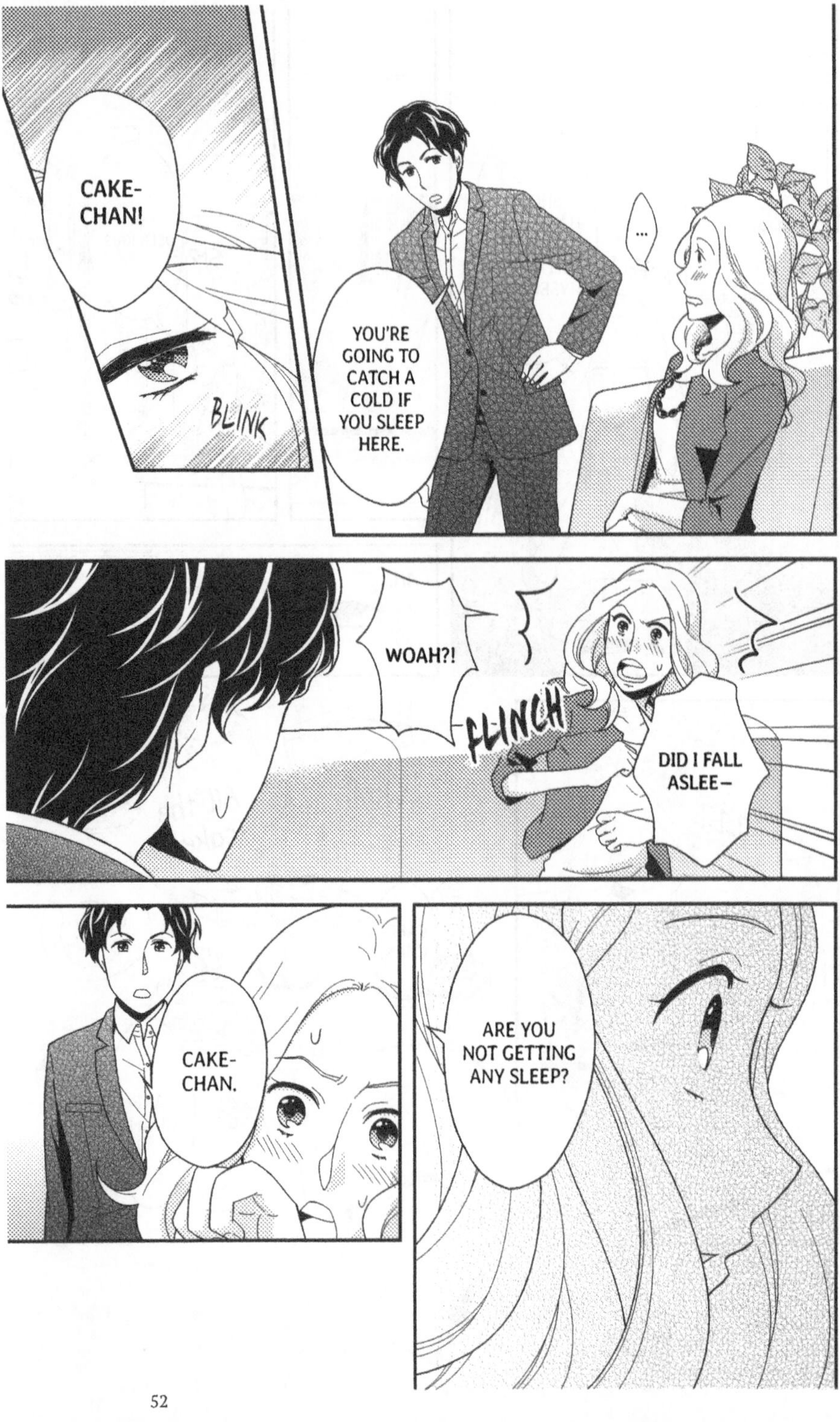
CAKE-CHAN!
BLINK
YOU'RE GOING TO CATCH A COLD IF YOU SLEEP HERE.
...
WOAH?!
FLINCH
DID I FALL ASLEE—
CAKE-CHAN.
ARE YOU NOT GETTING ANY SLEEP?

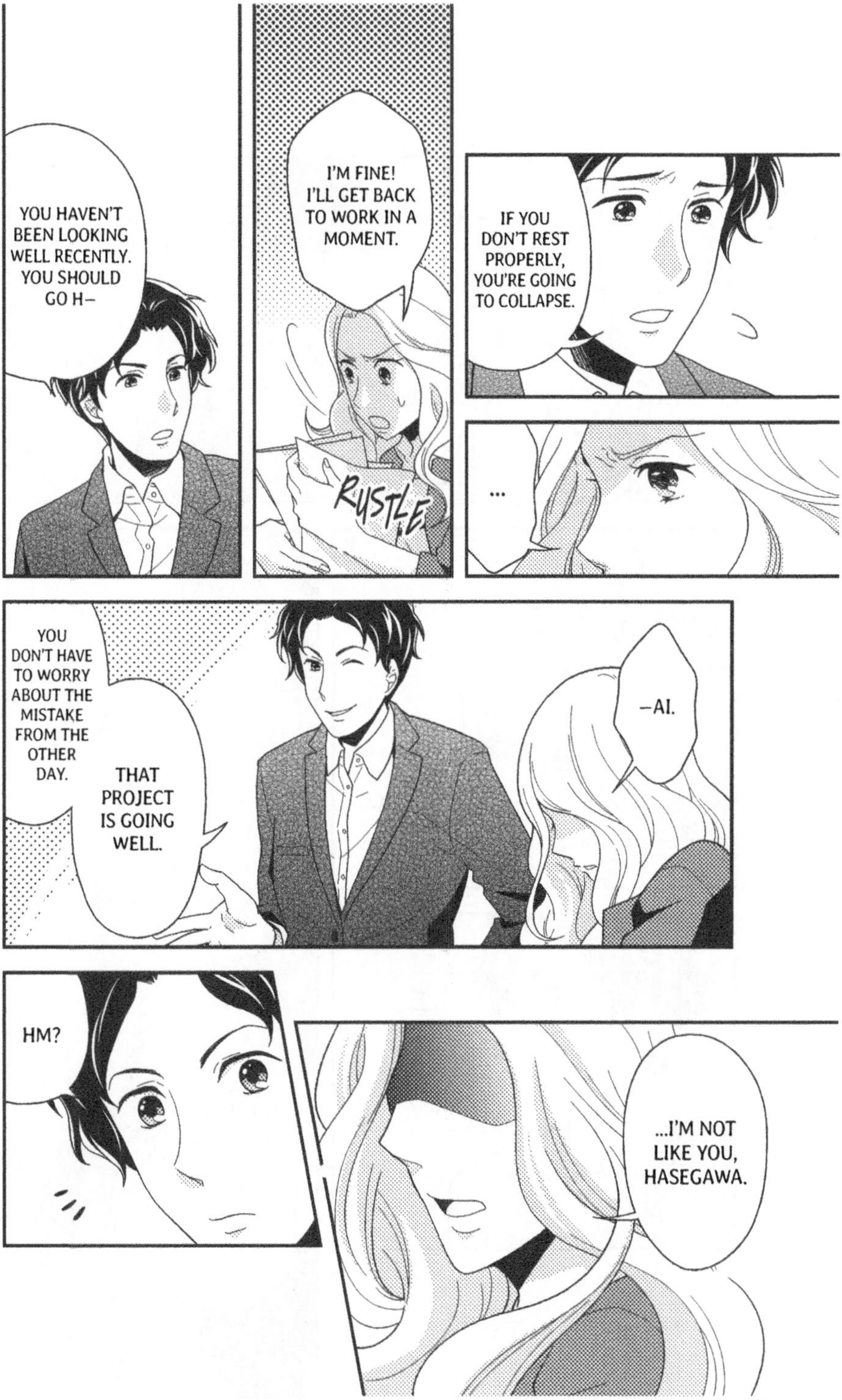
YOU HAVEN'T BEEN LOOKING WELL RECENTLY. YOU SHOULD GO H–
I'M FINE! I'LL GET BACK TO WORK IN A MOMENT.
RUSTLE
IF YOU DON'T REST PROPERLY, YOU'RE GOING TO COLLAPSE.
...
YOU DON'T HAVE TO WORRY ABOUT THE MISTAKE FROM THE OTHER DAY.
THAT PROJECT IS GOING WELL.
–AI.
HM?
...I'M NOT LIKE YOU, HASEGAWA.

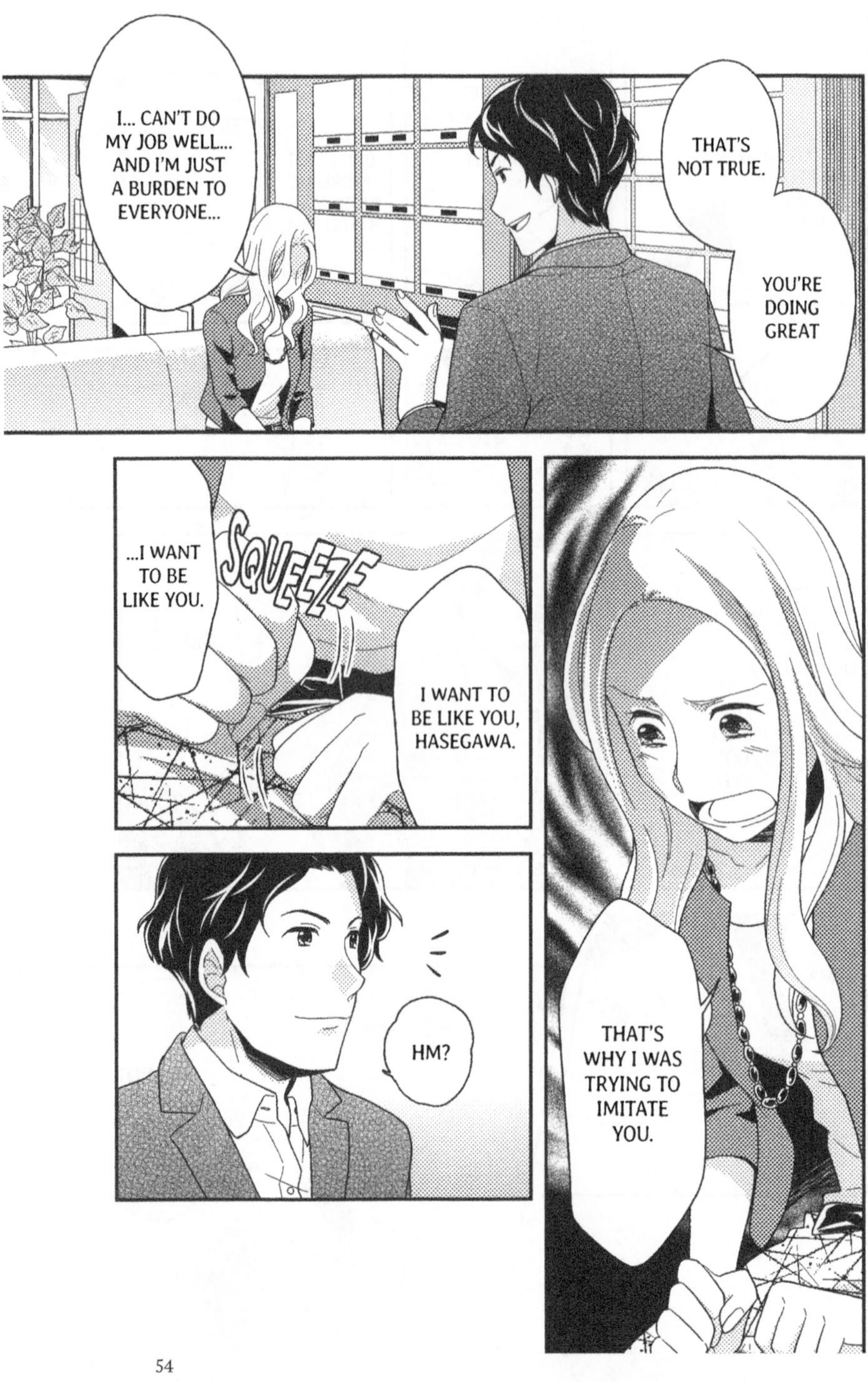

I... CAN'T DO MY JOB WELL... AND I'M JUST A BURDEN TO EVERYONE...
THAT'S NOT TRUE.
YOU'RE DOING GREAT
...I WANT TO BE LIKE YOU.
SQUEEZE
I WANT TO BE LIKE YOU, HASEGAWA.
THAT'S WHY I WAS TRYING TO IMITATE YOU.
HM?

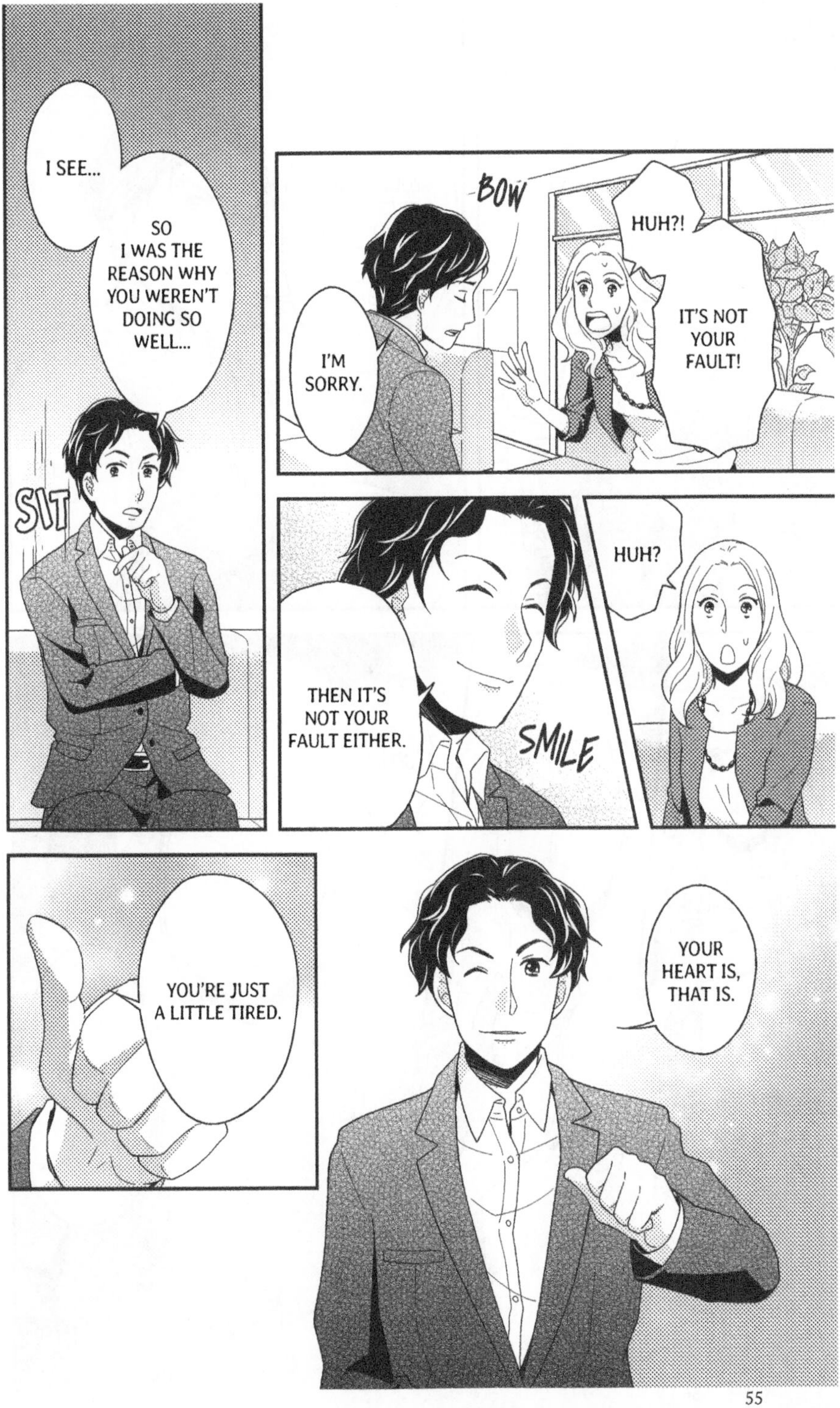
I SEE...
SO I WAS THE REASON WHY YOU WEREN'T DOING SO WELL...
SIT
BOW
I'M SORRY.
HUH?!
IT'S NOT YOUR FAULT!
THEN IT'S NOT YOUR FAULT EITHER.
SMILE
HUH?
YOUR HEART IS, THAT IS.
YOU'RE JUST A LITTLE TIRED.

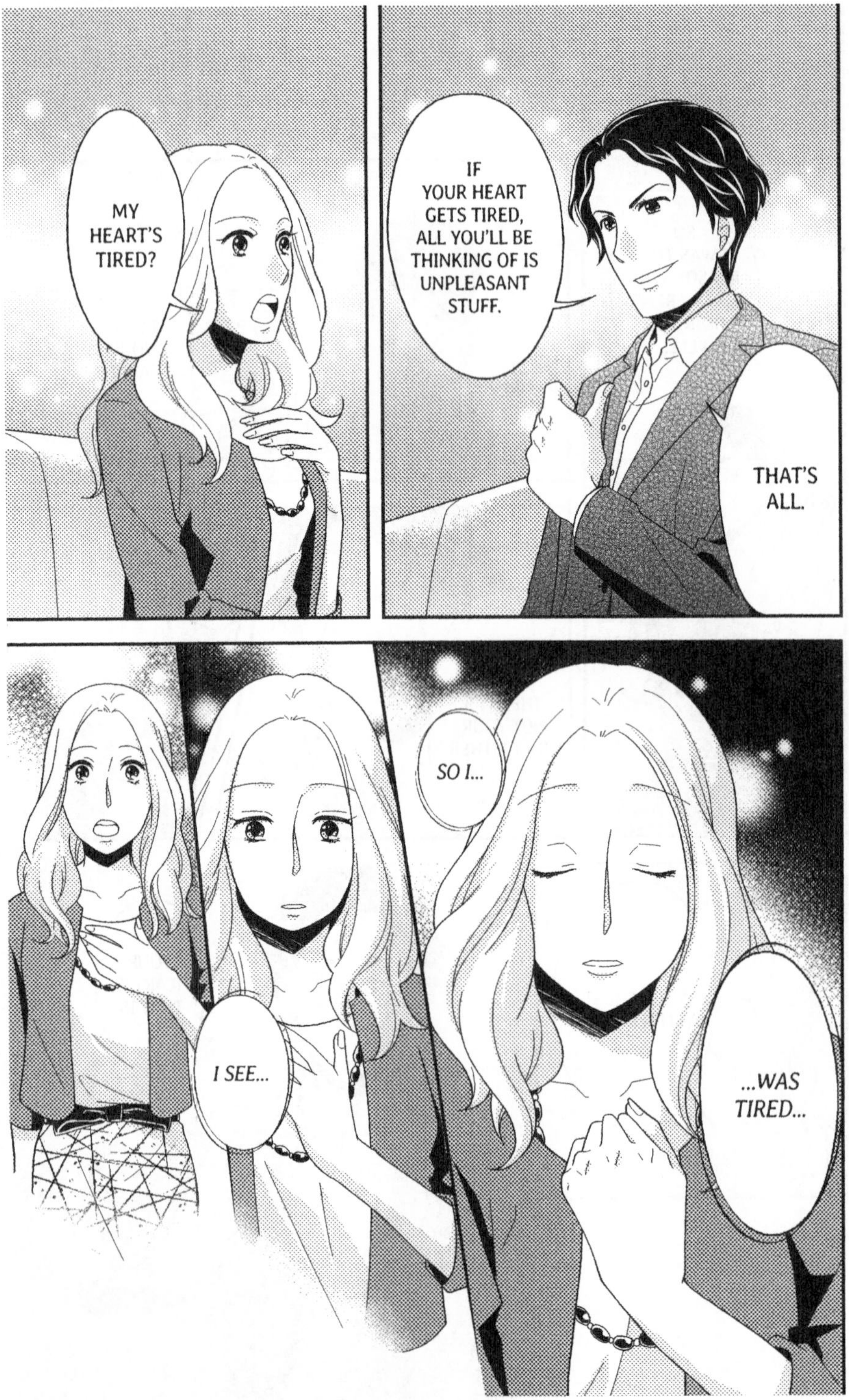

IF YOUR HEART GETS TIRED, ALL YOU'LL BE THINKING OF IS UNPLEASANT STUFF.
THAT'S ALL.
MY HEART'S TIRED?
SO I...
...WAS TIRED...
I SEE...

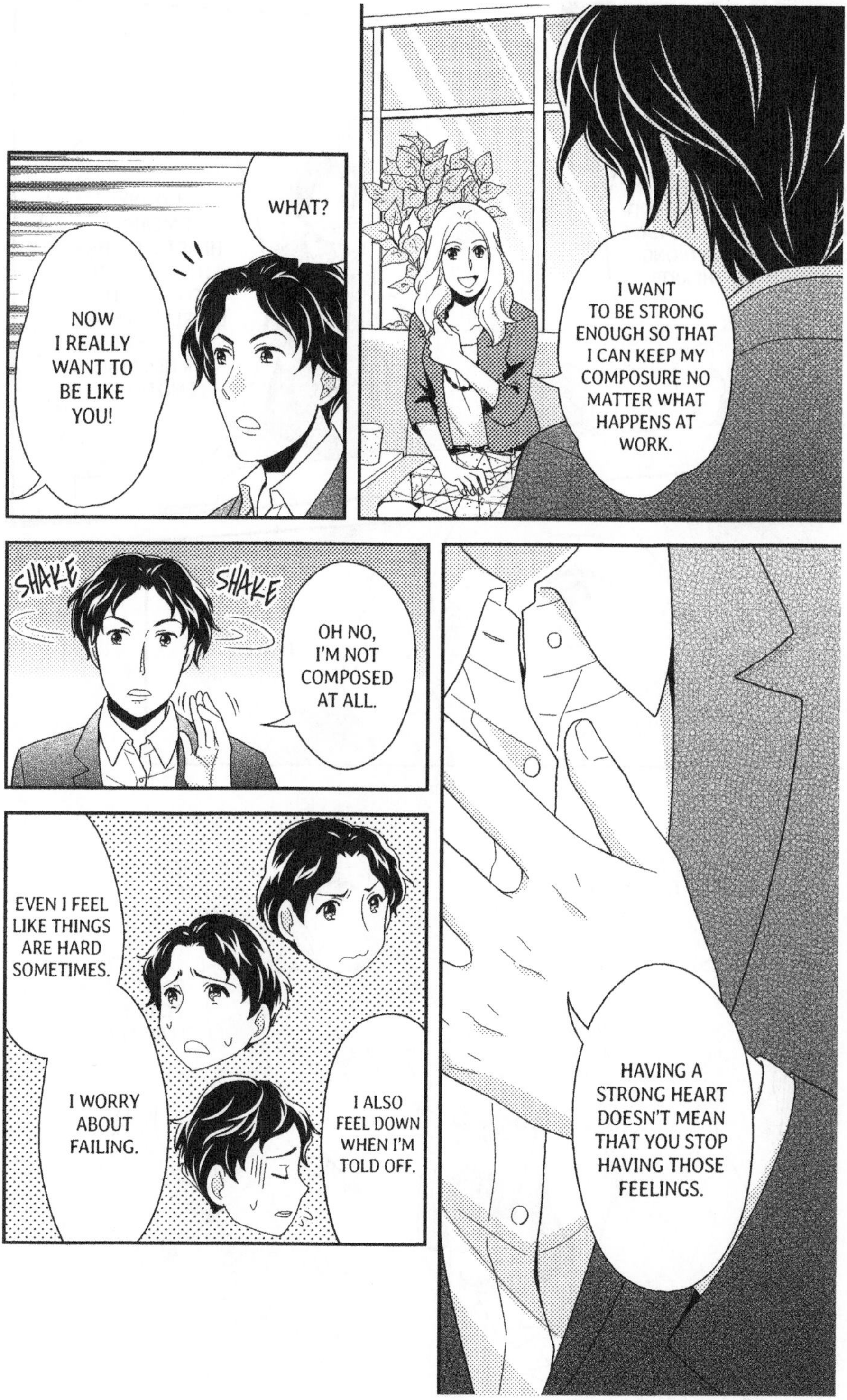
I WANT TO BE STRONG ENOUGH SO THAT I CAN KEEP MY COMPOSURE NO MATTER WHAT HAPPENS AT WORK.
NOW I REALLY WANT TO BE LIKE YOU!
WHAT?
SHAKE
SHAKE
OH NO, I'M NOT COMPOSED AT ALL.
EVEN I FEEL LIKE THINGS ARE HARD SOMETIMES.
I WORRY ABOUT FAILING.
I ALSO FEEL DOWN WHEN I'M TOLD OFF.
HAVING A STRONG HEART DOESN'T MEAN THAT YOU STOP HAVING THOSE FEELINGS.

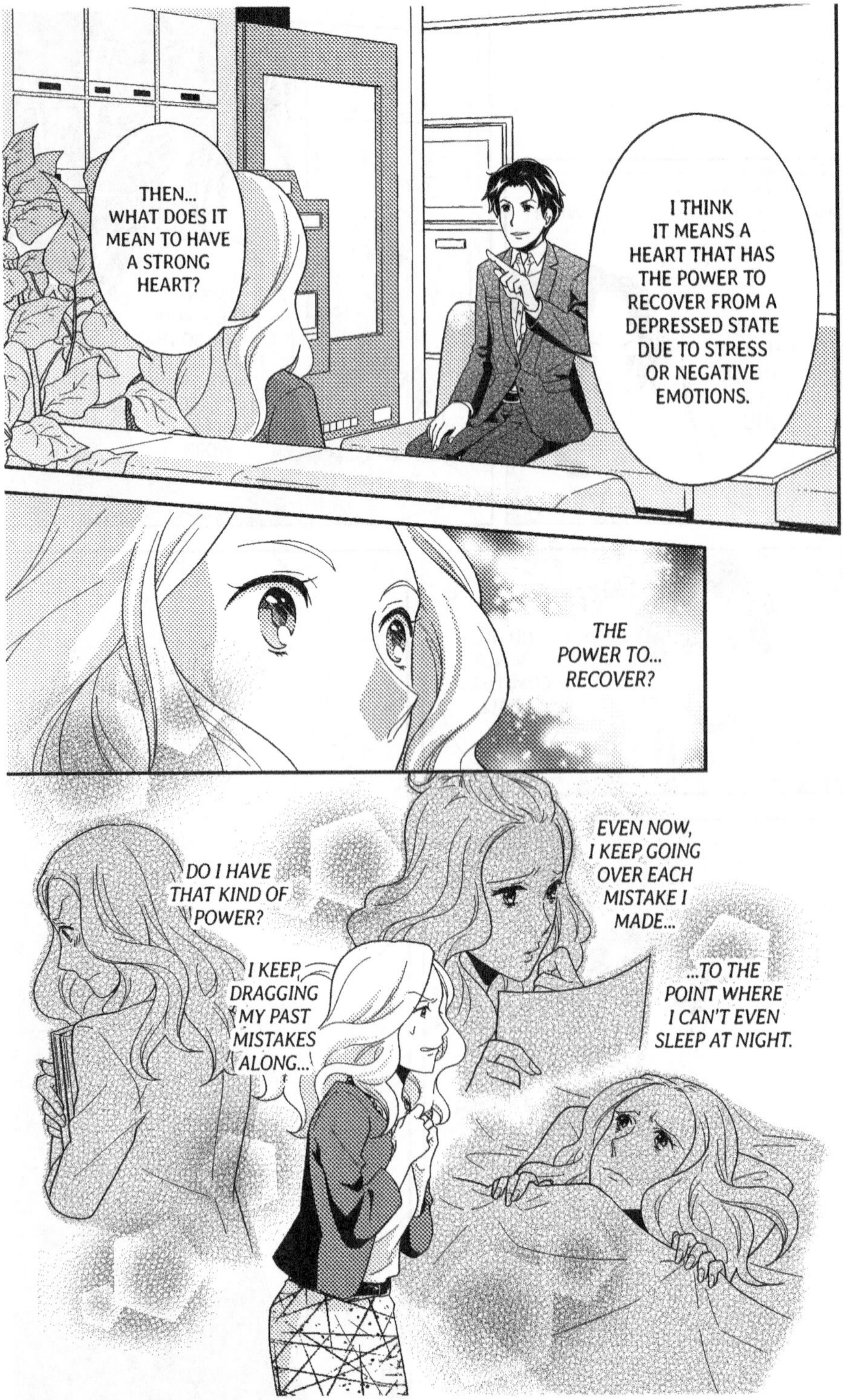
THEN... WHAT DOES IT MEAN TO HAVE A STRONG HEART?
I THINK IT MEANS A HEART THAT HAS THE POWER TO RECOVER FROM A DEPRESSED STATE DUE TO STRESS OR NEGATIVE EMOTIONS.
THE POWER TO... RECOVER?
EVEN NOW, I KEEP GOING OVER EACH MISTAKE I MADE...
...TO THE POINT WHERE I CAN'T EVEN SLEEP AT NIGHT.
DO I HAVE THAT KIND OF POWER?
I KEEP DRAGGING MY PAST MISTAKES ALONG...

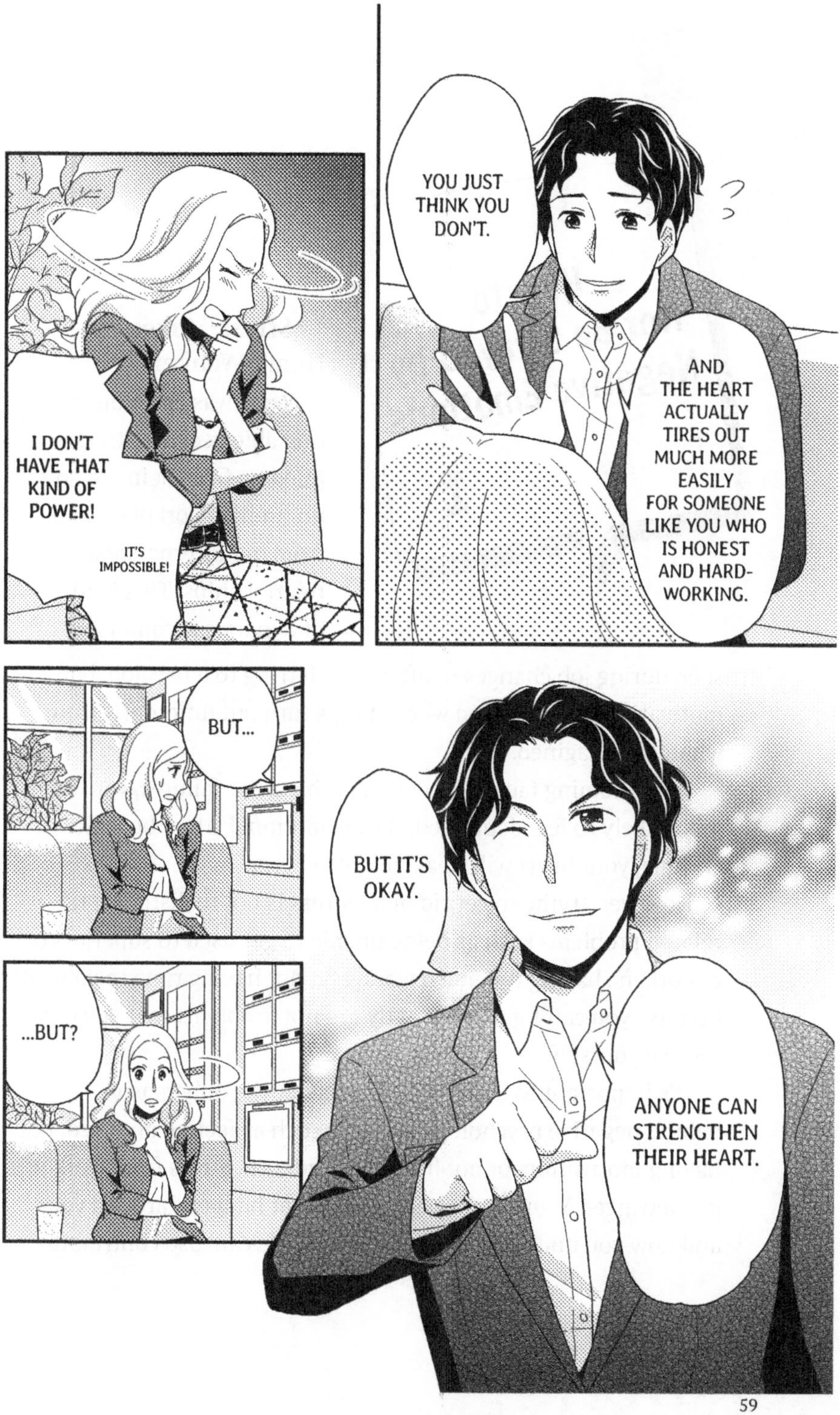
YOU JUST THINK YOU DON'T.
AND THE HEART ACTUALLY TIRES OUT MUCH MORE EASILY FOR SOMEONE LIKE YOU WHO IS HONEST AND HARD-WORKING.
I DON'T HAVE THAT KIND OF POWER!
IT'S IMPOSSIBLE!
BUT...
...BUT?
BUT IT'S OKAY.
ANYONE CAN STRENGTHEN THEIR HEART.

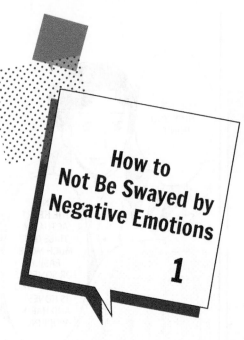

How to Not Be Swayed by Negative Emotions

1

⇨ **Stress Makes the Heart Weaker**

Reisa was emotionally unstable because stress piled up from being in an unfamiliar workplace and from her interpersonal relationships. This kind of dynamic is commonly seen during job changes or after transferring to a new job, but motivation can also drop when things turn out differently from what was imagined.

When coming face to face with problems or failures, you are more likely to feel depressed. If the emotional stress becomes chronic, your heart will weaken.

However, trying to get rid of all stress is not realistic. Work-related problems such as being unable to get used to superiors or coworkers, having too much work, and not having time to yourself because you can't get home early are not problems that you can resolve yourself.

It's important to note that stress is not the only reason behind negative psychological states such as feeling annoyed, not having motivation, or not having confidence. Stress from work is just a trigger. Your way of perceiving what happens around you and how you understand events in your life can also contribute

to negative psychological states. It is important to identify bad habits of thinking and modify them to help you become more resilient.

⇨ Emotions Can Be Controlled

Whether or not you can cut off a negative psychological state all depends on your ability to shift your focus from what you cannot control to what you can control.

If you think, "I can't do anything in this sort of situation," you will be overpowered by a sense of helplessness and fall into a state of depression. However, if you are able to shift your focus to what you are able to handle, that pessimism can turn into optimism, and despair can turn into hope.

ANNOYED
ANNOYED
UGH
UGH
ANNOYED

You can decide whether you want to be swung around by your emotions or whether you want to control them.

You may think, "I am often at the mercy of my emotions," but the truth is that you can control your emotions. You just need to learn how.

To learn to control your emotions and build a foundation of resilience, you must first understand the fundamentals of emotions.

⇨ Don't Seal Off Emotions

You may have been taught to not show your emotions. Even at work, there may be many who think that becoming emotional is a bad thing. It's true that if you let your emotions just burst, it could become an uncontrollable behavior problem.

However, if you get in the habit of holding back your emotions, you may find that other problems pop up in their place. People who engage in "emotional labor" are those who need to be the most cautious.

Emotional labor is work that requires you to modify your emotions for the sake of another's feelings. Some examples of emotional laborers are workers at call centers who need to cut off their own emotions to handle claims, flight attendants or nurses who are always expected to wear a smile, or workers in the service industry who are expected to provide the best hospitality.

The problem here is that if people continue sealing their emotions off for the sake of their work, they may forget their true selves or become violent because their stored up emotions explode. Some emotional laborers also experience *burnout syndrome*, when their hearts become exhausted and they can no longer continue to do their work effectively.

With interpersonal relationships both at work and in private, people may become *passive-aggressive* when they are unable to express their feelings openly. Unable to direct their anger openly toward others, passive-aggressive people may show their hostility by being silent or by ignoring the source of their anger. They may instead become sarcastic and critical. They may cause trouble by being late to work or by obstructing the work of others around them.

While such people actually have that pent-up anger boiling inside of them, they fear butting heads or have been told that it's important to cooperate and keep harmony. They have unconsciously sealed off their emotions.

Just because you suppress your emotions does not mean that they just disappear. If you do not release pent-up emotions, they may lead to health problems. By stifling negative emotions, you may also be suppressing the side of your brain that feels positive emotions such as joy and happiness.

To live in harmony with your emotions, you must learn the method that allows you to get along with them. In the text that follows, you will learn what you need to know to build resilience in the face of negative emotions.

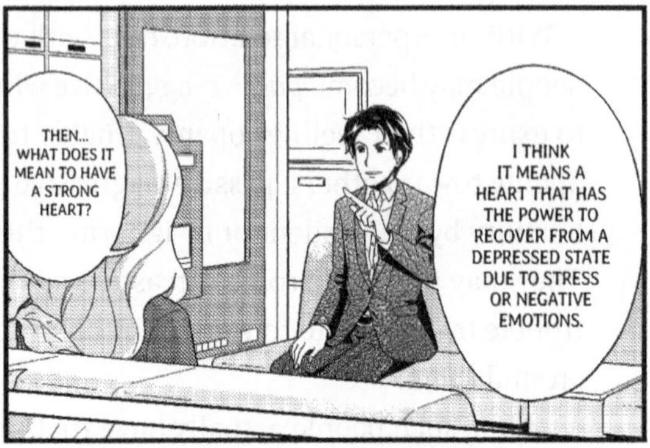
I THINK IT MEANS A HEART THAT HAS THE POWER TO RECOVER FROM A DEPRESSED STATE DUE TO STRESS OR NEGATIVE EMOTIONS.
THEN... WHAT DOES IT MEAN TO HAVE A STRONG HEART?

A strong heart does not mean you won't feel negative emotions at all. A strong heart is a heart that has the power to recover from a depressed state by being able to get along with emotions.

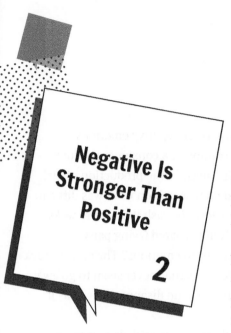

Negative Is Stronger Than Positive

2

⇨ The Rumination Phenomenon of Emotions

An important piece of knowledge when it comes to emotions is the **rumination phenomenon.** To ruminate means to repeat. It is a term that is also used to describe a cow munching on grass, but just as how it takes forever for a cow to stop chewing the grass, negative emotions seem to constantly cycle through our hearts.

Anger, worry, fear, depression, guilt, and embarrassment are some of the emotions that ruminate within us and don't exactly go away. Unfortunately, positive emotions such as joy and happiness disappear quite rapidly.

In other words, you are likely to remember negative experiences well, but you may not be able to recall positive ones as quickly. We call this phenomenon *negativity bias*.

Thinking about the persistence of negative emotions reminded me of when I was working at a consumer products company. At the time, I was involved in the production of dish soap. I would visit homes and do research on what was difficult to wash. The greasiest and hardest-to-wash items were woks. The least troublesome were Teflon-coated frying pans.

How does my experience relate to emotions? The grease stuck on woks is like the negative feelings that never seem to go away, while positive emotions wash away and disappear easily as if they were Teflon-coated.

In that way, negative emotions are more likely to remain as a memory compared to positive emotions. It's said that "bad people are stronger than good people," but this also goes for emotions. Negative emotions override positive emotions. Coming to understand this truth is the first step in getting along with your emotions.

This knowledge can also be used to form good personal relationships in the workplace or between spouses. According to specialists, married couples who are more likely to divorce in the future have the common element of no balance between their negative and positive emotions.

In order to have a good lasting relationship, it's ideal to have at least five times the positive emotions for each negative one. In other words, if you anger another person, it is important for you to go through a lot of positive experiences with them to mitigate that anger.

This observation applies to the workplace as well. Research has shown that high-performing teams receive six times as many positive feedback reviews compared to negative reviews. Poorly performing teams, on the other hand, receive three times the number of negative reviews as positive ones. With so many negative reviews, depression is likely to spread among members of a poorly performing team.

⇨ The Positive Brain and the Negative Brain

You have probably noticed that those who experience more positive feelings compared to negative ones are much happier. According to research, if you have three or more positive emotions for each negative one, you will have a higher level of happiness.

In order to increase your level of happiness, you need to control your negative emotions. In addition, if you have a habit that fills you with positive feelings, you should be able to experience a high level of happiness.

Why should this be the case? Because research has shown that positive and negative emotions are born from different parts of the brain. In an experiment conducted by placing numerous electrodes on test subjects' heads, electrical activity in the brain was measured. It was found that the left side of the brain was much more active than the right side for those who were optimistic. Those who were pessimistic showed a much lower sign of activity in the left side of the brain compared to the optimistic group.

According to research by neuroscientists, the amygdala, which is an almond-shaped part of the brain roughly the size of a thumbnail, plays an important role in the emotional experience of fear. The amygdala creates the neural pathways that connect to parts of the cerebral cortex, which has the ability to suppress emotions.

Normally, the amygdala, which is at the core of fear, and the cerebral cortex, which has the suppressor function, are in balance. However, the suppressor function is weaker in the cerebral cortex of people who are pessimistic and tend to think negatively about the future. Because of this, they may feel excess fear. In other words, their rationality is ruled by their emotions, and they are unable to take control of their anxieties or worries.

They may have been shaken to the point where they go "Oh no. What should I do?" or they may have felt some sort of fear because they feel like they have brought on trouble. "I've upset other people. What should I do now?"

These examples are situations where, due to fear, people's minds go blank, or they are no longer able to think rationally.

Whenever you make some sort of mistake, it's important to calm down and not panic. If you become emotionally unstable, you may act impulsively, which may aggravate the problem even further. In other words, it's important to calm yourself down without being led by your emotions.

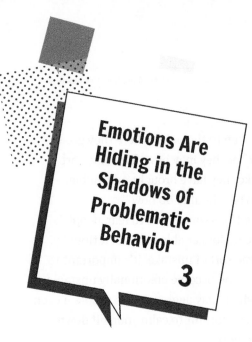

Emotions Are Hiding in the Shadows of Problematic Behavior

3

⇨ **The Mechanism of Emotions and Behaviors**

Behind impulsive behavior lies an emotional problem. The part of the brain that controls negative emotions instantaneously sends out specific commands to various parts of the body, causing the body to react subconsciously.

For example, the emotional feeling of anger may trigger aggressive behavior such as speaking in an abusive manner. When you are treated unfairly, the switch for the emotion of anger is flipped, leading to the activation of your aggressive instinct.

When you feel fear, you may want to escape. For example, you may have been afraid of giving a speech in front of others. You may have felt like you wanted to run away when you had to get up and make the presentation.

Part 1
Controlling Negative Emotions

That feeling of anxiety can show up as evasive behavior. For example, when someone is put in charge of a job for the first time, they may not be able to make a start because they think, "This is impossible for me" or "I can't do this on time." The feeling of anxiety is hiding in the shadows.

Embarrassment can trigger reclusive behavior. Being reprimanded by your superior in front of a large group of your colleagues, to the point where you become so embarrassed that your self-esteem crumbles, can make you want to avoid your superior or colleagues at work. Some people even withdraw completely from social situations as a result of being embarrassed this way at school as a child.

As you can see, emotions hide behind problematic behaviors. Coming to understand the relationship behind emotions and behaviors is the first step to resolving these problems.

Problematic Behavior Due to Negative Emotions

Anger
Aggression
Fear
Flight
Anxiety
Evasion
Embarrassment
Reclusion

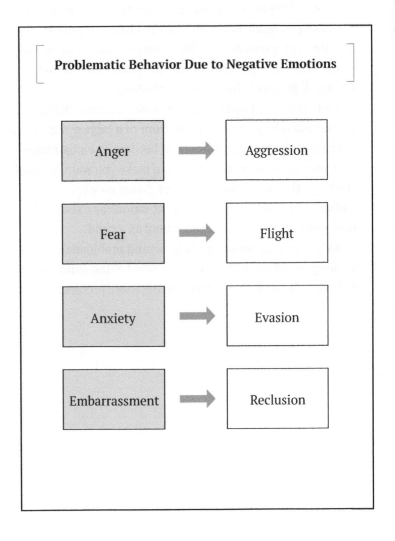

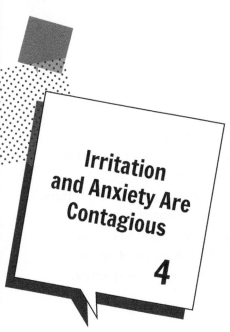

Irritation and Anxiety Are Contagious

4

⇨ **Beware of the Emotional Vampire**

Just like how the flu virus spreads inside an office, emotions can spread from person to person.

For example, have you ever found yourself feeling depressed when you were with someone who was insecure and pessimistic? Or if you had a leader who looked very anxious while working, did your entire team feel affected by the dull atmosphere created by the leader? Or if someone at your home was on edge, did you find everyone at home to be on edge?

As these examples illustrate, we can all be affected by what are known as **emotional vampires**. Those who have an emotional vampire near them need to be cautious. Emotional vampires are people who influence others' emotions and make them feel as if their energy was drained just by interacting with them.

Emotional vampires lower the self-esteem and energy of people around them by making them feel as if they are bad people or that their existence is insignificant.

In contrast to emotional vampires are **positive energizers**. They are people who make others feel happy and energized from just talking to them. They are viewed in a favorable manner because they increase the motivation of others. When a positive energizer takes on a leadership position, their teams become very activated.

⇨ Using Emotional Transmission Daily

Negative emotions are contagious. It's advisable to take care to not have your energy drained when you work with people who have such strong emotions. If you are in a situation where you can keep your distance from them, you should stay away from them as much as possible.

With that said, if you have an emotional vampire as your superior, subordinate, or family member, it may be difficult to keep your distance. In these cases, you will need to call on your resilience so as not to be controlled by negative emotions.

Negative emotions are not the only emotions that spread from person to person. Positive emotions spread as well. When one person is happy, their happiness can spread to others around them like ripples in water.

Knowing how emotions spread can help you realize how important it is to make good choices about the people you spend your time with. It is said that **your personality is made up of the average of the five people you spend the most time with.** The quickest way for you to become happy is to spend your time with people who are happy.

If you yourself have become the entity that drains the energy and motivation from others unconsciously, you should try hard to spread happiness to others rather than be the emotional vampire.

It is important for you to understand your emotional pattern and take control of your negative emotions. That is the foundation for resilience.

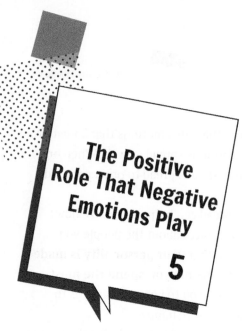

The Positive Role That Negative Emotions Play

5

⇨ **Learn How to Control Your Emotions**

So far, we've covered the problems with negative emotions. However, they're actually not all bad. Negative emotions are necessary in order to live.

What's important is that you do not despise negative emotions, but that you understand the traits of them and control them in a way that they become a plus for you.

Though we have focused our attention on the negative aspects of negative emotions, negative emotions do have positive aspects as well. For example, feeling anger about something that has distressed many people can instill a desire to seek justice, with the positive effect of benefiting society at large.

The Positive Roles Negative Emotions Play

Anger:	Demonstrates a sense of justice to maintain order. Anger becomes the driving force in raising motivation.

Fear:	Protects yourself from mental and physical risks. You gain motivation by having the feeling that you are not allowed to fail.

Anxiety:	Protects yourself from uncertain situations. You will know what to be careful of.

Embar-rassment:	Protects your self-esteem and self-worth. It can help you socially adapt.

Feelings of fear and anxiety can become an alarm to protect you from harm. The sense of urgency that comes from these emotions can push you forward and motivate you to take action.

Feelings of embarrassment may lead you to want to hide, which is a reaction to protect yourself from the criticism of others. But if, instead of running away, you put in the effort to think and act rationally, you will be able to adapt to challenging situations more readily.

In other words, people with high resilience not only have the ability to control the negative aspects of their emotions, but also have the ability to be flexible with the positive aspects of their emotions.

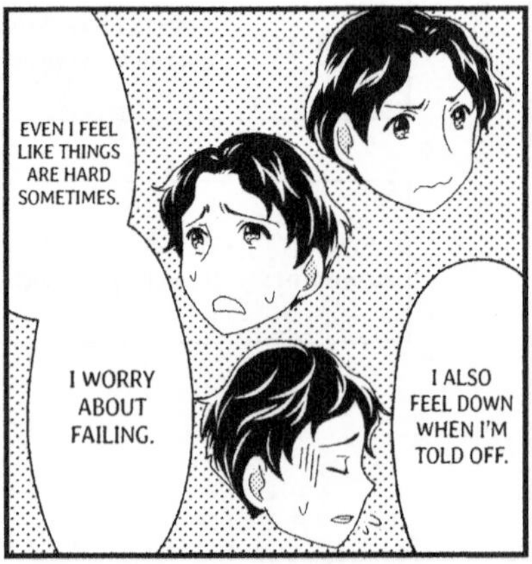
EVEN I FEEL LIKE THINGS ARE HARD SOMETIMES.
I WORRY ABOUT FAILING.
I ALSO FEEL DOWN WHEN I'M TOLD OFF.

One of the skills of resilience is being able to adapt to the positive aspects of negative emotions without being overwhelmed by them.

The Three Methods of Controlling Emotions

6

⇨ **Cool Your Emotions Down with Breathing Exercises**

Three effective methods can be used to handle negative emotions:

1. Cooling your emotions down with breathing exercises
2. Labeling your emotions
3. Finding a diversion from your emotions

To begin, it's important to cool your emotions down. The power of thinking is not enough to calm down your emotions. In order to calm yourself down safely, you can use a breathing technique such as the **three-minute mindful breathing meditation**, which has been proven scientifically to work. The graphic on the next page demonstrates the method.

First, you let your body relax by taking a seat in a quiet place. It's up to you whether you keep your eyes open or shut, but it's important to pay attention to your breathing and to breathe slowly. This method is effective at relieving stress.

I have personally made it a habit to calm myself down with this technique before I talk in front of a crowd.

⇨ Label Your Emotions

Next up is **labeling your emotions.** The goal is to label emotions that result from stress or failures and to take a step back to look at them from a distance. By doing so, you should be able to effectively control them.

Adding labels to your emotions allows you to visualize the mixed-up emotions inside you.

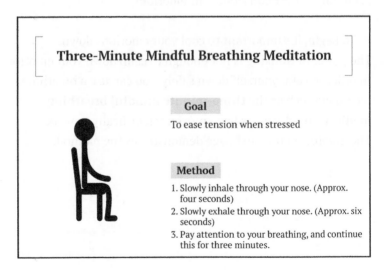

Three-Minute Mindful Breathing Meditation

Goal

To ease tension when stressed

Method

1. Slowly inhale through your nose. (Approx. four seconds)
2. Slowly exhale through your nose. (Approx. six seconds)
3. Pay attention to your breathing, and continue this for three minutes.

Regardless of the problem, in order to effectively handle the situation, it's necessary to figure out what the target emotion is. In other words, to handle emotions, you need to figure out what the emotion is by labeling it.

Neuroscience studies have shown that simply labeling a thought or image that comes to mind can activate the brain's suppressor function, the cerebral cortex, and calm the core of fear, the amygdala.

By repeating this training over and over, the brain should be able to regain its original balance and should be able to calm down emotional reactions such as anxiety and fear.

A single emotion can trigger multiple emotions like a chain reaction. For example, whenever I personally feel irritation or dissatisfaction, I then feel disappointed in myself for not being able to suppress my anger, and then I feel fatigued.

Whenever you label your emotions, it would be good to look at the different emotional patterns that come from the first emotion, second emotion, and so on and not just focus on a single emotion. In this way, you should be able to deepen your understanding of yourself and prevent yourself from unconsciously acting emotionally as shown on page 70.

It may become a little easier to add labels to emotions if you consult friends or family members you can trust. I recommend you confirm your feelings with others by asking, "How did you feel at that time?"

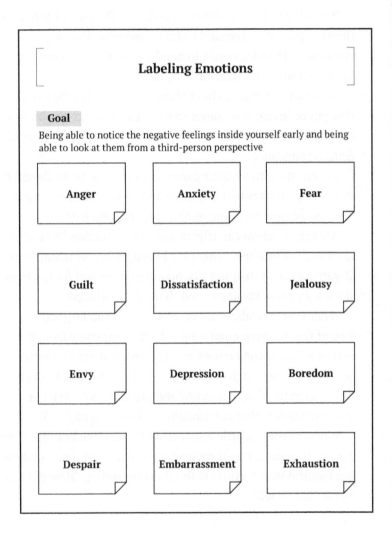

Labeling Emotions

Goal

Being able to notice the negative feelings inside yourself early and being able to look at them from a third-person perspective

Anger	Anxiety	Fear
Guilt	Dissatisfaction	Jealousy
Envy	Depression	Boredom
Despair	Embarrassment	Exhaustion

⇨ Find a Diversion from Your Negative Emotions

The final step in effectively handling negative stress is to **find a diversion** from the emotions that keep coming back. Emotions like anger and anxiety can weaken your heart if left alone and can spread to people around you. That's why it's important to let off steam as soon as possible.

As an example, imagine that you annoyed your coworkers at a meeting. You might find yourself repeating the incident endlessly in your mind. Simply trying to stop this negative mindset might not work. This is where finding a diversion comes in.

Four types of activities have been proven effective as ways to divert attention from your negative thinking:

1. Physical activity: Exercise, dance, various sports, etc.
2. Music: Instrumental performance/appreciation, karaoke, etc.
3. Breathing: Yoga, meditation, speed walking, etc.
4. Writing: Writing stories or poems, journaling, letter writing, etc.

Other methods of diverting attention can be just as effective. They are things you are able to immerse yourself in. They could be a hobby, something you like, or anything at all. The more your concentration heightens and you forget about the passing of time, you will enter a psychological state called the *flow state*. This allows you to change your emotional mindset.

When possible, it is best to find and activate a diversion on the same day as the negative incident. Negative emotions have an adverse effect on sleep and result in an unpleasant morning when you wake up the next day. It's important that you don't hold on to stress overnight. If you are too busy and unable to deal with it on the same day, I recommend putting it into practice as soon as possible.

Diversions for Negative Emotions

Physical Activity	Exercise, dance, various sports	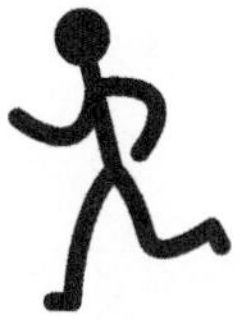
Music	Music performance, music appreciation, karaoke	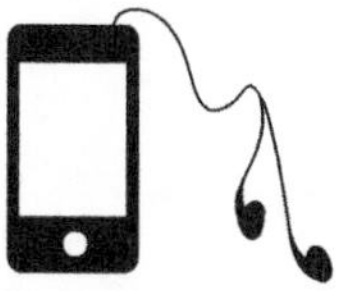
Breathing	Yoga, meditation, speed walking	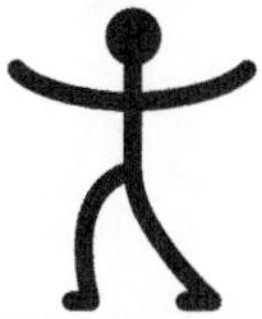
Writing	Writing stories or poems, journaling, writing letters	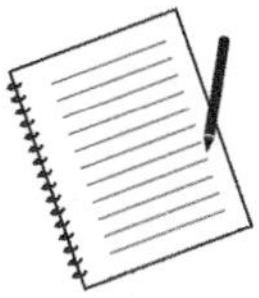

Activities that allow you to immerse yourself to reach a flow state will be most effective.

It's good to have several diversion tactics that you can activate. The point is to quickly take care of things with a diversion. Feel free to test it out.

Taming Negative Assumptions

IT'S BECAUSE YOU'VE EXPERIENCED SADNESS IN THE PAST.
EXPERIENCED?

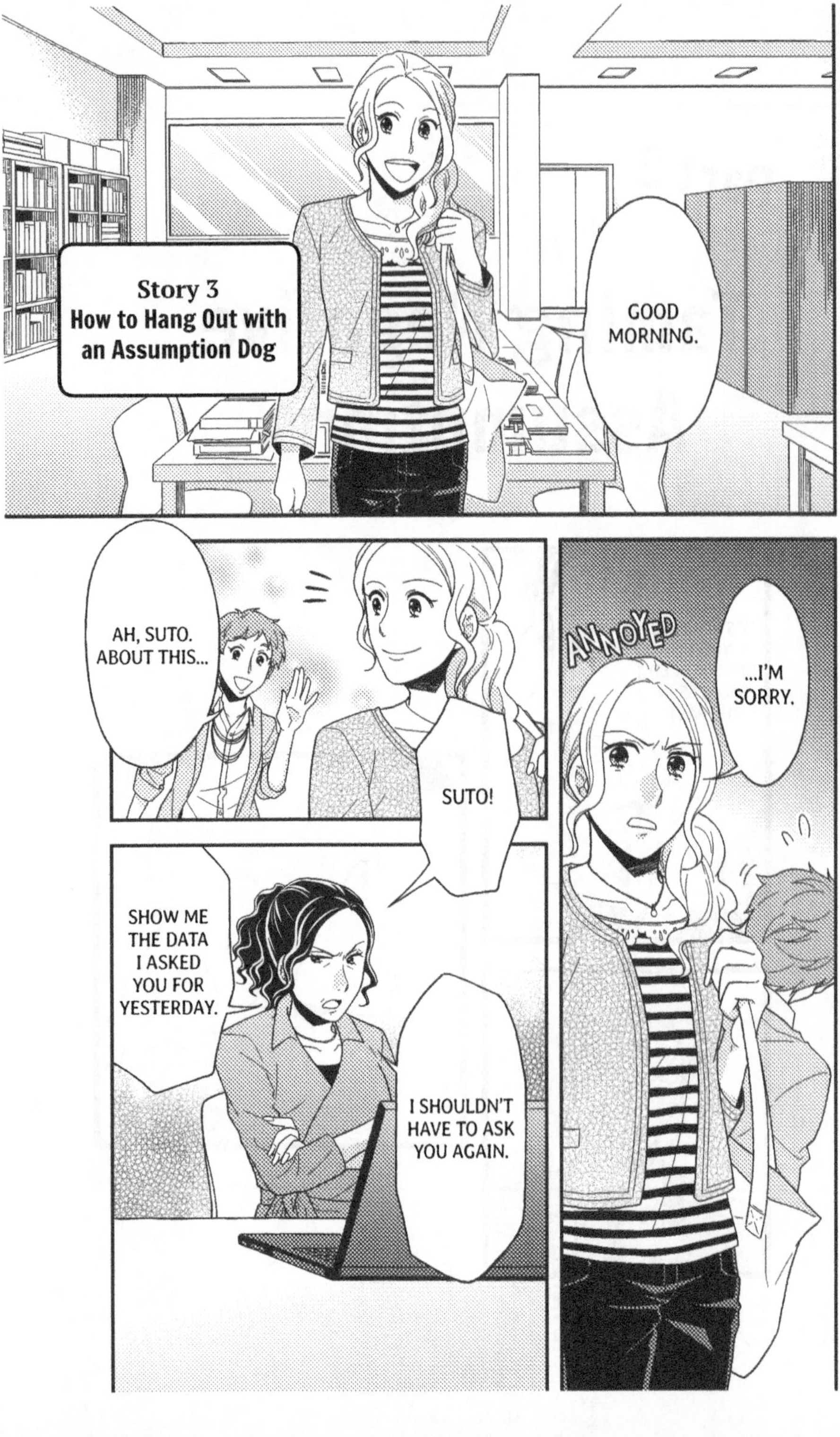
Story 3
How to Hang Out with an Assumption Dog
GOOD MORNING.
AH, SUTO. ABOUT THIS...
SUTO!
SHOW ME THE DATA I ASKED YOU FOR YESTERDAY.
I SHOULDN'T HAVE TO ASK YOU AGAIN.
ANNOYED
...I'M SORRY.

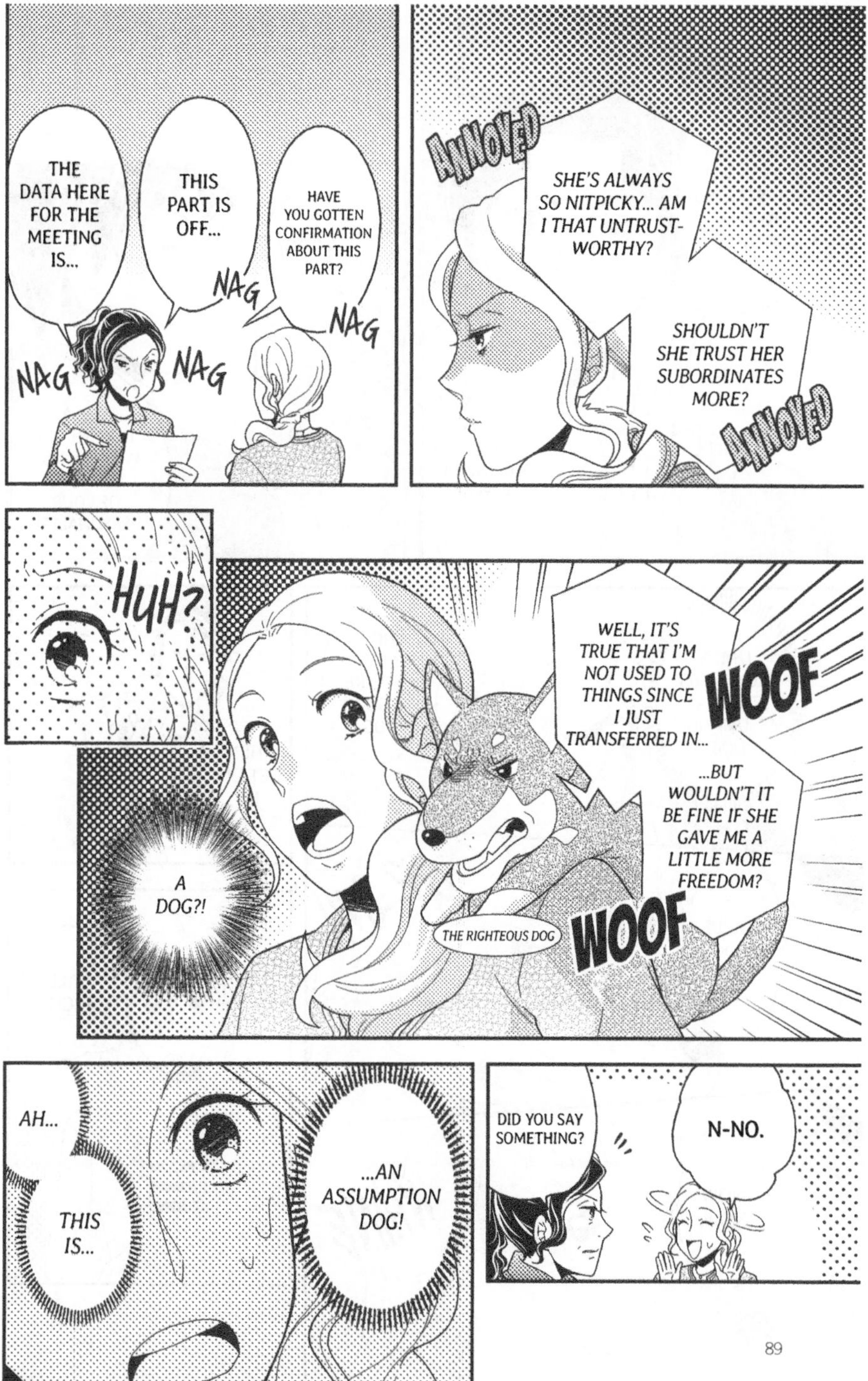

THE DATA HERE FOR THE MEETING IS...
THIS PART IS OFF...
HAVE YOU GOTTEN CONFIRMATION ABOUT THIS PART?
NAG
NAG
NAG
NAG
ANNOYED
SHE'S ALWAYS SO NITPICKY... AM I THAT UNTRUST-WORTHY?
SHOULDN'T SHE TRUST HER SUBORDINATES MORE?
ANNOYED
HUH?
A DOG?!
WELL, IT'S TRUE THAT I'M NOT USED TO THINGS SINCE I JUST TRANSFERRED IN...
...BUT WOULDN'T IT BE FINE IF SHE GAVE ME A LITTLE MORE FREEDOM?
WOOF
WOOF
THE RIGHTEOUS DOG
AH...
THIS IS...
...AN ASSUMPTION DOG!
DID YOU SAY SOMETHING?
N-NO.

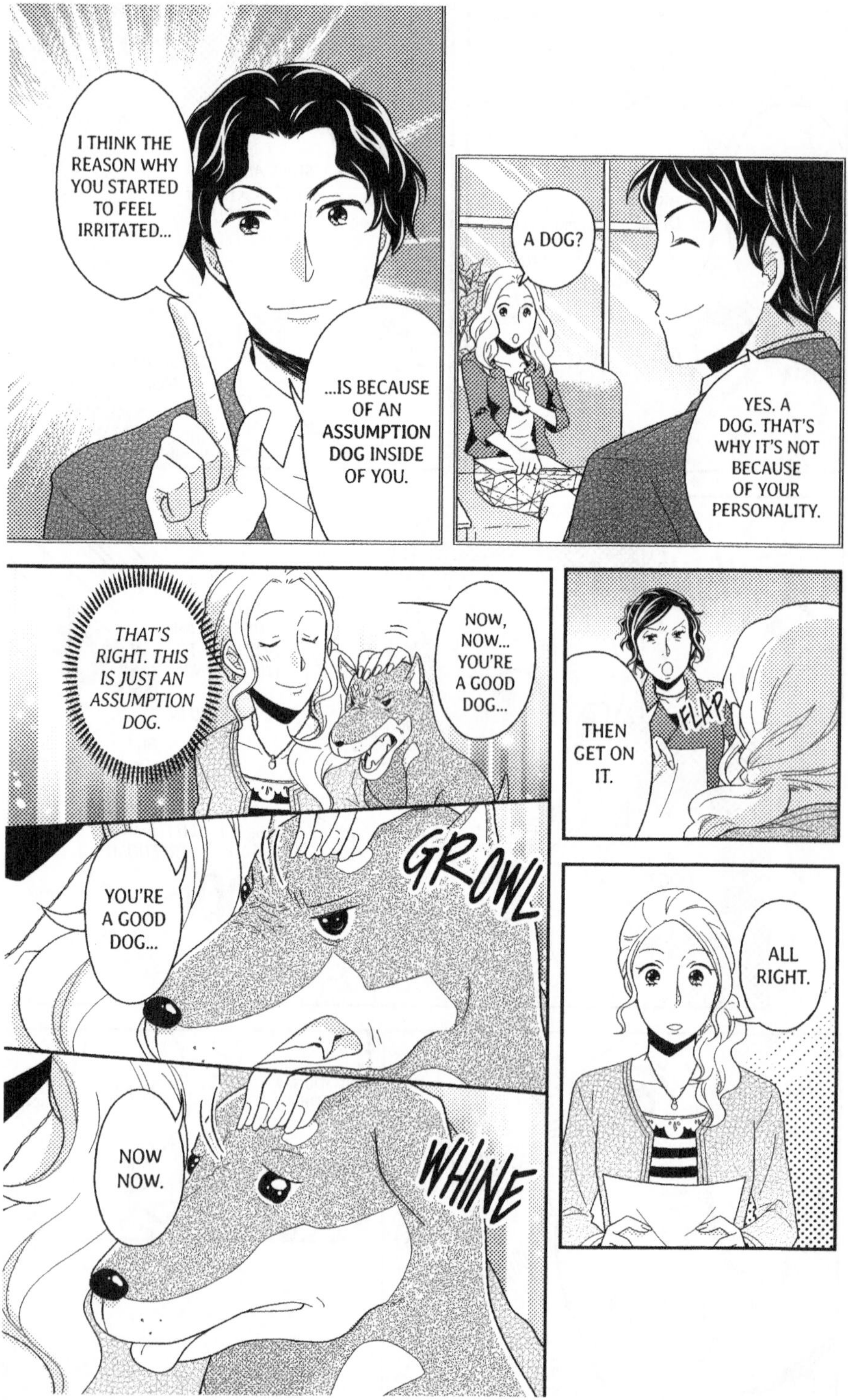
I THINK THE REASON WHY YOU STARTED TO FEEL IRRITATED...
...IS BECAUSE OF AN ASSUMPTION DOG INSIDE OF YOU.
A DOG?
YES. A DOG. THAT'S WHY IT'S NOT BECAUSE OF YOUR PERSONALITY.
THAT'S RIGHT. THIS IS JUST AN ASSUMPTION DOG.
NOW, NOW... YOU'RE A GOOD DOG...
THEN GET ON IT.
FLAP
YOU'RE A GOOD DOG...
GROWL
ALL RIGHT.
NOW NOW.
WHINE

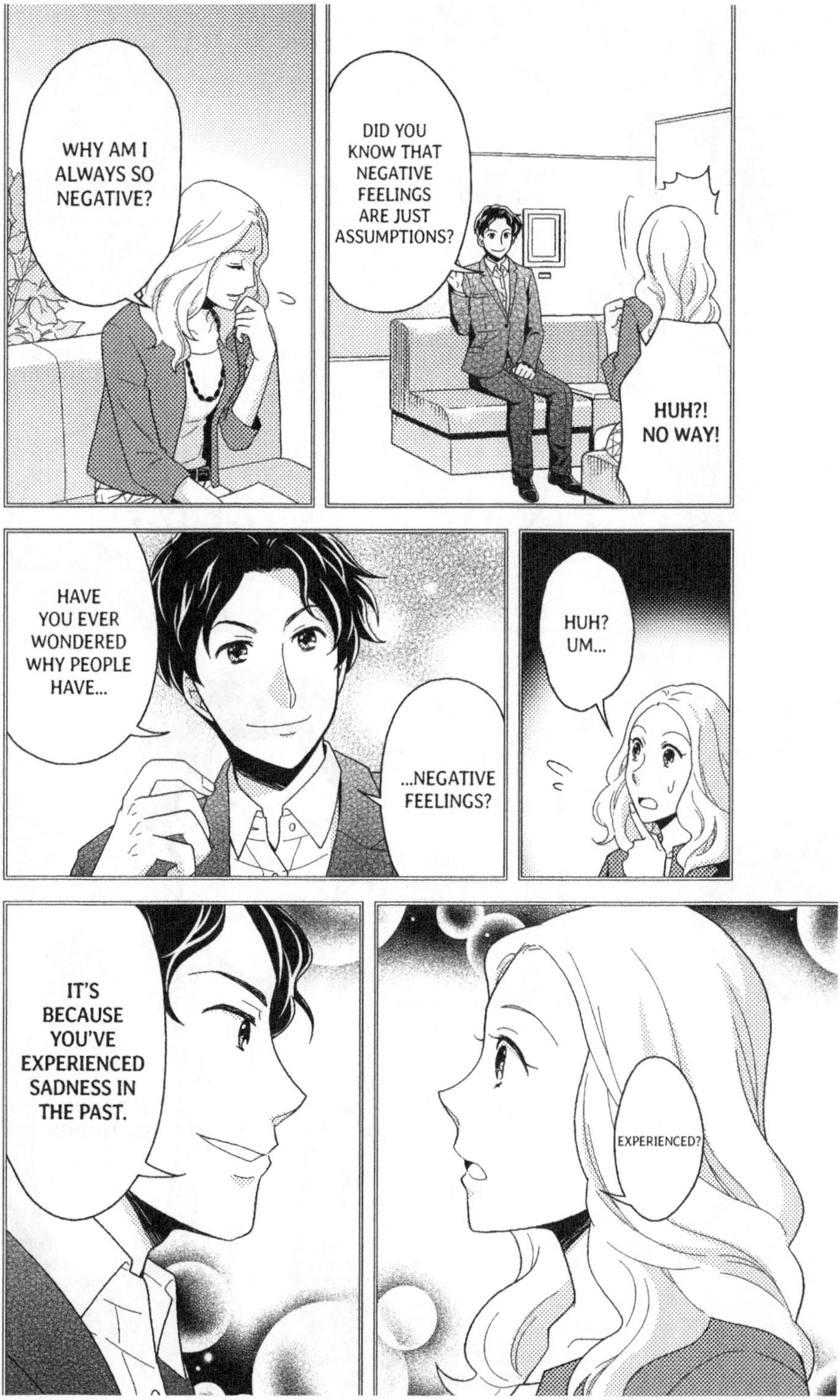
WHY AM I ALWAYS SO NEGATIVE?
DID YOU KNOW THAT NEGATIVE FEELINGS ARE JUST ASSUMPTIONS?
HUH?! NO WAY!
HAVE YOU EVER WONDERED WHY PEOPLE HAVE...
...NEGATIVE FEELINGS?
HUH? UM...
IT'S BECAUSE YOU'VE EXPERIENCED SADNESS IN THE PAST.
EXPERIENCED?

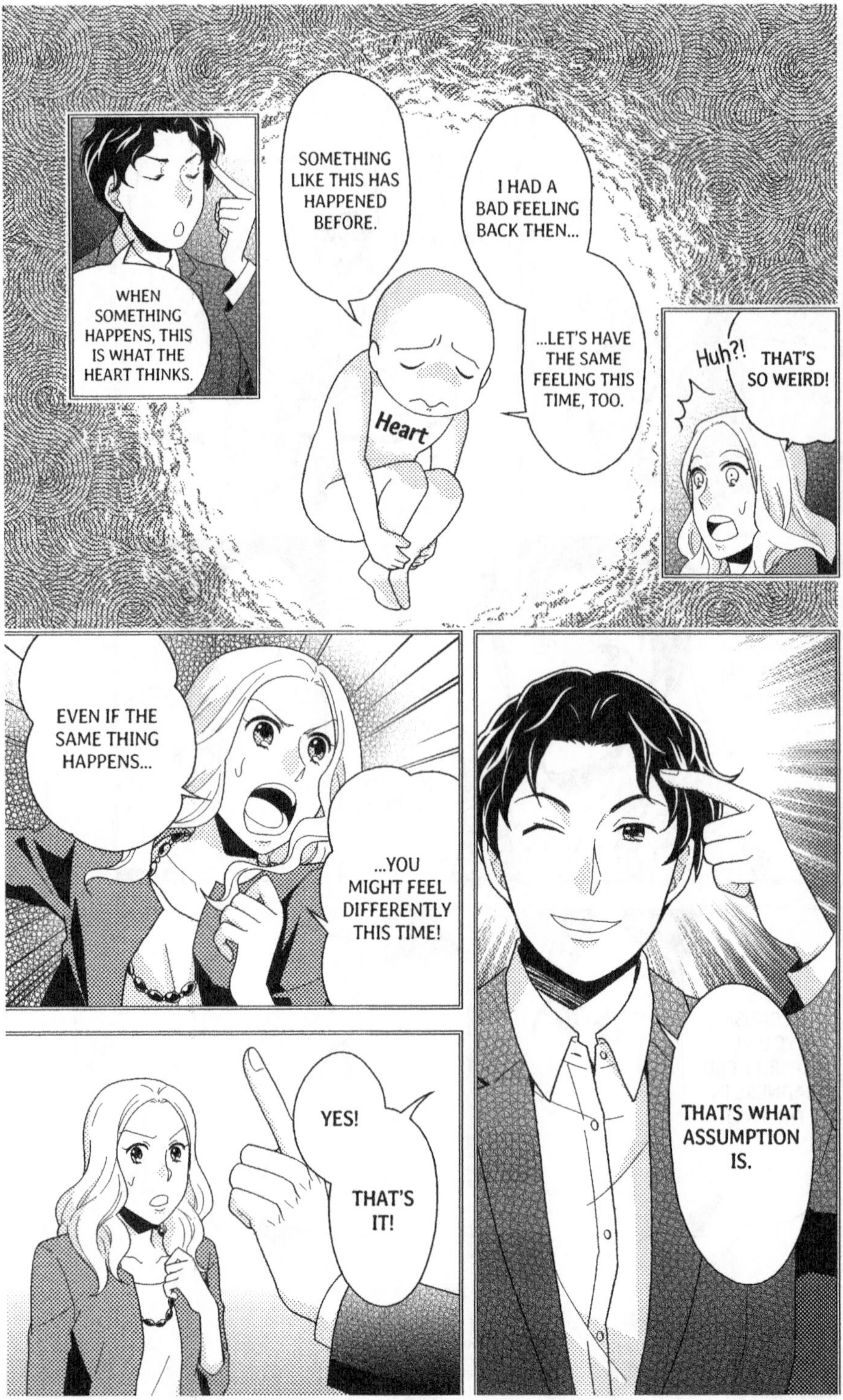
WHEN SOMETHING HAPPENS, THIS IS WHAT THE HEART THINKS.
SOMETHING LIKE THIS HAS HAPPENED BEFORE.
I HAD A BAD FEELING BACK THEN...
...LET'S HAVE THE SAME FEELING THIS TIME, TOO.
Heart
Huh?!
THAT'S SO WEIRD!
EVEN IF THE SAME THING HAPPENS...
...YOU MIGHT FEEL DIFFERENTLY THIS TIME!
THAT'S WHAT ASSUMPTION IS.
YES!
THAT'S IT!

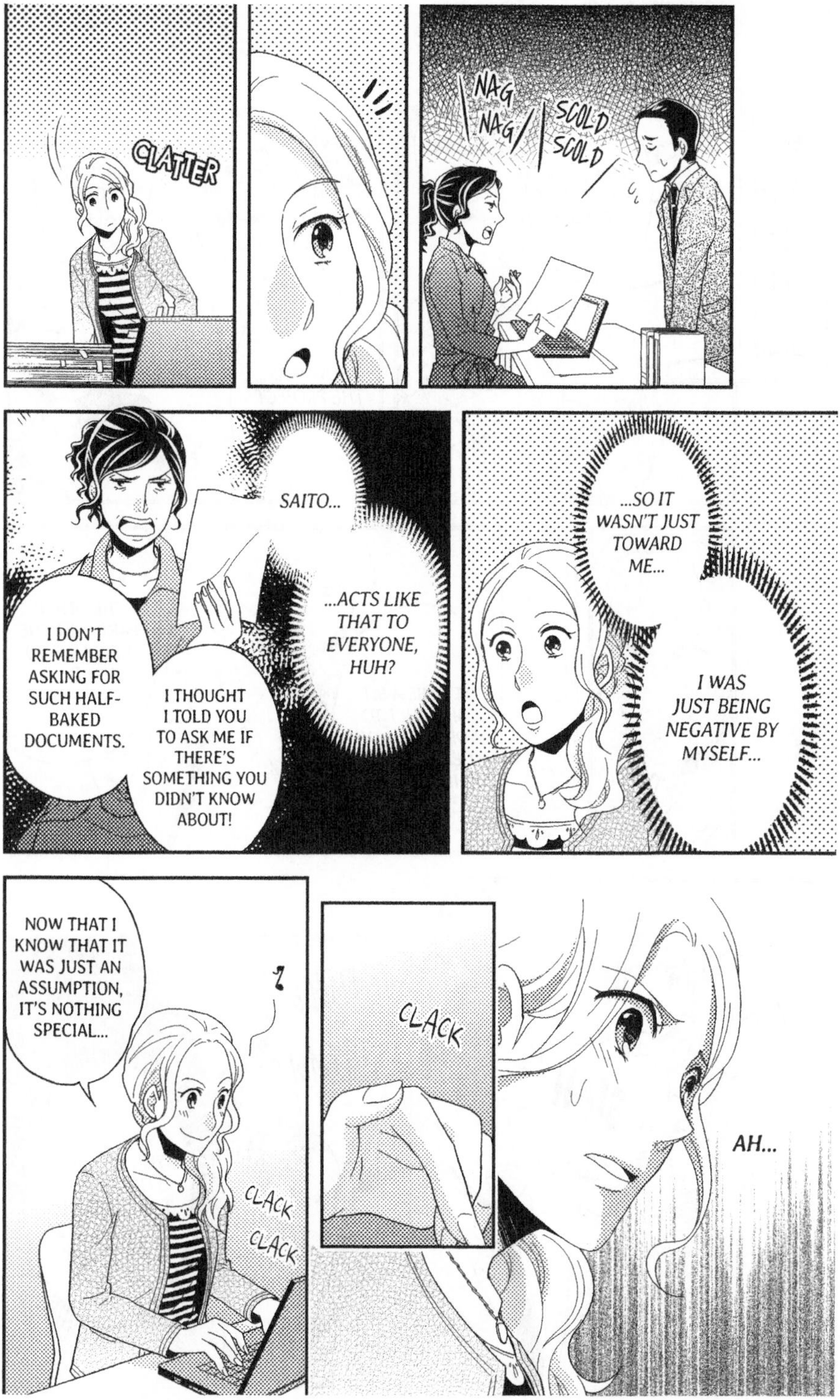
CLATTER
NAG NAG
SCOLD SCOLD
SAITO...
...ACTS LIKE THAT TO EVERYONE, HUH?
I DON'T REMEMBER ASKING FOR SUCH HALF-BAKED DOCUMENTS.
I THOUGHT I TOLD YOU TO ASK ME IF THERE'S SOMETHING YOU DIDN'T KNOW ABOUT!
...SO IT WASN'T JUST TOWARD ME...
I WAS JUST BEING NEGATIVE BY MYSELF...
NOW THAT I KNOW THAT IT WAS JUST AN ASSUMPTION, IT'S NOTHING SPECIAL...
CLACK
CLACK
CLACK
AH...

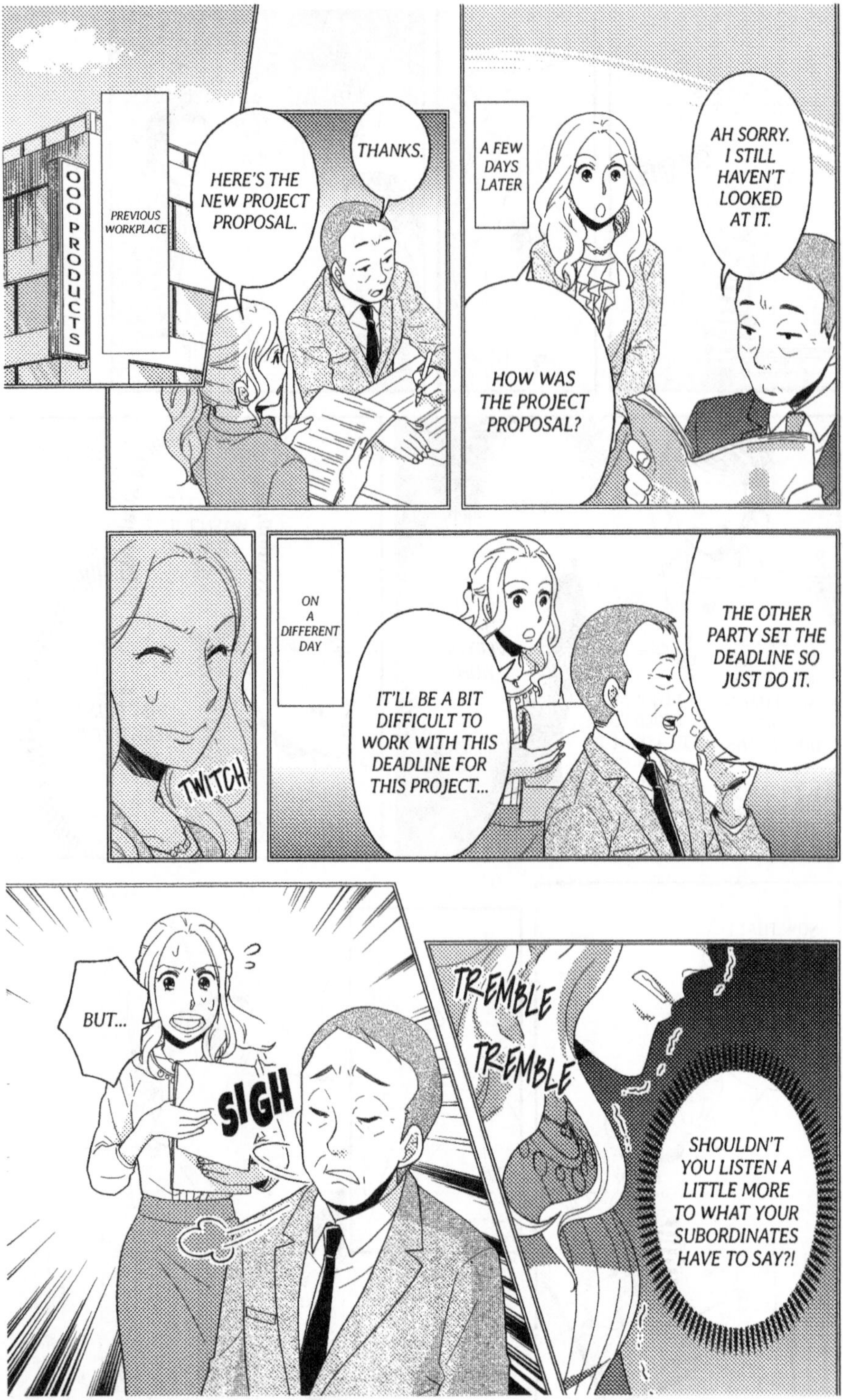
OOO PRODUCTS
PREVIOUS WORKPLACE
HERE'S THE NEW PROJECT PROPOSAL.
THANKS.
A FEW DAYS LATER
HOW WAS THE PROJECT PROPOSAL?
AH SORRY. I STILL HAVEN'T LOOKED AT IT.
ON A DIFFERENT DAY
IT'LL BE A BIT DIFFICULT TO WORK WITH THIS DEADLINE FOR THIS PROJECT...
THE OTHER PARTY SET THE DEADLINE SO JUST DO IT.
TWITCH
BUT...
SIGH
TREMBLE
TREMBLE
SHOULDN'T YOU LISTEN A LITTLE MORE TO WHAT YOUR SUBORDINATES HAVE TO SAY?!

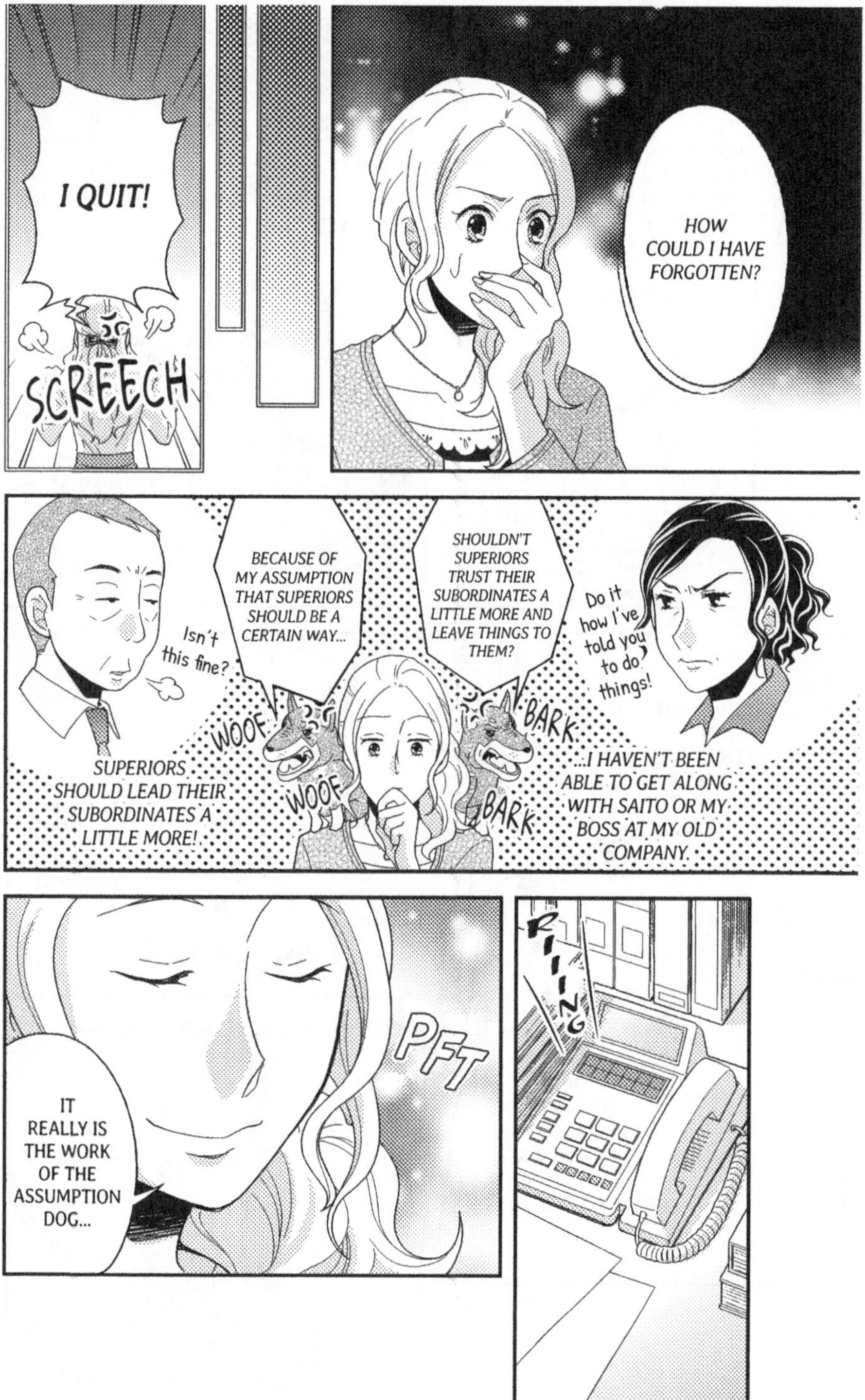
HOW COULD I HAVE FORGOTTEN?
I QUIT!
SCREECH
Do it how I've told you to do things!
SHOULDN'T SUPERIORS TRUST THEIR SUBORDINATES A LITTLE MORE AND LEAVE THINGS TO THEM?
BECAUSE OF MY ASSUMPTION THAT SUPERIORS SHOULD BE A CERTAIN WAY...
Isn't this fine?
BARK
BARK
WOOF
WOOF
...I HAVEN'T BEEN ABLE TO GET ALONG WITH SAITO OR MY BOSS AT MY OLD COMPANY.
SUPERIORS SHOULD LEAD THEIR SUBORDINATES A LITTLE MORE!
RIIING
PFT
IT REALLY IS THE WORK OF THE ASSUMPTION DOG...

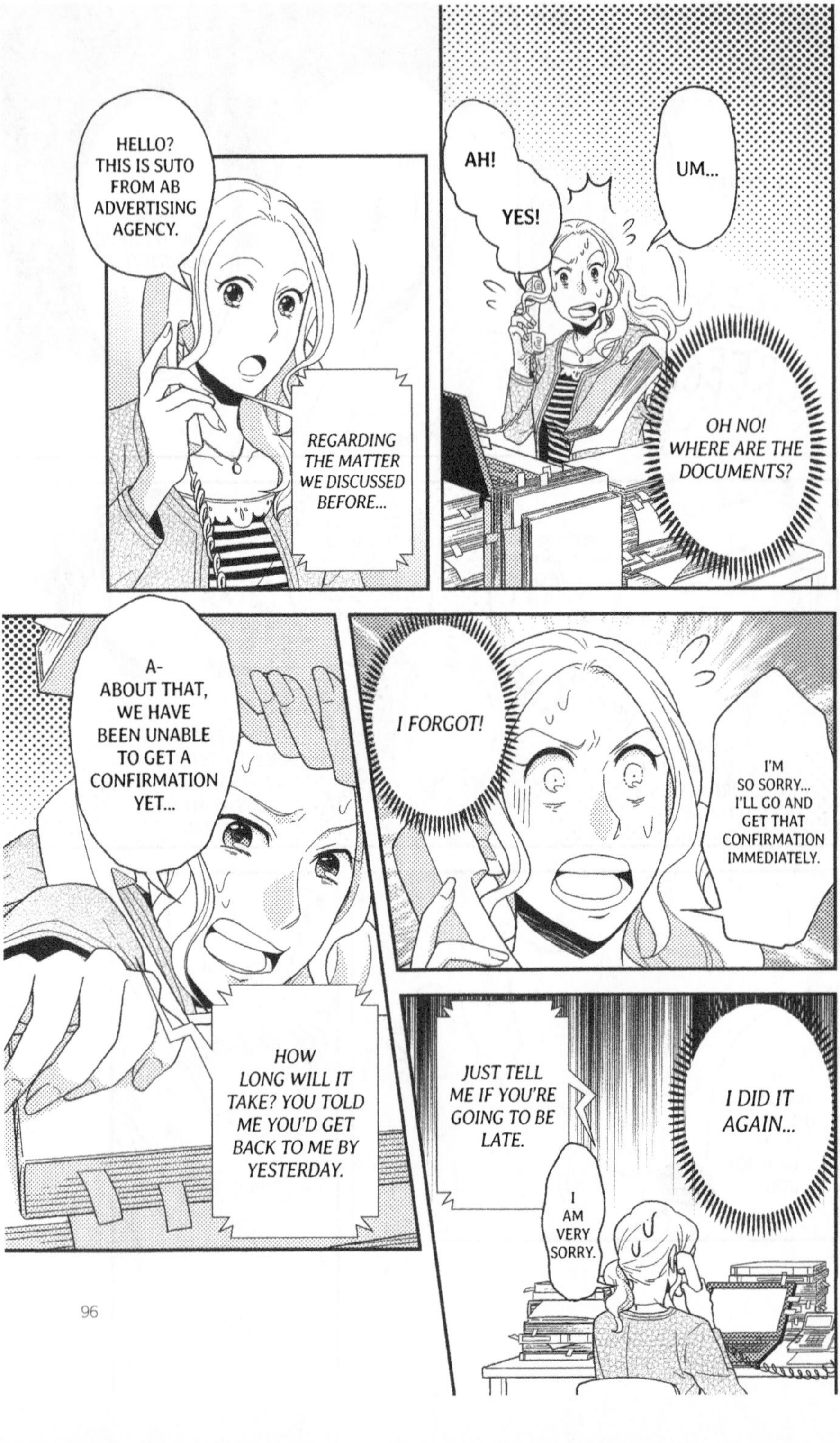
HELLO? THIS IS SUTO FROM AB ADVERTISING AGENCY.
REGARDING THE MATTER WE DISCUSSED BEFORE...
UM...
AH!
YES!
OH NO! WHERE ARE THE DOCUMENTS?
A- ABOUT THAT, WE HAVE BEEN UNABLE TO GET A CONFIRMATION YET...
HOW LONG WILL IT TAKE? YOU TOLD ME YOU'D GET BACK TO ME BY YESTERDAY.
I FORGOT!
I'M SO SORRY... I'LL GO AND GET THAT CONFIRMATION IMMEDIATELY.
JUST TELL ME IF YOU'RE GOING TO BE LATE.
I AM VERY SORRY.
I DID IT AGAIN...

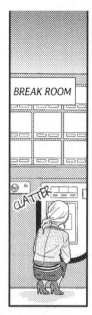

BREAK ROOM

CLATTER

I'M SO BAD AT MY JOB...

WHINE WHINE

LOSER DOG

I'M AWFUL AT HANDLING THINGS... I'M REALLY NO GOOD.

WHAT'S WRONG? NOT SLEEPING WELL AGAIN?

HASEGAWA.

NO...

I JUST MADE ANOTHER MISTAKE AT WORK...

SO THAT'S WHY YOU'RE FEELING DOWN RIGHT NOW?

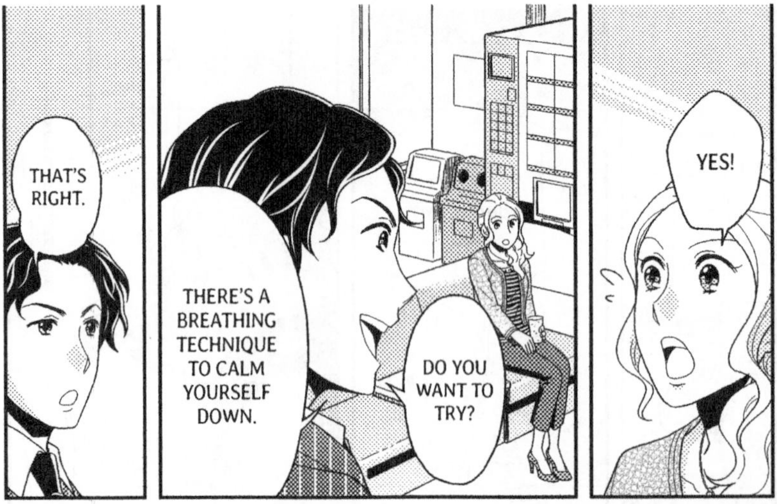
THAT'S RIGHT.
THERE'S A BREATHING TECHNIQUE TO CALM YOURSELF DOWN.
DO YOU WANT TO TRY?
YES!

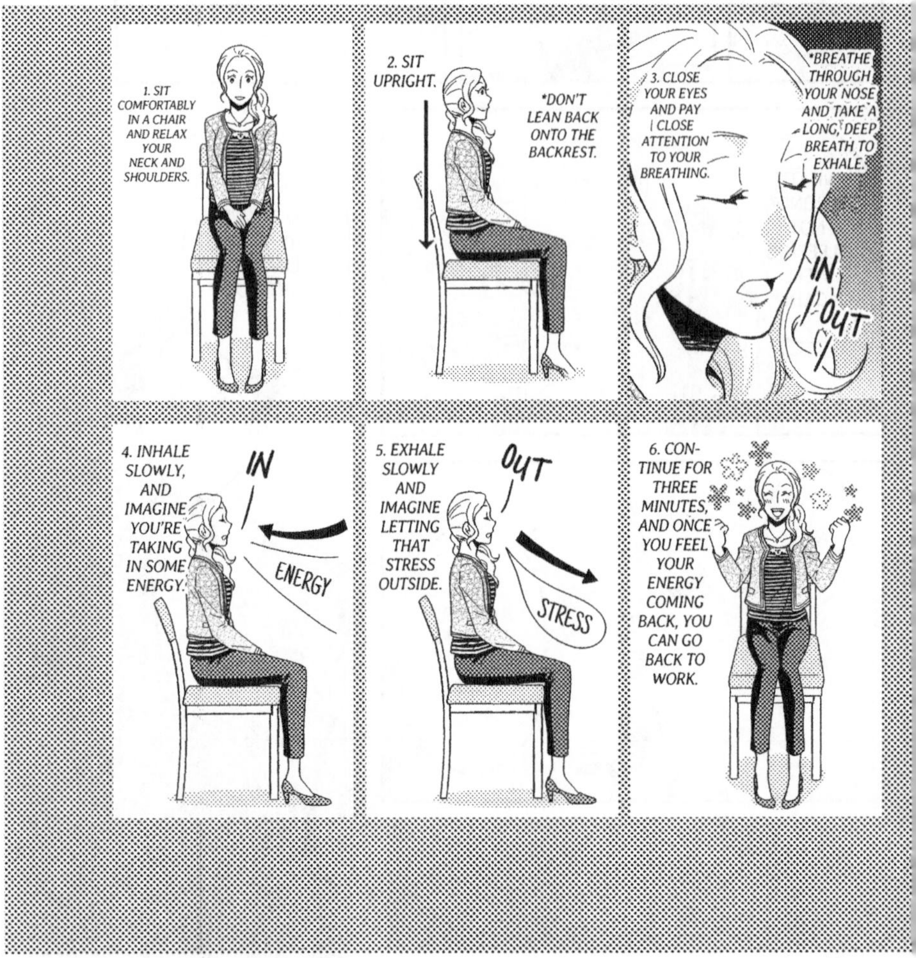
1. SIT COMFORTABLY IN A CHAIR AND RELAX YOUR NECK AND SHOULDERS.
2. SIT UPRIGHT.
*DON'T LEAN BACK ONTO THE BACKREST.
3. CLOSE YOUR EYES AND PAY CLOSE ATTENTION TO YOUR BREATHING.
*BREATHE THROUGH YOUR NOSE AND TAKE A LONG, DEEP BREATH TO EXHALE.
IN
OUT
4. INHALE SLOWLY, AND IMAGINE YOU'RE TAKING IN SOME ENERGY.
IN
ENERGY
5. EXHALE SLOWLY AND IMAGINE LETTING THAT STRESS OUTSIDE.
OUT
STRESS
6. CONTINUE FOR THREE MINUTES, AND ONCE YOU FEEL YOUR ENERGY COMING BACK, YOU CAN GO BACK TO WORK.

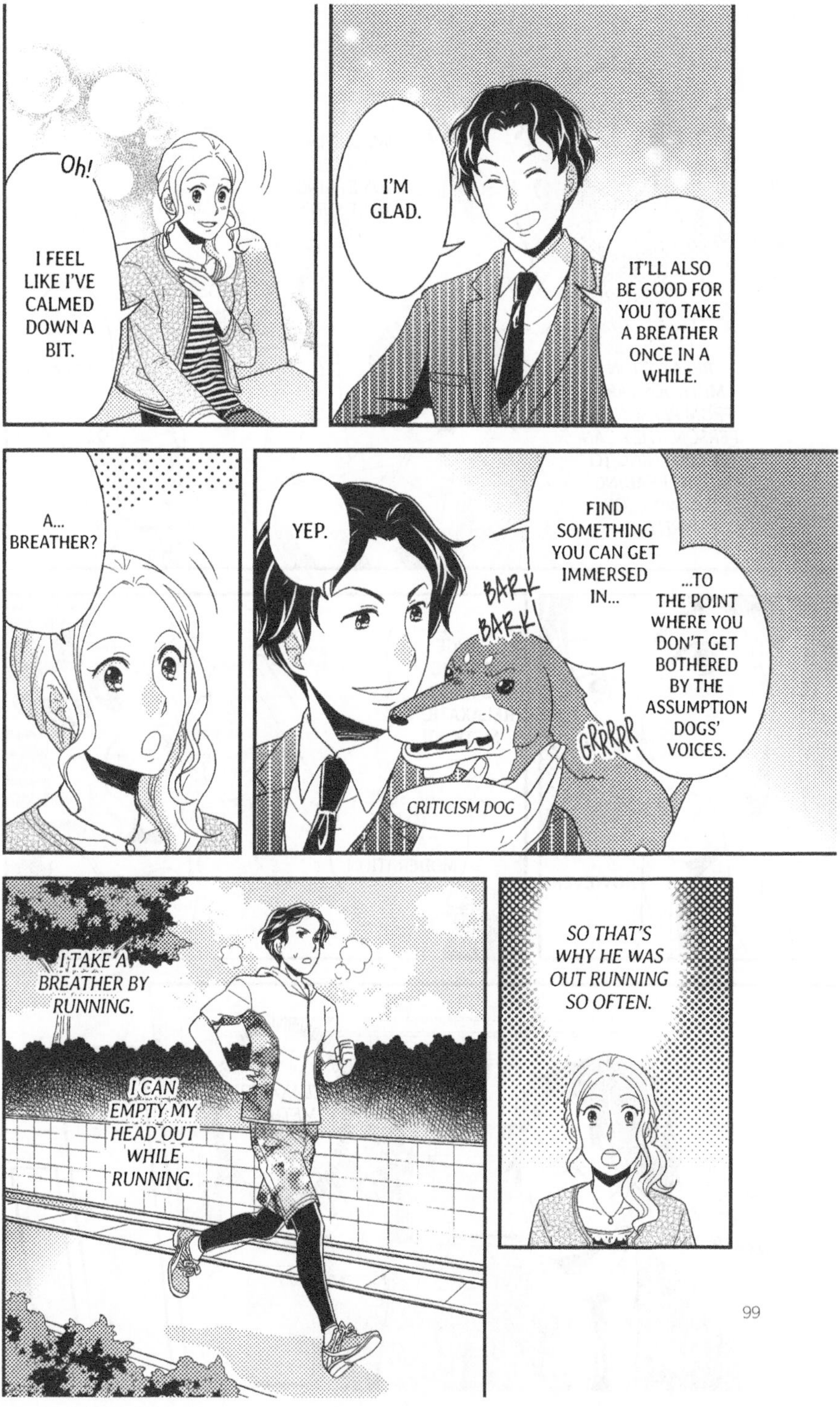
Oh!
I FEEL LIKE I'VE CALMED DOWN A BIT.
I'M GLAD.
IT'LL ALSO BE GOOD FOR YOU TO TAKE A BREATHER ONCE IN A WHILE.
A... BREATHER?
YEP.
FIND SOMETHING YOU CAN GET IMMERSED IN...
...TO THE POINT WHERE YOU DON'T GET BOTHERED BY THE ASSUMPTION DOGS' VOICES.
BARK BARK
GRRRRR
CRITICISM DOG
I TAKE A BREATHER BY RUNNING.
I CAN EMPTY MY HEAD OUT WHILE RUNNING.
SO THAT'S WHY HE WAS OUT RUNNING SO OFTEN.

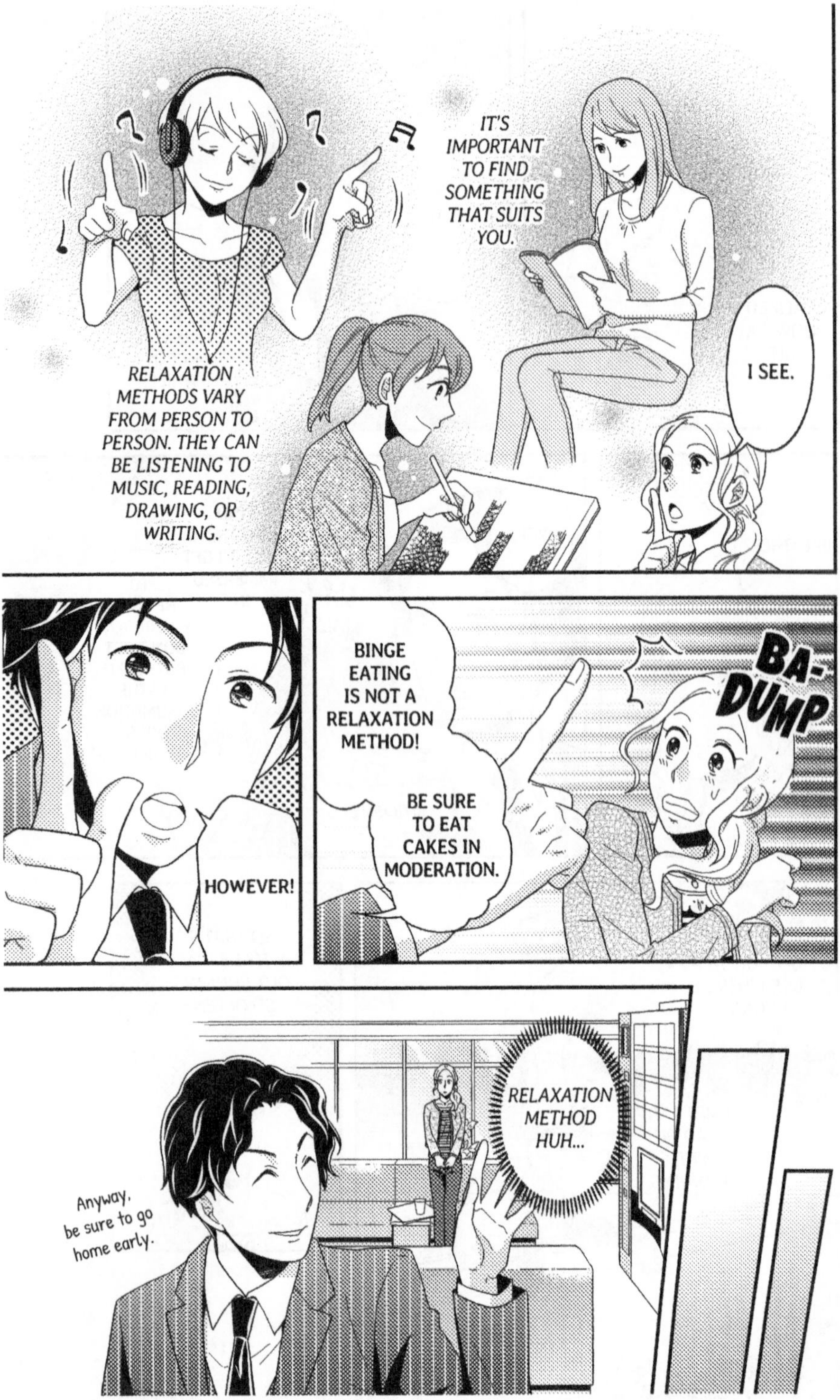

RELAXATION METHODS VARY FROM PERSON TO PERSON. THEY CAN BE LISTENING TO MUSIC, READING, DRAWING, OR WRITING.
IT'S IMPORTANT TO FIND SOMETHING THAT SUITS YOU.
I SEE.
HOWEVER!
BINGE EATING IS NOT A RELAXATION METHOD!
BE SURE TO EAT CAKES IN MODERATION.
BA-DUMP
Anyway, be sure to go home early.
RELAXATION METHOD HUH...

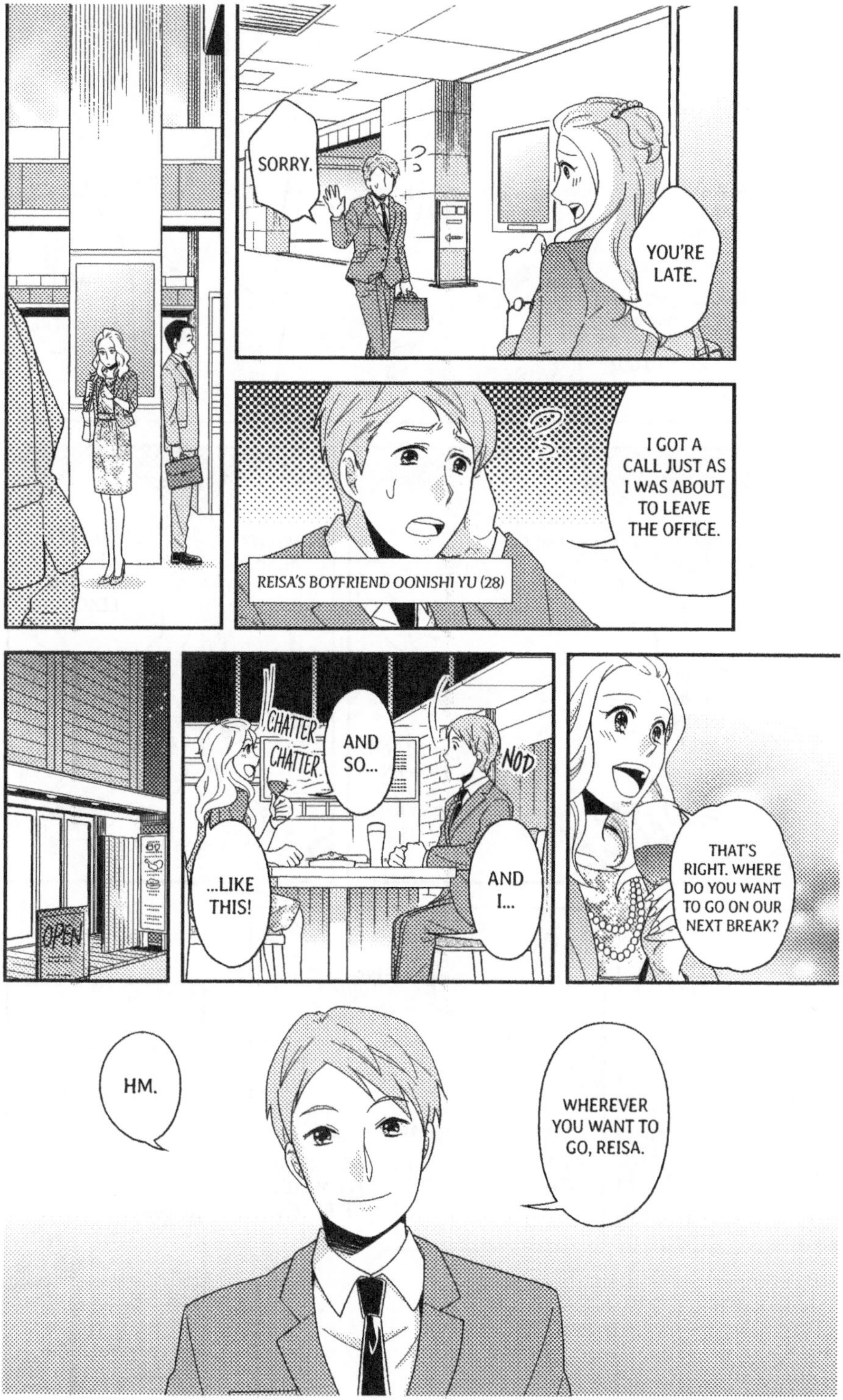
SORRY.
YOU'RE LATE.
I GOT A CALL JUST AS I WAS ABOUT TO LEAVE THE OFFICE.
REISA'S BOYFRIEND OONISHI YU (28)
CHATTER CHATTER
AND SO...
...LIKE THIS!
NOD
AND I...
THAT'S RIGHT. WHERE DO YOU WANT TO GO ON OUR NEXT BREAK?
HM.
WHEREVER YOU WANT TO GO, REISA.
OPEN

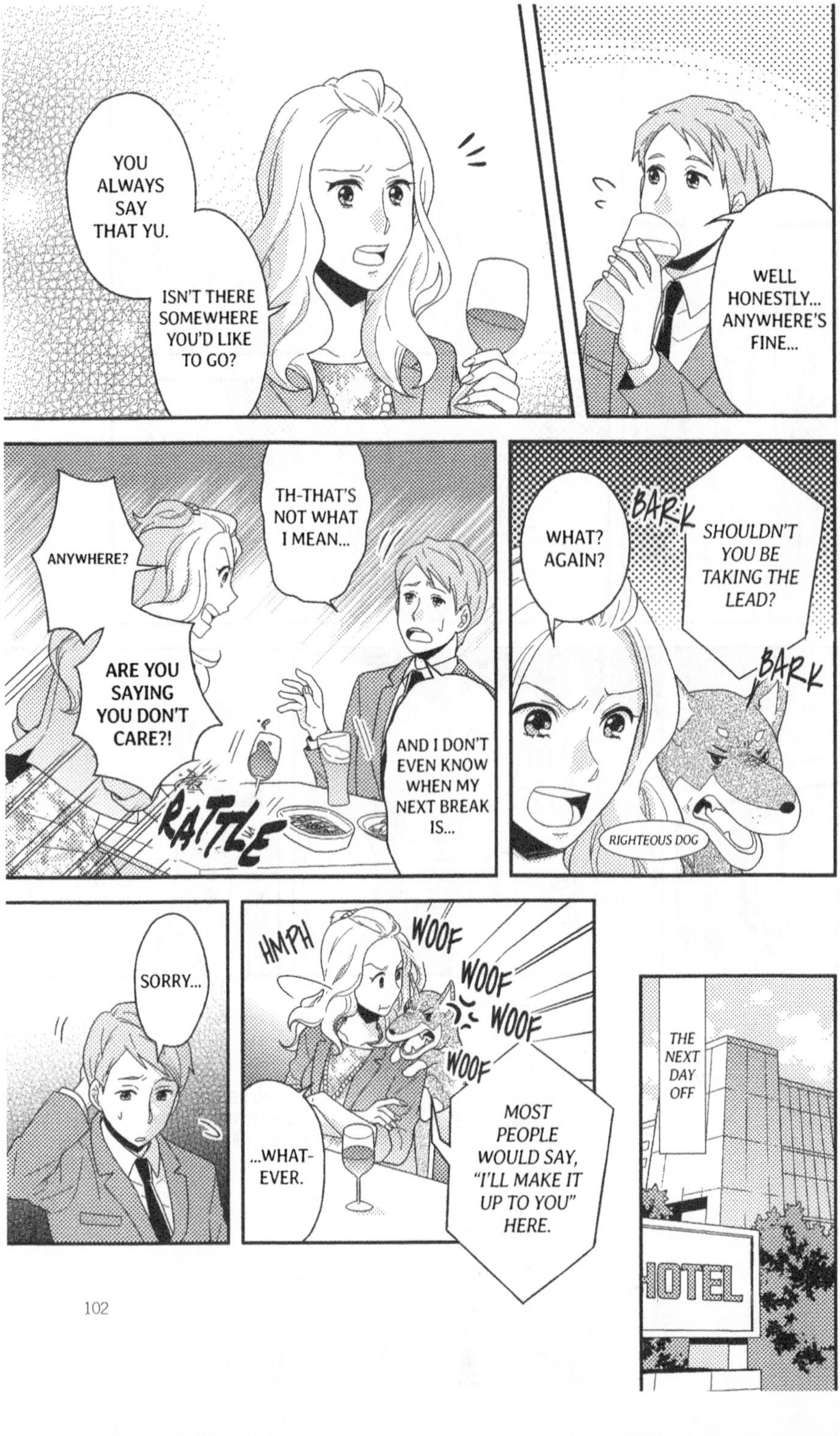
YOU ALWAYS SAY THAT YU.
ISN'T THERE SOMEWHERE YOU'D LIKE TO GO?
WELL HONESTLY... ANYWHERE'S FINE...
ANYWHERE?
ARE YOU SAYING YOU DON'T CARE?!
TH-THAT'S NOT WHAT I MEAN...
AND I DON'T EVEN KNOW WHEN MY NEXT BREAK IS...
RATTLE
WHAT? AGAIN?
BARK
SHOULDN'T YOU BE TAKING THE LEAD?
BARK
RIGHTEOUS DOG
SORRY...
HMPH
WOOF
WOOF
WOOF
WOOF
...WHAT-EVER.
MOST PEOPLE WOULD SAY, "I'LL MAKE IT UP TO YOU" HERE.
THE NEXT DAY OFF
HOTEL

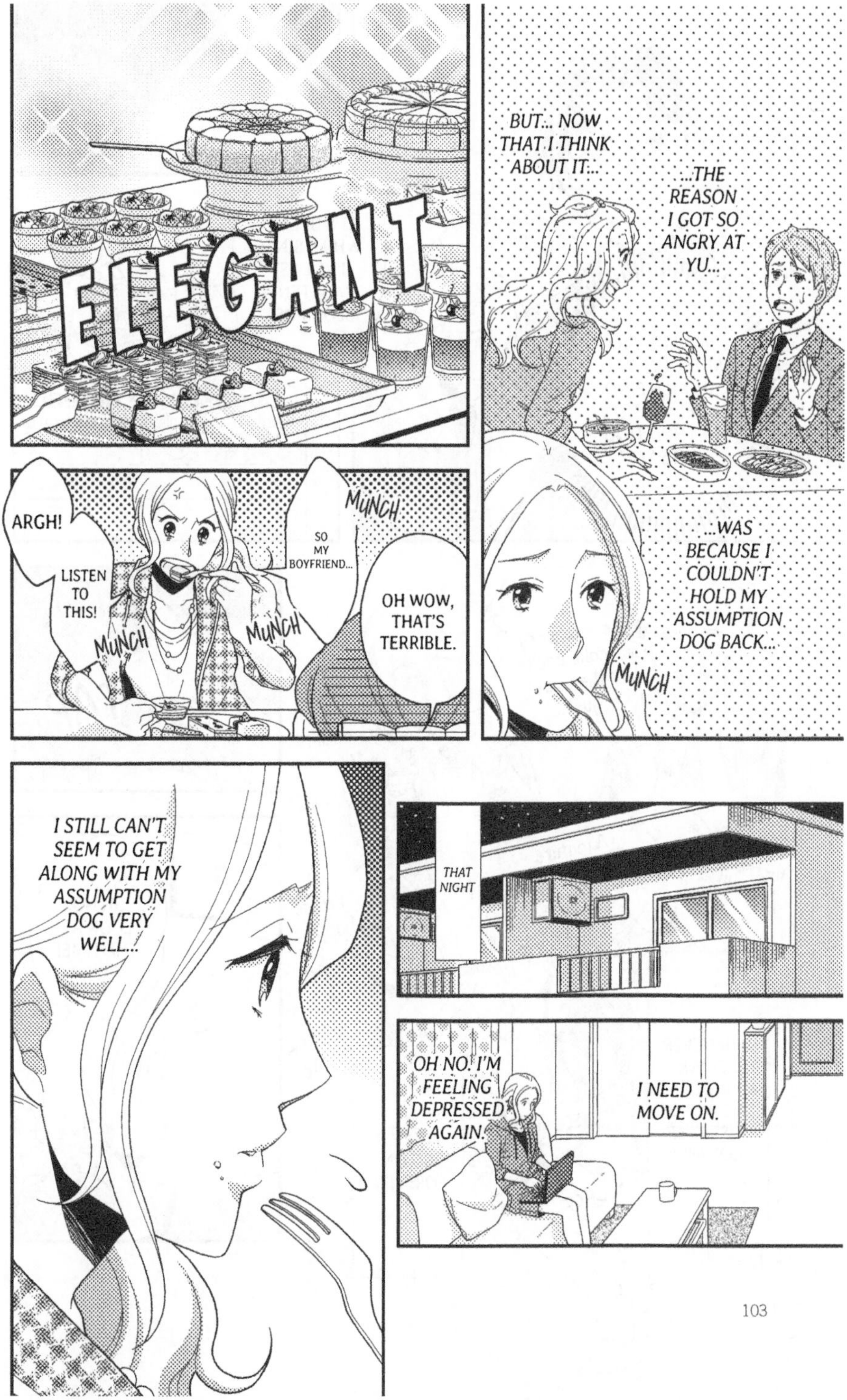
ELEGANT
BUT... NOW THAT I THINK ABOUT IT...
...THE REASON I GOT SO ANGRY AT YU...
ARGH!
LISTEN TO THIS!
MUNCH
SO MY BOYFRIEND...
MUNCH
MUNCH
OH WOW, THAT'S TERRIBLE.
...WAS BECAUSE I COULDN'T HOLD MY ASSUMPTION DOG BACK...
MUNCH
I STILL CAN'T SEEM TO GET ALONG WITH MY ASSUMPTION DOG VERY WELL...
THAT NIGHT
OH NO. I'M FEELING DEPRESSED AGAIN.
I NEED TO MOVE ON.

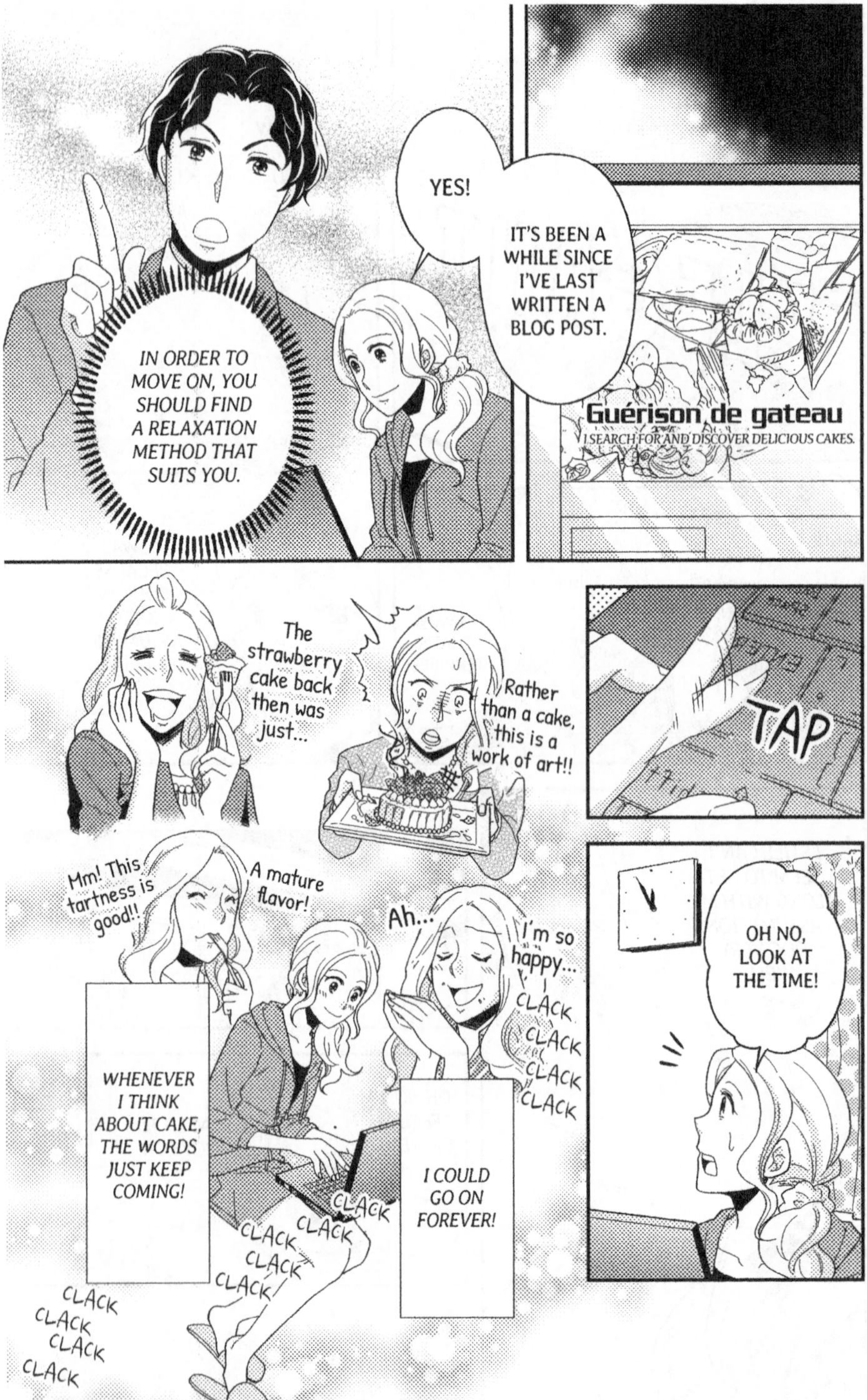
IN ORDER TO MOVE ON, YOU SHOULD FIND A RELAXATION METHOD THAT SUITS YOU.
YES!
IT'S BEEN A WHILE SINCE I'VE LAST WRITTEN A BLOG POST.
Guérison de gateau
I SEARCH FOR AND DISCOVER DELICIOUS CAKES.
TAP
The strawberry cake back then was just...
Rather than a cake, this is a work of art!!
Mm! This tartness is good!!
A mature flavor!
Ah...
I'm so happy...
CLACK CLACK CLACK CLACK
WHENEVER I THINK ABOUT CAKE, THE WORDS JUST KEEP COMING!
I COULD GO ON FOREVER!
CLACK CLACK CLACK CLACK CLACK
CLACK CLACK CLACK CLACK
OH NO, LOOK AT THE TIME!

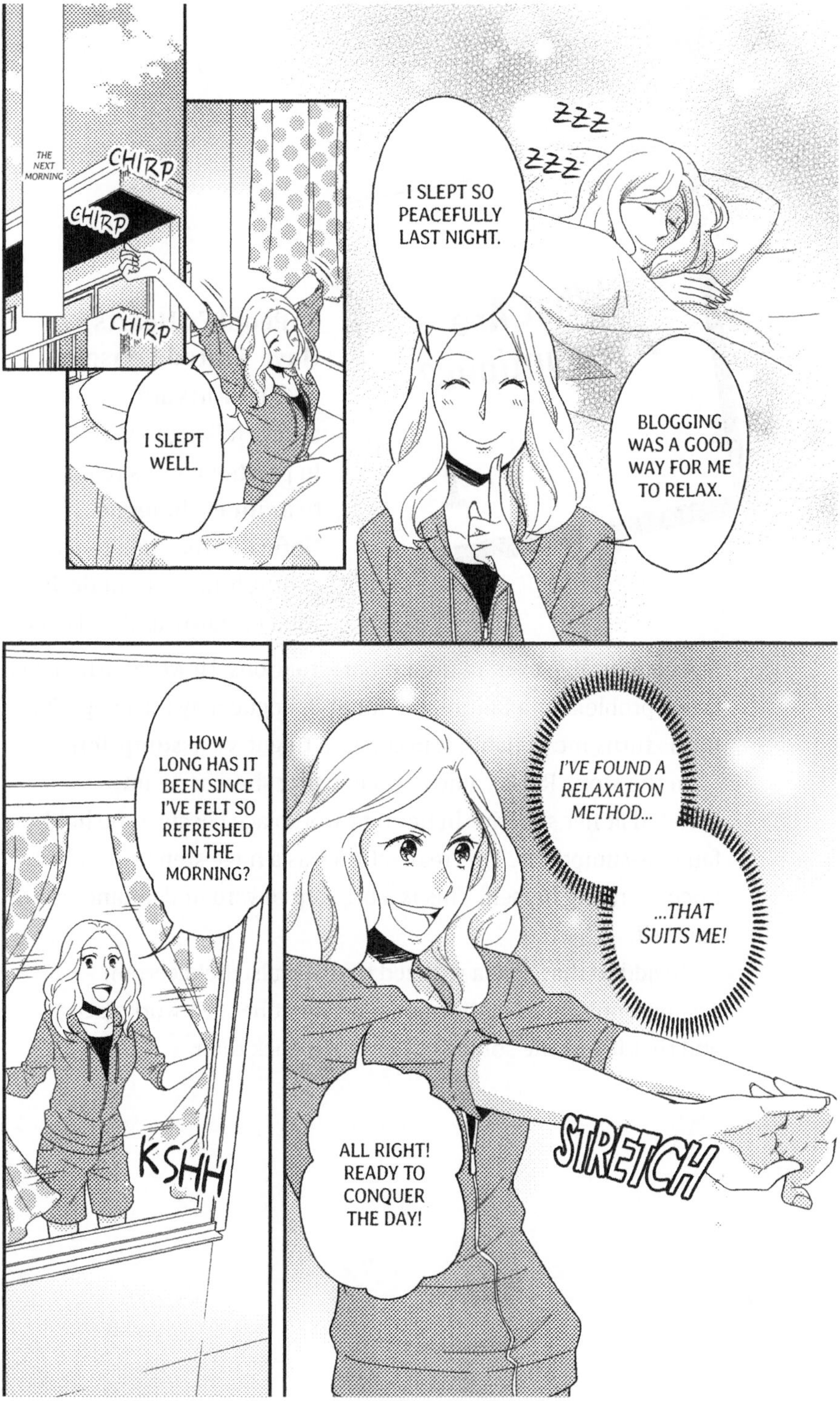
THE NEXT MORNING
CHIRP
CHIRP
CHIRP
I SLEPT WELL.
ZZZ
ZZZ
I SLEPT SO PEACEFULLY LAST NIGHT.
BLOGGING WAS A GOOD WAY FOR ME TO RELAX.
HOW LONG HAS IT BEEN SINCE I'VE FELT SO REFRESHED IN THE MORNING?
KSHH
I'VE FOUND A RELAXATION METHOD...
...THAT SUITS ME!
STRETCH
ALL RIGHT! READY TO CONQUER THE DAY!

What Are Assumptions?

1

⇨ **People's Hearts Have Tinted Lenses**

Our hearts are always talking to us. In psychology, it's referred to as **inner dialogue**. Normally, they talk to us gently, bring out our desires, calm us down, and make us feel comfortable even in unfamiliar situations. However, when you face a problem or a failure, the inner dialogue may turn negative. If this turns into a habit, it becomes a **negative assumption**.

In the story, Reisa came to realize that she was feeling irritated at her superior in her new workplace because she held faulty assumptions. This realization was a huge step toward her understanding herself. This is a big step toward understanding yourself.

To add to that, Reisa realized that she also held certain assumptions about her former superior at her last workplace and that it was the source of her stress back then.

If you start to understand your assumption patterns toward others, you may be able to come to a better understanding of your interpersonal relationships.

Occurrences are neutral, neither good nor bad. However, depending on the person, the way they view them varies. Even if they face the same situation, they may react or behave differently.

Imagine that there are tinted lenses inside the heart. We interpret various situations through them. The colors of these lenses differ from person to person, so even if someone goes through the same experience, they may interpret that experience differently. Some things that don't mean anything to you could be stressful for others.

⇨ The Mechanisms of Assumptions and Emotions

Let us take a look at what Reisa went through at her workplace.

Situation: Reisa's boss gave some very detailed criticism about the way she works.

Interpretation: She thinks, "A superior should trust her subordinates a little more."

Emotion: She feels irritated, and the feeling of anger is born.

Action: Her dissatisfaction is shown on her face and in her attitude.

Reisa was irritated by her boss who nitpicks. I can sympathize with that irritation. I don't do too well with superiors who micromanage. There were times when I wondered, "Why do they have to nitpick that much?"

But my colleague, who was also working under the same person, simply replied with "Understood" when they were warned about their performance. They just honestly accepted it, and it didn't seem like they paid much mind to it. I asked why, and they just responded with, "I think they're just pointing out the areas I'm lacking in, while thinking about my growth."

Other colleagues lost confidence and fell into a slump after being warned. They would ask, "Am I going to be able to keep working for this company?"

People interpret things differently. Emotions and attitudes vary from person to person. People look at the world with their own assumptions, as if they are wearing glasses with tinted lenses.

Both positive and negative assumptions about other people's behavior can become triggers for anger and anxiety. These assumptions are engraved into your memory from past experiences. If you have experienced painful heartbreaks, huge failures, situations that brought hopelessness or despair, you may have had some negative assumptions created inside of you.

⇨ Learn to Control Your Emotions

The more emotional a person is, the more likely that they will have their minds controlled by negative assumptions. As a result, they may be troubled by impulsive actions they are unable to control.

In order to not let negative emotions turn into a vicious cycle, it is important to recognize the negative assumption that is at the root of the emotion. This is the first step in getting better control over your emotions. On top of that, you will need to handle your emotions rationally.

Taming
Assumptions

2

⇨ **The Seven Types of Negative Assumptions**

The psychologist Dr. Ilona Boniwell put assumptions into seven categories. To make it easier to remember them, I have added "dog" to the end of each name.

By adding the word *dog* to the end of the assumptions, I have tried to simplify how you look at them. You were not born with assumptions. Consequently, you can view them in a carefree manner. For example, you can tell yourself, "The assumption dog just happened to settle down inside my heart." Isn't it a bit easier to accept an assumption if you view it as just an assumption, and not the personality you were born with?

There may be several assumption dogs that have settled inside your heart from things you have gone through in your past. Whenever you encounter a problem, they bark inside of your heart and make you feel unsettled. They then develop some negative emotions that can become the trigger to problematic actions.

Anyone can have assumption dogs. However, it's up to each and every one of us to decide on how to handle these dogs. Let's take a look at the various assumption dogs.

⇨ The Righteous Dog (The "Should Be" Mindset)

This assumption's trait is that it thinks that things should be a certain way. This righteous dog was living inside Reisa's head. The "should be" mindset of the righteous dog causes stubborn views to cycle inside your head. The following are examples of negative self-talk that the righteous dog generates:

- You shouldn't do that.
- That's unfair.
- That sort of thinking is wrong.

As a result of this thinking, you may become irritated by another person and show negative emotions such as anger and jealousy.

Those who have these "should be" thoughts strongly believe that others should be a certain way and may feel irked by those who don't meet their expectations. Their relationships may especially worsen with those who also have the same righteous dog type of thinking. In Reisa's case, her superior also had a righteous dog inside her head, so the irritation from both sides heated up.

Even with child-rearing, parents who strongly believe that things should be a certain way may feel constant irritation toward their child. You also might end up feeling irritated at yourself because of the high hurdles you have set for yourself. If the righteous dog barks a little too much, you may need to even discard it.

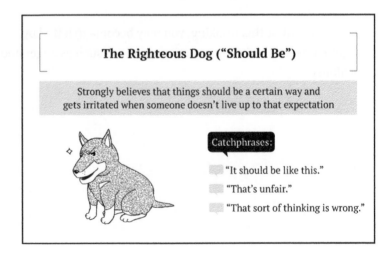

The Righteous Dog ("Should Be")

Strongly believes that things should be a certain way and gets irritated when someone doesn't live up to that expectation

Catchphrases:

"It should be like this."

"That's unfair."

"That sort of thinking is wrong."

Taming Negative Assumptions

⇨ The Loser Dog (The Devaluing Mindset)

Losing confidence because you're concerned about what you can't do or what skills you lack or having devaluing assumptions that come from negative emotions such as sadness, depression, and embarrassment are traits of the loser dog. People with assumptions of this type often say these things:

• "I'm a useless human being."
• "Others can do much better than I can."
• "I'm so pathetic. I can't even do something like this."

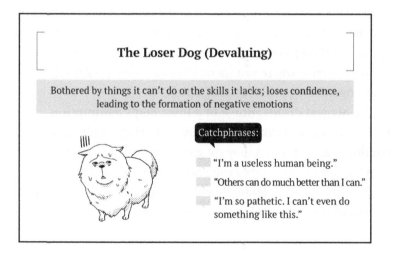

The Loser Dog (Devaluing)

Bothered by things it can't do or the skills it lacks; loses confidence, leading to the formation of negative emotions

Catchphrases:

"I'm a useless human being."

"Others can do much better than I can."

"I'm so pathetic. I can't even do something like this."

113

In our story, Reisa, who was unable to get used to the work at her new workplace, had this assumption going around in her head. Her mindset was so overwhelmed by the loser dog that it caused her heart to get tired so much so that she couldn't even sleep at night.

If you are caught by this assumption, you may become bothered by thoughts such as "Won't others laugh at me if I fail?" "Won't I receive a bad evaluation?" You may become excessively wary about the eyes of others and avoid failure as much as possible.

When things don't go well, you may think that you're no good, and your confidence may drop even lower. You may also compare yourself to your colleagues and develop an inferiority complex.

When you feel inferior to others, your self-esteem falls and you end up with an extreme fear of being compared to others. You may also avoid doing work that requires you to state your opinion or doing a presentation in front of others. You may end up in a dilemma where you spend too much time preparing, resulting in being unable to take action.

The **biggest disadvantage of a loser dog's assumption is that they avoid taking action because they don't have confidence.** Even when they are given a great chance, if they turn it down by saying they can't do it, then they will not be able to show off their true strength and consequently will not be able to demonstrate personal or professional growth.

The loser dog inside the heart becomes an internal obstacle and may cause you to abandon your efforts toward personal growth. You should get rid of the loser dog if you have one!

⇨ The Worrywart Dog (The Pessimistic Mindset)

The worrywart assumption dog has fears about the future and makes you worry that things won't go well. If something doesn't go well, you may become anxious, thinking that things will fail from now on too. This pessimistic thinking turns into a habit.

Anxiety leads to the distrust of your own ability and makes you lose hope for the future. The worrywart dog fills your head with thoughts such as these:

- "Nothing's going well."
- "I'm sure this problem will spread to other things."
- "Things probably won't go well if I date this person."

According to research, the three main sources of stress in the workplace are personal relationships, nerve-wracking jobs, and overwork. Additional reasons for stress include worries about the future of the company, post-retirement concerns, and issues related to promotions and raises.

People who have jobs that require them to predict what's up ahead are most at risk of falling victim to the worrywart dog. Constantly focusing on what might happen in the future can be extremely stressful. If they end up predicting a negative future, they may end up with the habit of thinking pessimistically.

The worrywart dog may become an assumption habit for those who work jobs in accounting, finance, legal affairs, safety management, and administration.

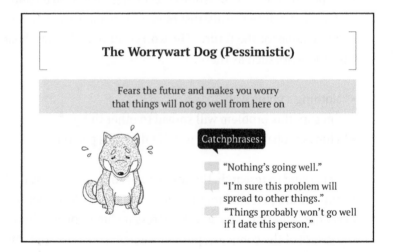

The Worrywart Dog (Pessimistic)

Fears the future and makes you worry that things will not go well from here on

Catchphrases:

"Nothing's going well."

"I'm sure this problem will spread to other things."

"Things probably won't go well if I date this person."

In addition, if you bring the worrywort dog mindset into your private life, you may excessively worry about family finances or your children's education. This may result in distressing family members, so you may need to take action to get rid of this dog.

⇨ The Abandoning Dog (The Powerless Mindset)

A core trait of the powerless mindset is a negative assumption that disheartens you from doing what you want to do. When an abandoning dog lives inside your head, you end up making a baseless conclusion that you are unable to take control of any problem that pops up.

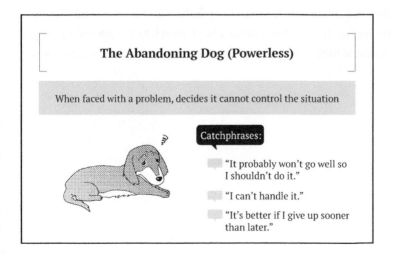

The Abandoning Dog (Powerless)

When faced with a problem, decides it cannot control the situation

Catchphrases:

"It probably won't go well so I shouldn't do it."

"I can't handle it."

"It's better if I give up sooner than later."

The following phrases repeat inside your heart:

• "It probably won't go well so I shouldn't do it."
• "I can't handle it."
• "It's better if I give up sooner than later."

When this assumption becomes a habit, it can produce negative emotions such as ambiguous anxiety, depression, helplessness, and fatigue. You may become discouraged and may give up before you even try to take on new challenges.

⇨ The Apologetic Dog (The Self-Accusing Mindset)

Many people who have an apologetic assumption dog think that they are the reason behind every failure and have a tendency to apologize. In our story, Reisa's boyfriend has the apologetic dog inside of him. This is typical of people who lack self-confidence.

People who have this negative assumption, tend to say the following things:

- "It was my fault that we failed."
- "I'm to blame for inconveniencing others."
- "I'm a failure in this role."

This sort of self-accusing mindset is especially common in those who are serious and hard-working. You may take on too much responsibility and blame yourself excessively. Negative emotions such as guilt and shame may lower your self-worth and extend to your work performance.

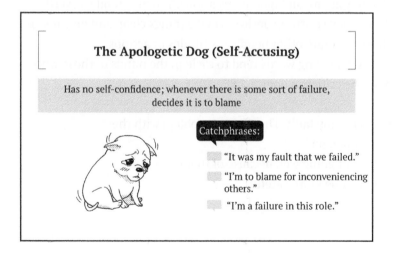

The Apologetic Dog (Self-Accusing)

Has no self-confidence; whenever there is some sort of failure, decides it is to blame

Catchphrases:

"It was my fault that we failed."

"I'm to blame for inconveniencing others."

"I'm a failure in this role."

It is very rare for a mistake to be a single person's fault. More often, mistakes are the result of many people's collective action.

Nonetheless, if you experience failure, you may end up in a near panic state and lose the ability to see things rationally. The apologetic dog will continue to bark inside your mind, saying that it was your own fault, making it harder to remain calm.

⇨ The Criticism Dog (The Blaming Others Mindset)

Whenever an unexpected problem occurs, unlike the apologetic dog who excessively blames themselves, the criticism dog often blames and criticizes others. If you have this assumption, you may be stubborn, may not change your mind easily, and may not be able to tolerate ambiguous situations. You may tend to overthink things, have a strong desire to make things clear, and may not be able to tolerate other people's attitudes or actions.

The following words tend to cycle in the minds of those who have the criticism dog:

- "It's not my fault. There was a problem with the other person."
- "It's not going well because of them."
- "I must be more careful."

There are two main problems with this mindset. First, you may lash out at others and end up destroying your interpersonal relationships. If the mindset of blaming others becomes excessive, it may become impossible for you to tolerate others. A superior may feel irritated by a subordinate who is not able to become fully fledged. A parent may feel frustrated by their child who isn't showing any improvement academically, athletically, or in whatever lessons they are taking. As a result, relationships are strained and the people around you lose their motivation and confidence.

Second, you may direct your criticism at yourself. This is called *self-criticism* and can be as destructive as criticism directed at others.

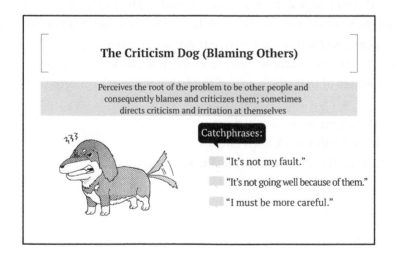

The Criticism Dog (Blaming Others)

Perceives the root of the problem to be other people and consequently blames and criticizes them; sometimes directs criticism and irritation at themselves

Catchphrases:

"It's not my fault."

"It's not going well because of them."

"I must be more careful."

When the criticism is directed at yourself, you may feel irritated and wonder, "Why can't I even do something like this?" The most obvious difference compared to the self-accusing apologetic dog is that rather than feeling guilt and shame, you feel dissatisfaction and irritation toward yourself.

When self-criticism becomes a habit, the feeling of anger can trigger the production of noradrenaline, or what is also known as the anger hormone. When the amount of noradrenaline increases drastically, blood pressure rises and can cause arteriosclerosis to progress. Blood vessels may clog, leading to strokes or heart attacks, so you must be vigilant.

⇨ The Apathetic Dog (The Irresponsible Mindset)

The apathetic dog says, "This has nothing to do with me." This sort of response can be seen as defiant. You aren't serious enough to worry over self-accusations, but you are also not judgmental enough to blame others. You are simply irresponsible because regardless of the issue, you just think that it doesn't concern you:

• "There's no point in panicking."
• "It'll probably work itself out."
• "It's not like it matters to me. Do what you want."

People who have these assumptions dislike getting involved in difficult problems and prefer to remain on the sidelines. Even when something fails, they don't care.

If this assumption becomes a habit, you may not feel motivated to do anything and may become chronically fatigued. Because you may try to avoid troublesome personal relationships, be absent from meetings that don't interest you, and turn down jobs that could become demanding, people may question your attitude as a working adult.

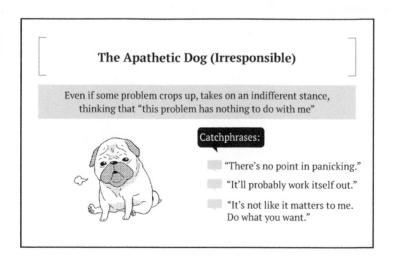

The Apathetic Dog (Irresponsible)

Even if some problem crops up, takes on an indifferent stance, thinking that "this problem has nothing to do with me"

Catchphrases:

"There's no point in panicking."

"It'll probably work itself out."

"It's not like it matters to me. Do what you want."

⇨ Become Aware of Your Assumptions

In our discussion of the seven types of negative assumptions that trigger negative emotions, were you able to find an assumption dog inside of you? The first step in taming assumptions is becoming aware of your assumption pattern.

Of course, it is not easy to recognize assumptions as they often surface in a moment and drift away just as quickly. To become aware of your assumption dogs, you will need to understand the negative emotion patterns that trigger them. Because emotions leave a strong impression in your heart, you should be able to notice them if you look for them. Knowing your negative emotions will lead you to the assumption dogs that arise from them.

Feel free to refer to the comparison table of negative emotions and assumptions on the following page.

The Negative Emotion That Becomes the Root of Negative Assumptions

Negative Emotion	Assumption Type	Thinking Habit
Anger/Jealousy	Righteous Dog	"Should Be" Mindset
Sadness/Depression/Envy	Loser Dog	Devaluing Mindset
Anxiety/Fear	Worrywart Dog	Pessimistic Mindset
Anxiety/Depression/Powerlessness	Abandoning Dog	Powerless Mindset
Guilt/Shame	Apologetic Dog	Self-Accusing Mindset
Anger/Dissatisfaction/Resentment	Criticism Dog	Blaming Others Mindset
Exhaustion	Apathetic Dog	Irresponsible Mindset

Three Ways to Deal with Assumption Dogs

3

⇨ **Dealing with Negative Assumptions**

Once you become aware of your negative assumptions, the next step is to deal with them independently. The independence here refers to you yourself. Assumptions just happen to be the dogs that settled inside of your heart. There are several methods you can use to deal with your assumption dogs.

⇨ Banish the Assumption Dog

The first option is to banish the assumption. If it is a useless and disadvantageous assumption, it may hold you back. When the time comes, it may make you anxious and prevent you from having a confident attitude. In such a situation, it might be wise to just let go of that assumption dog.

What has been imprinted on us after birth can be discarded by the power of our own will. We call this *unlearning*. Let go of it, as if you were deleting unnecessary files on your computer. Imagine that you are connected to the assumption dog inside your heart with a chain. Open up the hand that is holding that chain and let it go.

After that, don't give any attention to the assumption dog regardless of what it says. That's no longer a dog you own. It's just a stray, so pay no mind to it.

⇨ Accept the Assumption Dog

The second option is to accept it. If what the assumption dog is saying is realistic, it may be rational to accept its words. Once you accept it, pay no mind to it afterward.

⇨ Train/Tame the Assumption Dog

The final option is to train or tame the assumption dog. If you are hesitant to either banish it or accept it, make up your mind to get along with it from now on. You must learn how to tame the assumption dog, whenever it barks excessively.

You must be flexible in your approach to taming an assumption dog. You can try three types of approaches to see what works for you:

- Make a different choice. Try to see if there are other possible causes for what you are experiencing. Ask yourself, "Are there any other ways to look at this?"
- Change your viewpoint. Change how you think about what you are experiencing. Ask yourself, "Am I seeing this as it really is?"
- Verify. Take a closer look at the situation. Ask yourself, "Is there anything I could change?"

There's no right or wrong answer in the method you choose to take. It's fine as long as it's something you are satisfied with. The important point is that you treat the assumption as a dog that has just happened to settle down inside of your heart. Because it is just an assumption and not something that is a part of your personality, you should be able to handle it.

Three Ways to Deal with an Assumption Dog

1. Banish it...

• ...if the dog's opinion is unreasonable and has no evidence.
• ...if the dog's words are questionable and seem untrustworthy.

2. Accept it...

• ...if the dog's opinion is realistic and has evidence.
• ...if it seems like you can accept and trust the dog's words.

3. Train/tame it...

• ...if it's hard to figure out if you can trust the dog's words.
• ...when you're able to have a different viewpoint.

Three Ways to Deal with an Aggressive Dog

1. Touch it

2. Accept it

3. Tolerate it

Part 3

Get Social Support

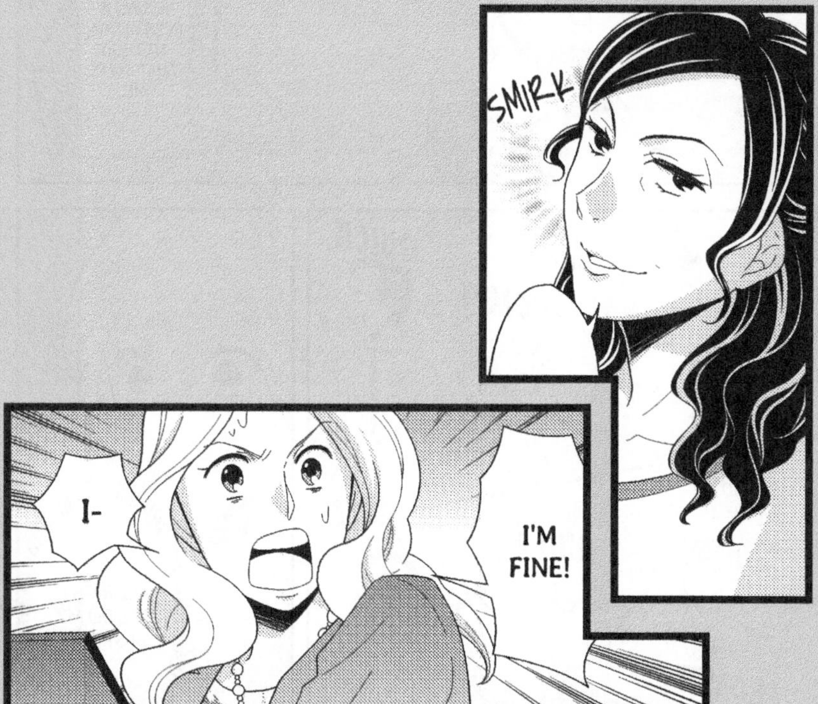
SMIRK
I-
I'M FINE!

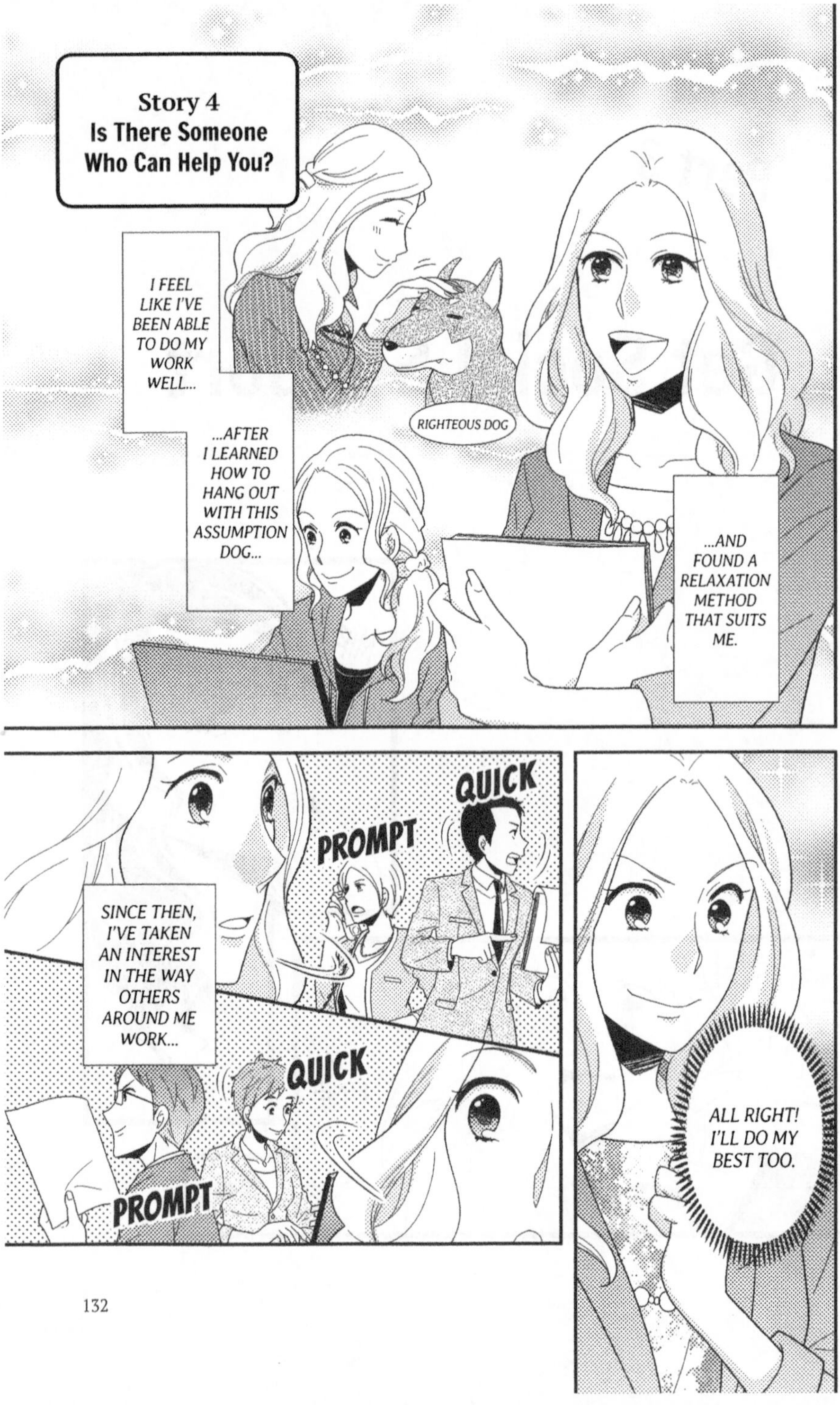
Story 4
Is There Someone Who Can Help You?
I FEEL LIKE I'VE BEEN ABLE TO DO MY WORK WELL...
...AFTER I LEARNED HOW TO HANG OUT WITH THIS ASSUMPTION DOG...
RIGHTEOUS DOG
...AND FOUND A RELAXATION METHOD THAT SUITS ME.
SINCE THEN, I'VE TAKEN AN INTEREST IN THE WAY OTHERS AROUND ME WORK...
PROMPT
QUICK
QUICK
PROMPT
ALL RIGHT! I'LL DO MY BEST TOO.

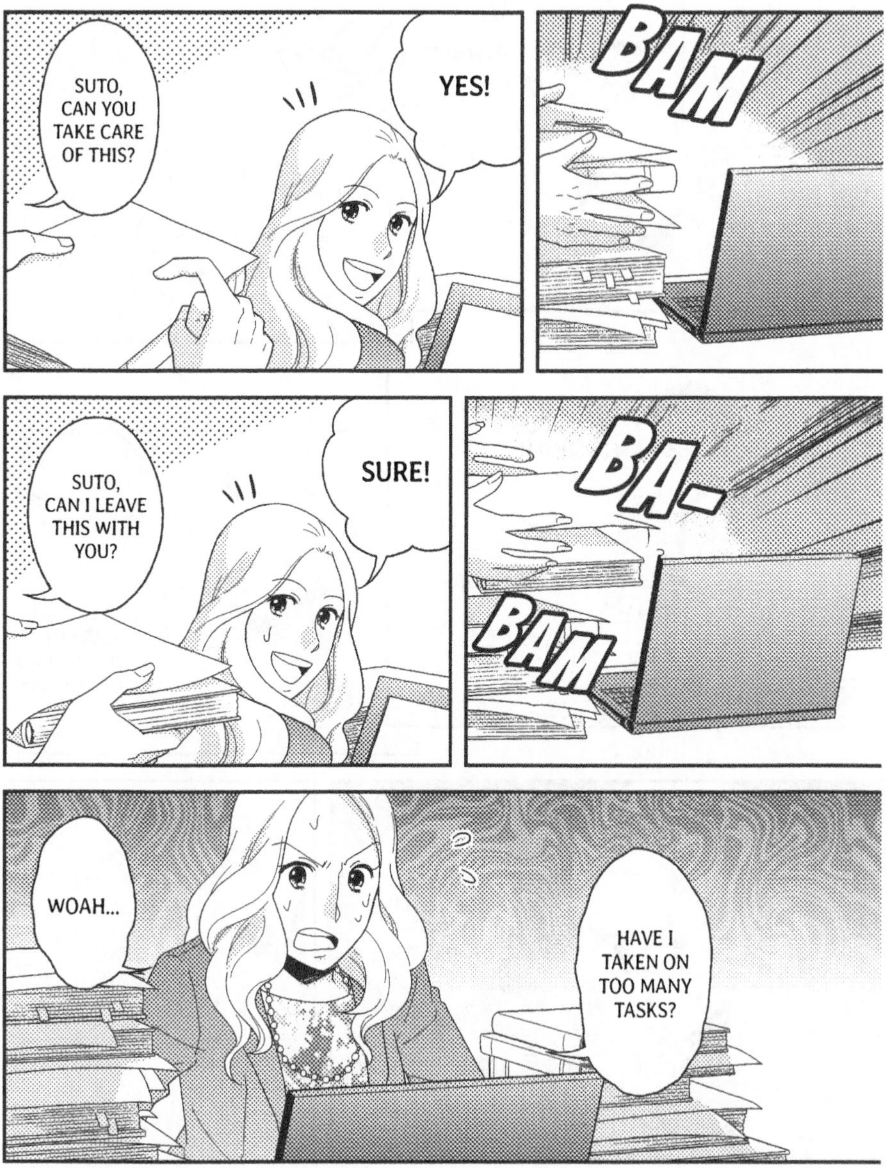
SUTO, CAN YOU TAKE CARE OF THIS?
YES!
BAM
SUTO, CAN I LEAVE THIS WITH YOU?
SURE!
BA-
BAM
WOAH...
HAVE I TAKEN ON TOO MANY TASKS?

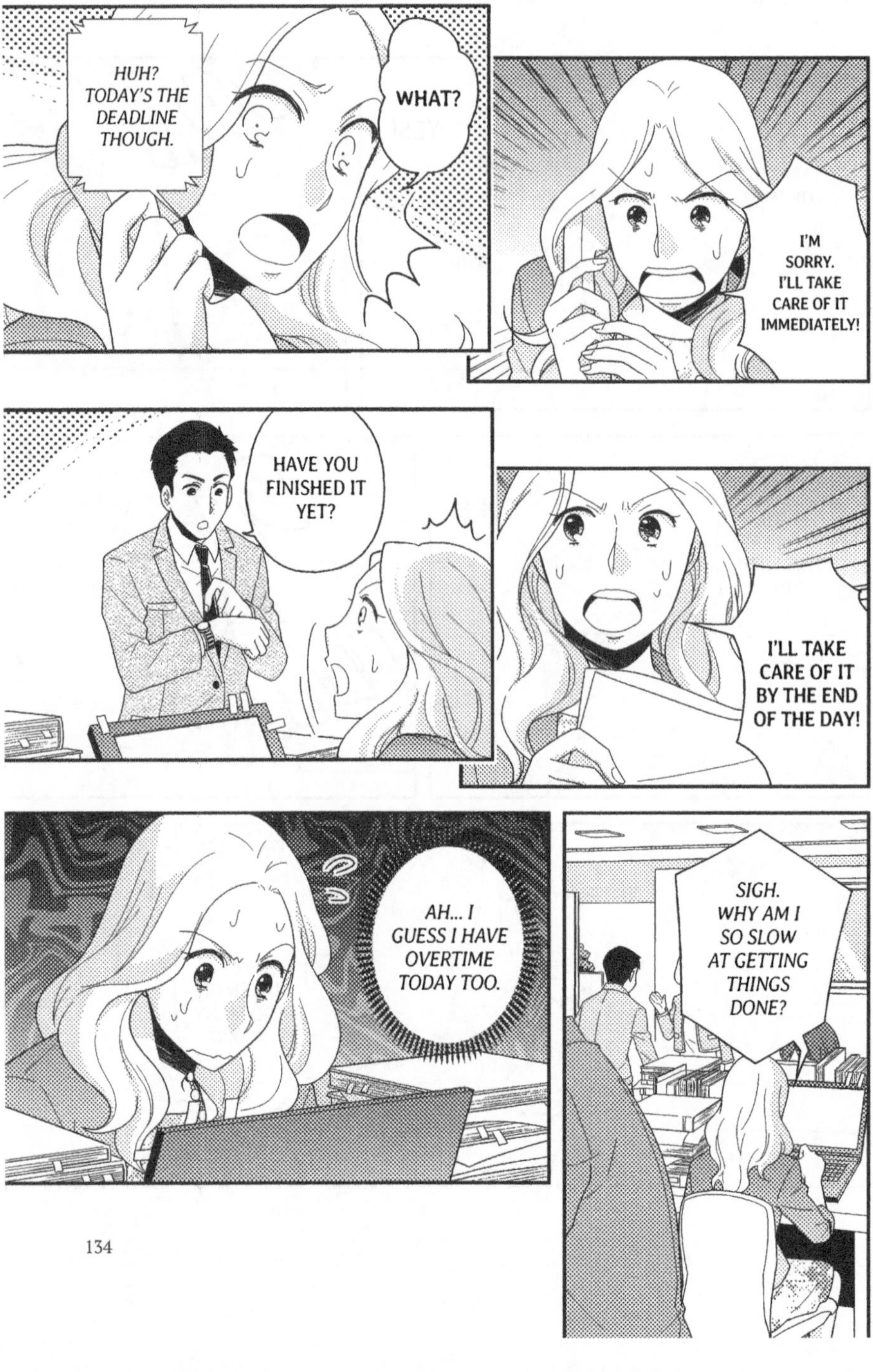
HUH? TODAY'S THE DEADLINE THOUGH.
WHAT?
I'M SORRY. I'LL TAKE CARE OF IT IMMEDIATELY!
HAVE YOU FINISHED IT YET?
I'LL TAKE CARE OF IT BY THE END OF THE DAY!
AH... I GUESS I HAVE OVERTIME TODAY TOO.
SIGH. WHY AM I SO SLOW AT GETTING THINGS DONE?

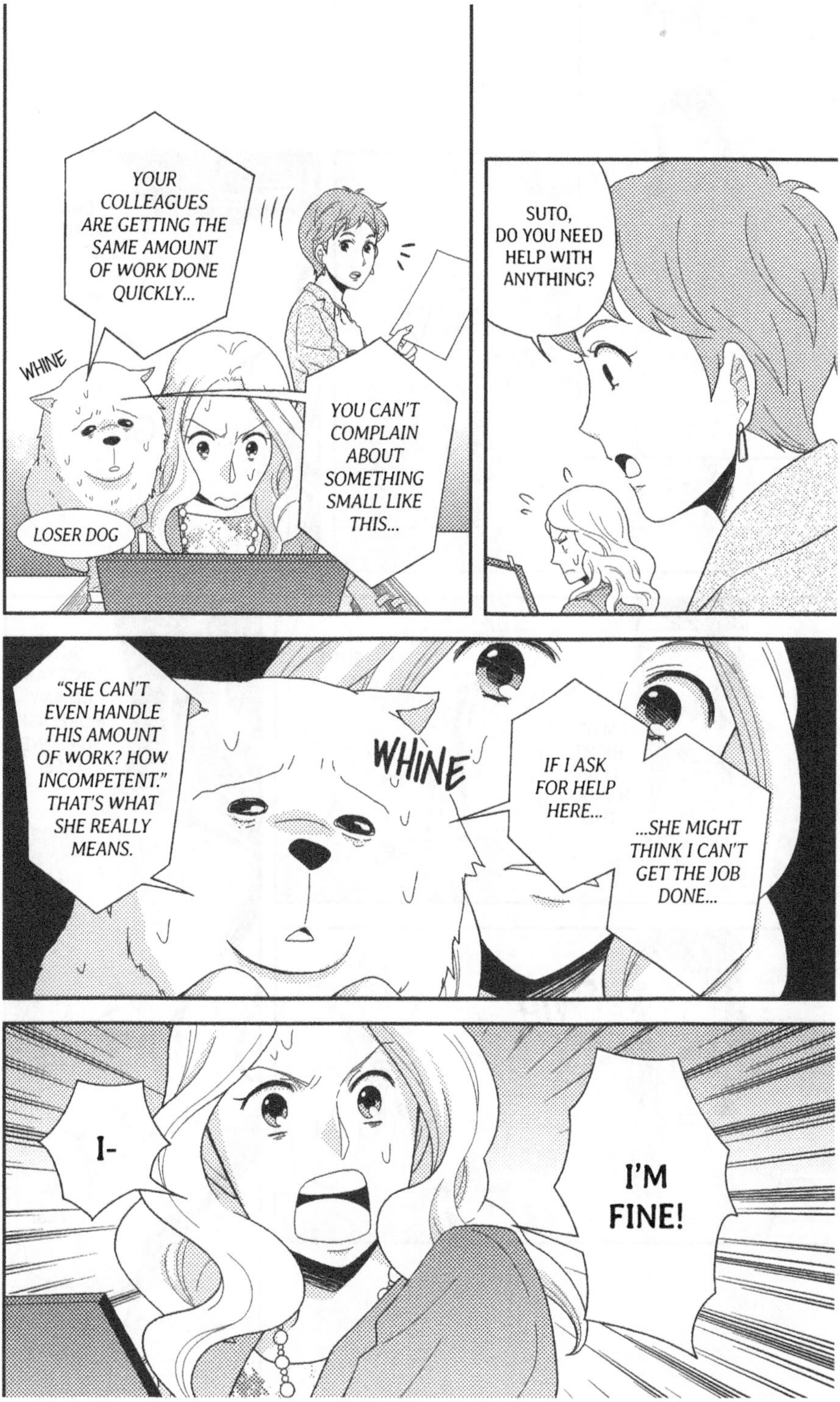
YOUR COLLEAGUES ARE GETTING THE SAME AMOUNT OF WORK DONE QUICKLY...
WHINE
LOSER DOG
YOU CAN'T COMPLAIN ABOUT SOMETHING SMALL LIKE THIS...
SUTO, DO YOU NEED HELP WITH ANYTHING?
"SHE CAN'T EVEN HANDLE THIS AMOUNT OF WORK? HOW INCOMPETENT." THAT'S WHAT SHE REALLY MEANS.
WHINE
IF I ASK FOR HELP HERE...
...SHE MIGHT THINK I CAN'T GET THE JOB DONE...
I-
I'M FINE!

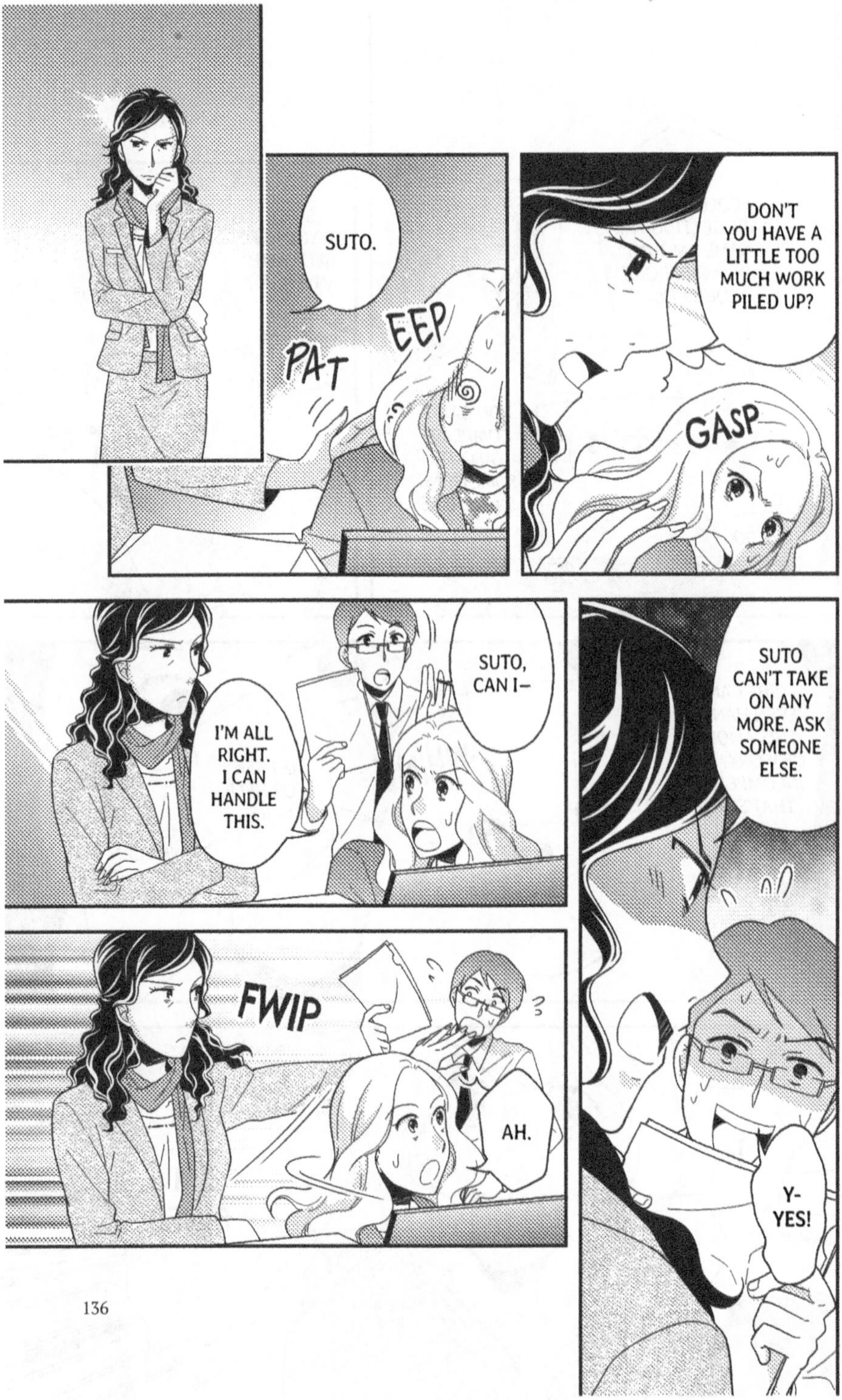
SUTO.
PAT
EEP
DON'T YOU HAVE A LITTLE TOO MUCH WORK PILED UP?
GASP
SUTO, CAN I–
I'M ALL RIGHT. I CAN HANDLE THIS.
FWIP
AH.
SUTO CAN'T TAKE ON ANY MORE. ASK SOMEONE ELSE.
Y- YES!

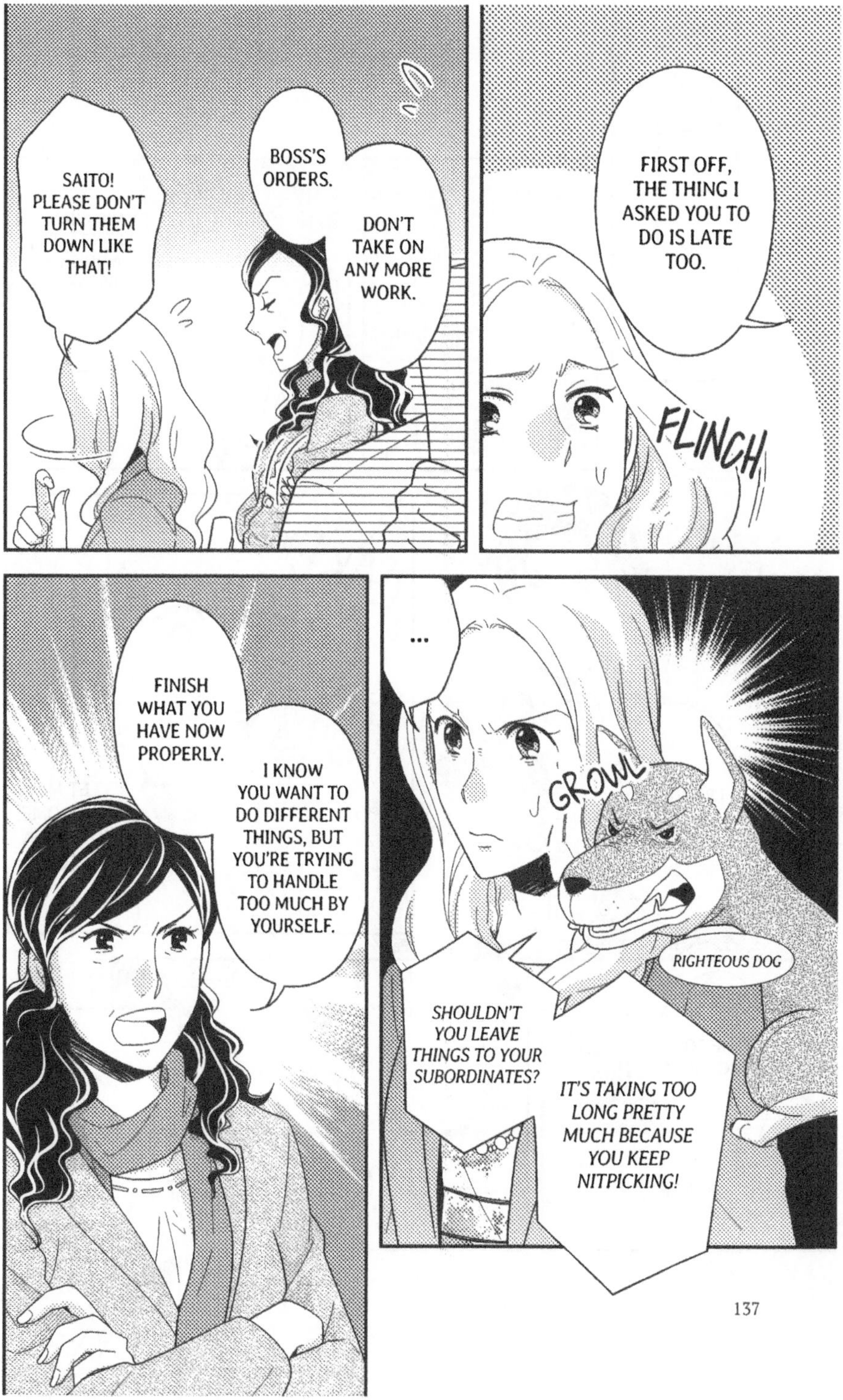
BOSS'S ORDERS.
DON'T TAKE ON ANY MORE WORK.
SAITO! PLEASE DON'T TURN THEM DOWN LIKE THAT!
FIRST OFF, THE THING I ASKED YOU TO DO IS LATE TOO.
FLINCH
FINISH WHAT YOU HAVE NOW PROPERLY.
I KNOW YOU WANT TO DO DIFFERENT THINGS, BUT YOU'RE TRYING TO HANDLE TOO MUCH BY YOURSELF.
...
GROWL
RIGHTEOUS DOG
SHOULDN'T YOU LEAVE THINGS TO YOUR SUBORDINATES?
IT'S TAKING TOO LONG PRETTY MUCH BECAUSE YOU KEEP NITPICKING!

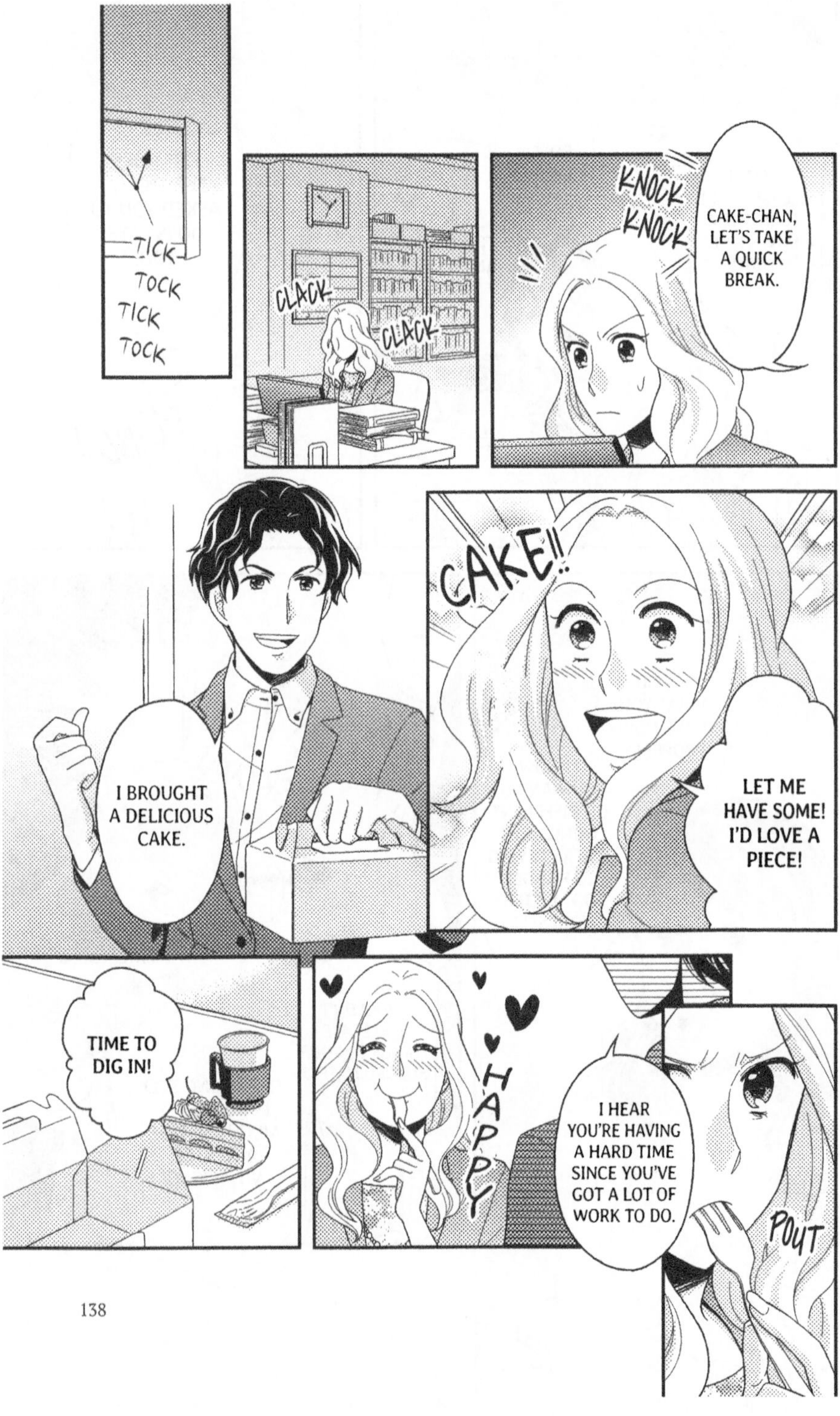
TICK
TOCK
TICK
TOCK
CLACK
CLACK
KNOCK
KNOCK
CAKE-CHAN, LET'S TAKE A QUICK BREAK.
I BROUGHT A DELICIOUS CAKE.
CAKE!!
LET ME HAVE SOME! I'D LOVE A PIECE!
TIME TO DIG IN!
HAPPY
I HEAR YOU'RE HAVING A HARD TIME SINCE YOU'VE GOT A LOT OF WORK TO DO.
POUT

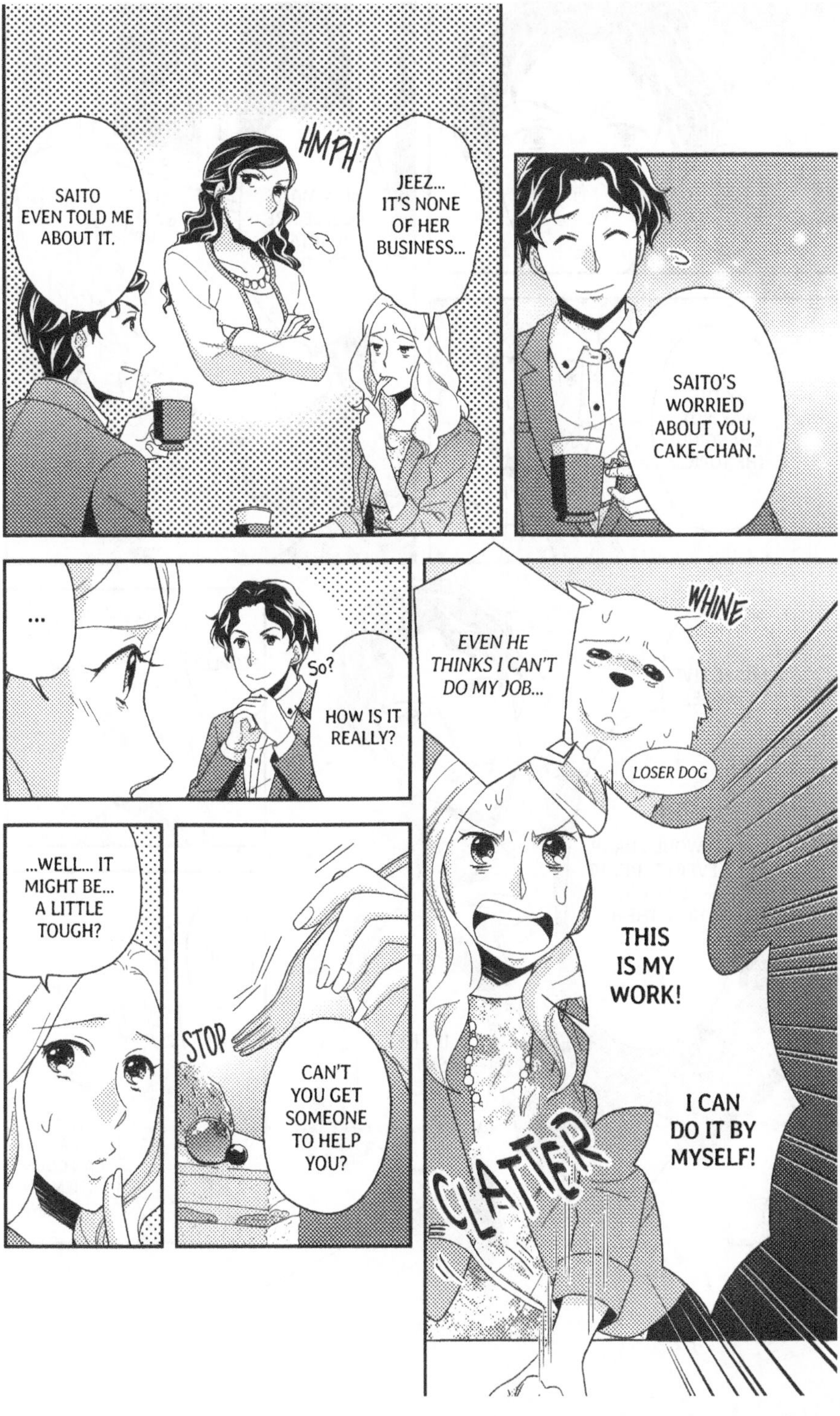
SAITO EVEN TOLD ME ABOUT IT.
HMPH
JEEZ... IT'S NONE OF HER BUSINESS...
SAITO'S WORRIED ABOUT YOU, CAKE-CHAN.
...
So?
HOW IS IT REALLY?
...WELL... IT MIGHT BE... A LITTLE TOUGH?
STOP
CAN'T YOU GET SOMEONE TO HELP YOU?
EVEN HE THINKS I CAN'T DO MY JOB...
WHINE
LOSER DOG
THIS IS MY WORK!
CLATTER
I CAN DO IT BY MYSELF!

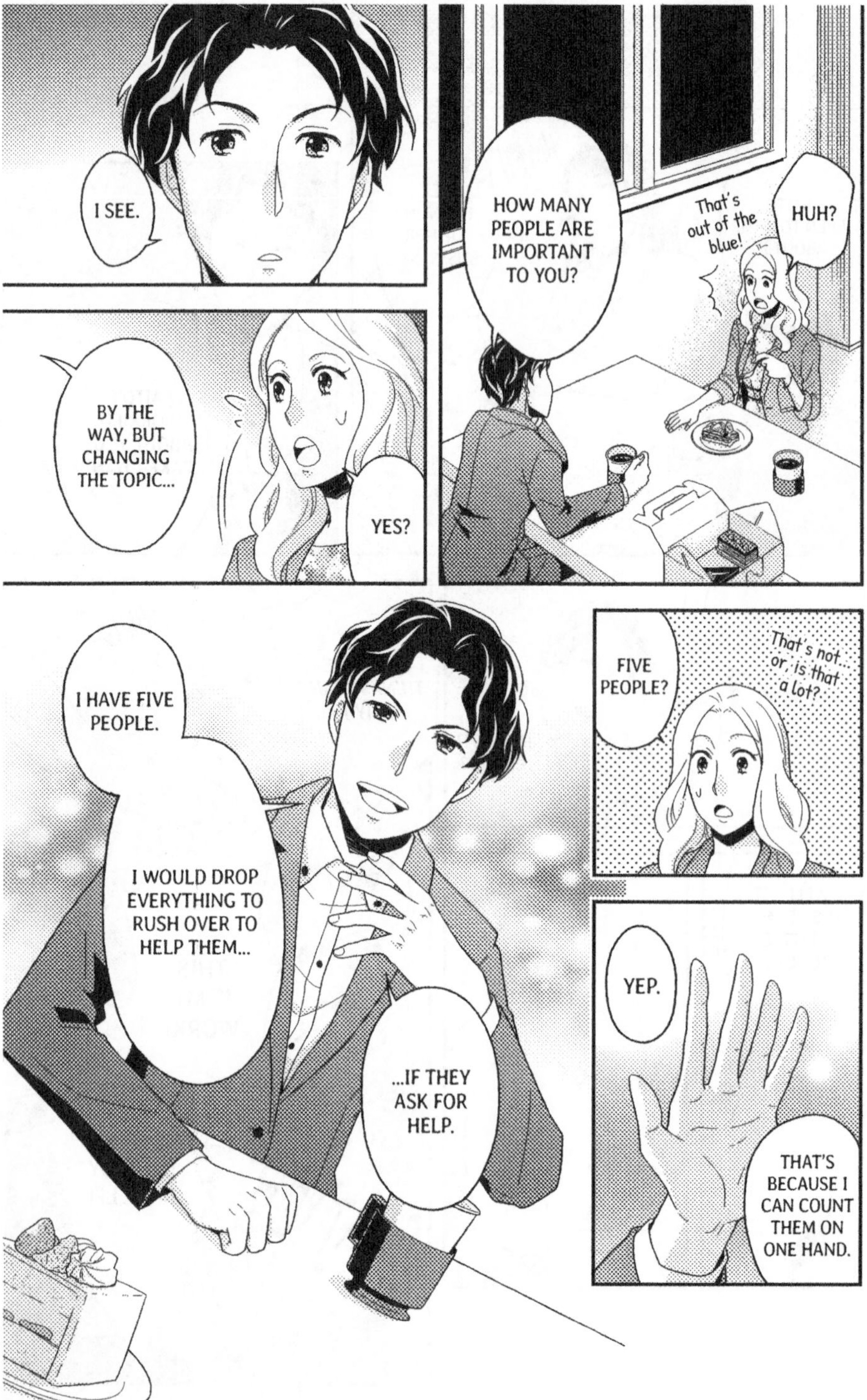
I SEE.
HOW MANY PEOPLE ARE IMPORTANT TO YOU?
HUH?
That's out of the blue!
BY THE WAY, BUT CHANGING THE TOPIC...
YES?
I HAVE FIVE PEOPLE.
I WOULD DROP EVERYTHING TO RUSH OVER TO HELP THEM...
...IF THEY ASK FOR HELP.
FIVE PEOPLE?
That's not... or, is that a lot?
YEP.
THAT'S BECAUSE I CAN COUNT THEM ON ONE HAND.

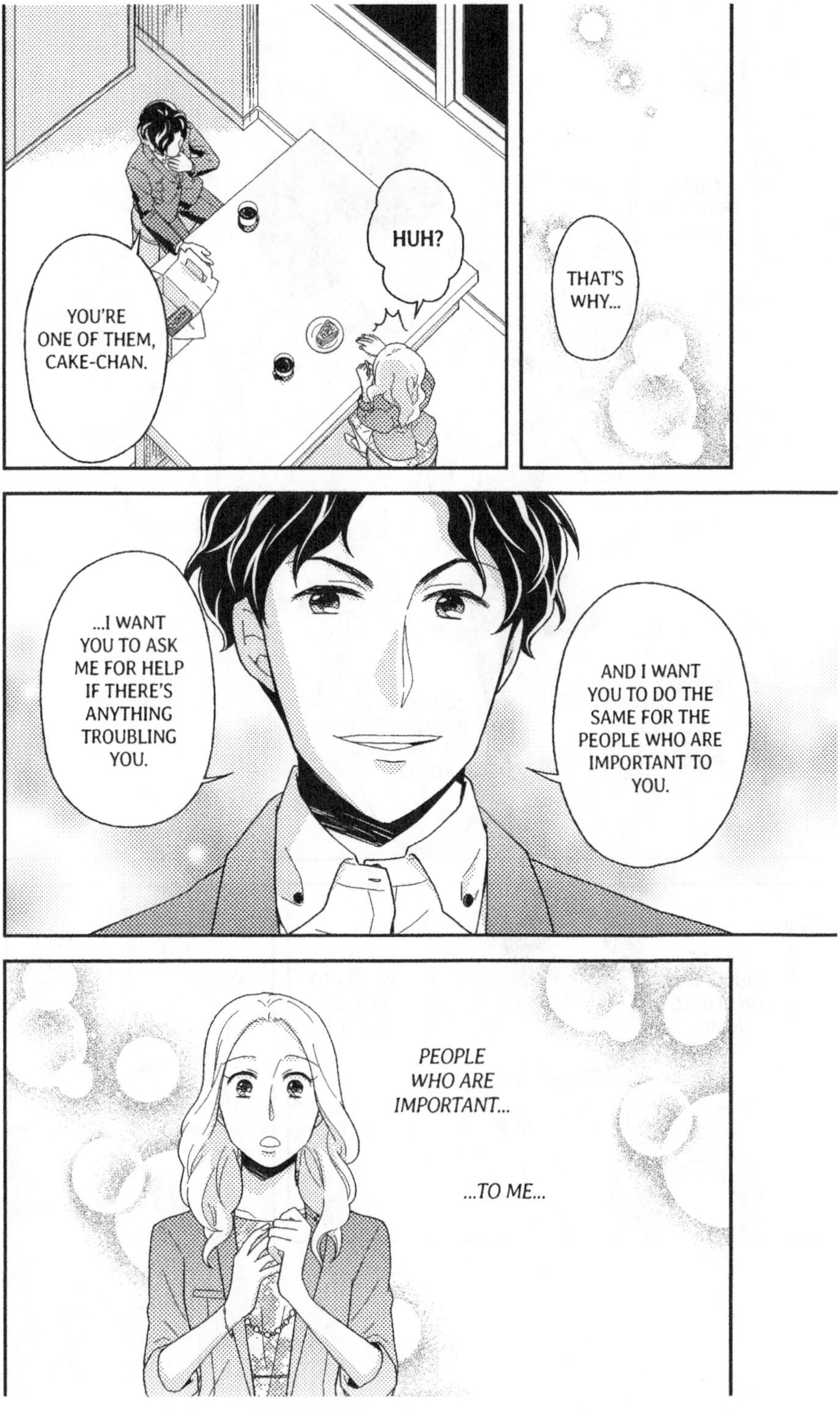
THAT'S WHY...
HUH?
YOU'RE ONE OF THEM, CAKE-CHAN.
AND I WANT YOU TO DO THE SAME FOR THE PEOPLE WHO ARE IMPORTANT TO YOU.
...I WANT YOU TO ASK ME FOR HELP IF THERE'S ANYTHING TROUBLING YOU.
PEOPLE WHO ARE IMPORTANT...
...TO ME...

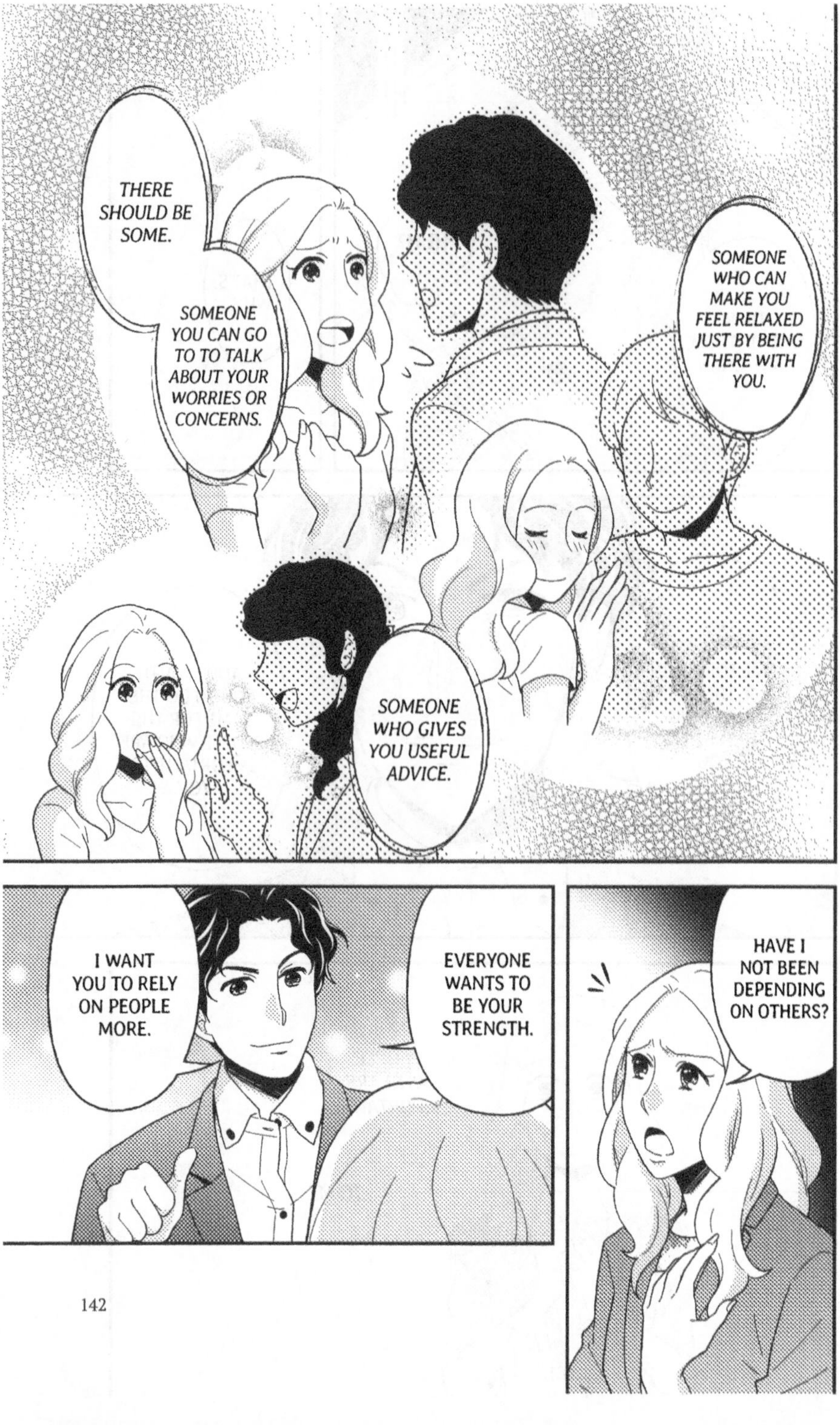
THERE SHOULD BE SOME.
SOMEONE YOU CAN GO TO TO TALK ABOUT YOUR WORRIES OR CONCERNS.
SOMEONE WHO CAN MAKE YOU FEEL RELAXED JUST BY BEING THERE WITH YOU.
SOMEONE WHO GIVES YOU USEFUL ADVICE.
EVERYONE WANTS TO BE YOUR STRENGTH.
I WANT YOU TO RELY ON PEOPLE MORE.
HAVE I NOT BEEN DEPENDING ON OTHERS?

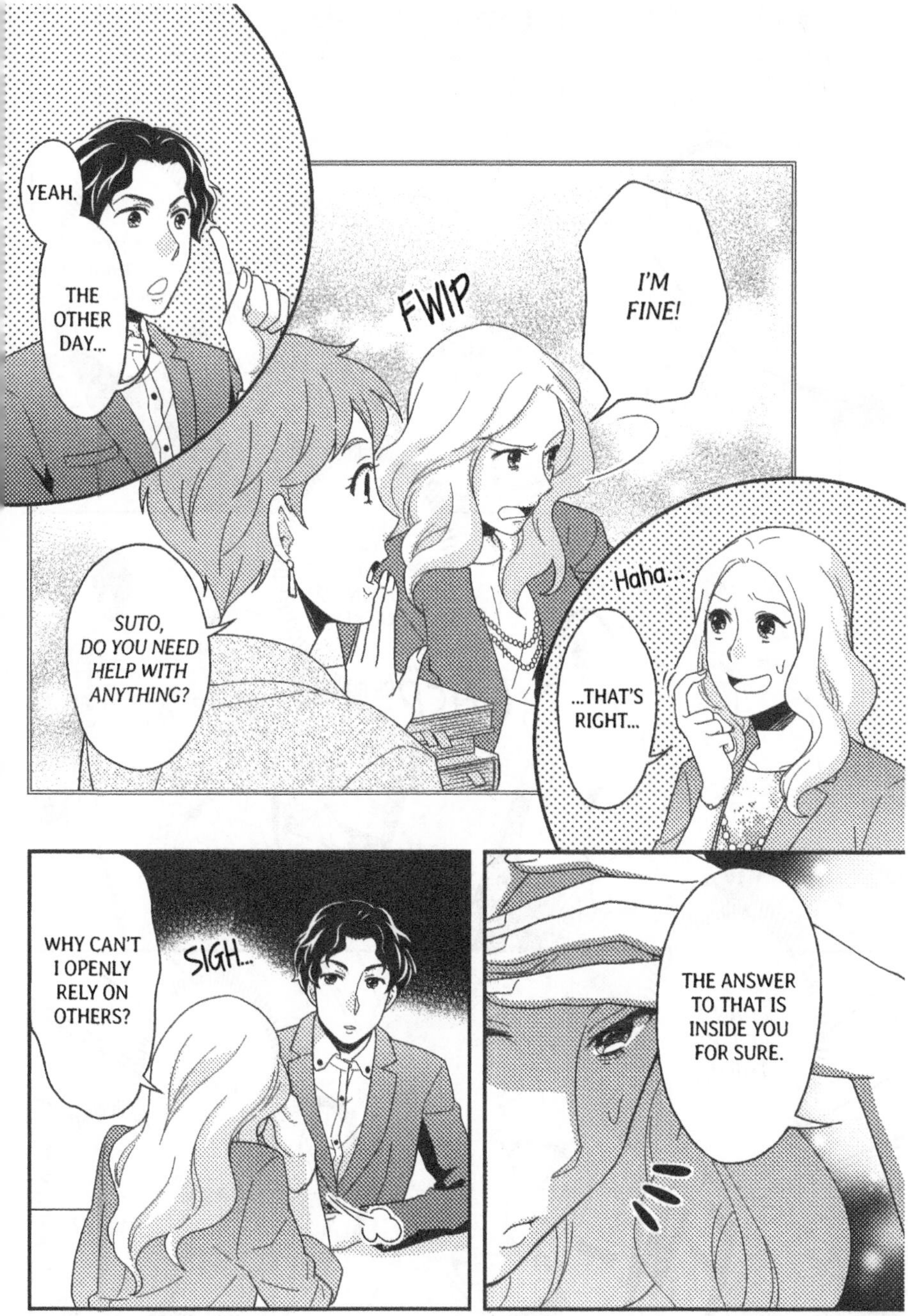
YEAH.
THE OTHER DAY...
FWIP
I'M FINE!
SUTO, DO YOU NEED HELP WITH ANYTHING?
Haha...
...THAT'S RIGHT...
WHY CAN'T I OPENLY RELY ON OTHERS?
SIGH...
THE ANSWER TO THAT IS INSIDE YOU FOR SURE.

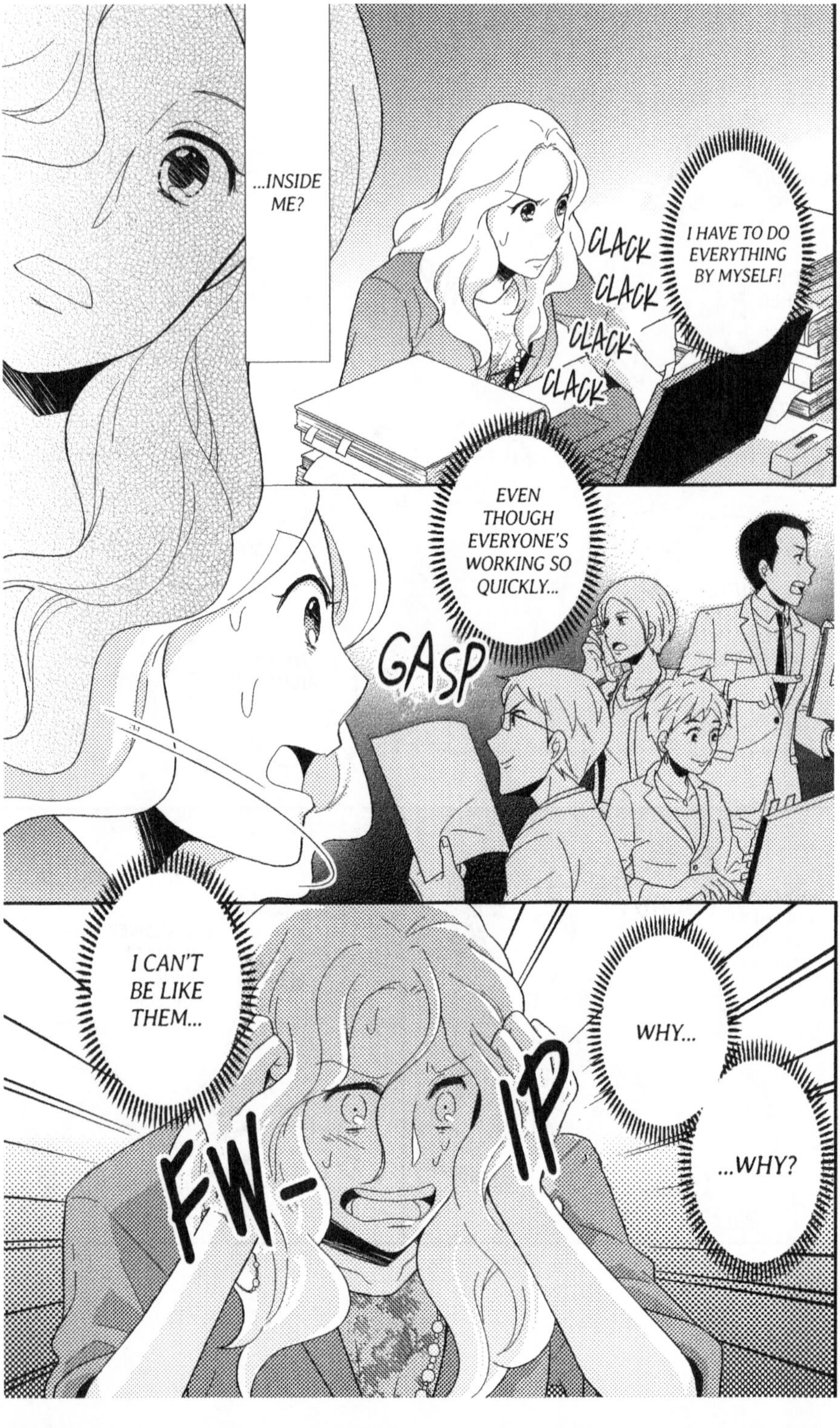

...INSIDE ME?
I HAVE TO DO EVERYTHING BY MYSELF!
CLACK
CLACK
CLACK
CLACK
EVEN THOUGH EVERYONE'S WORKING SO QUICKLY...
GASP
I CAN'T BE LIKE THEM...
WHY...
...WHY?
FW-IP

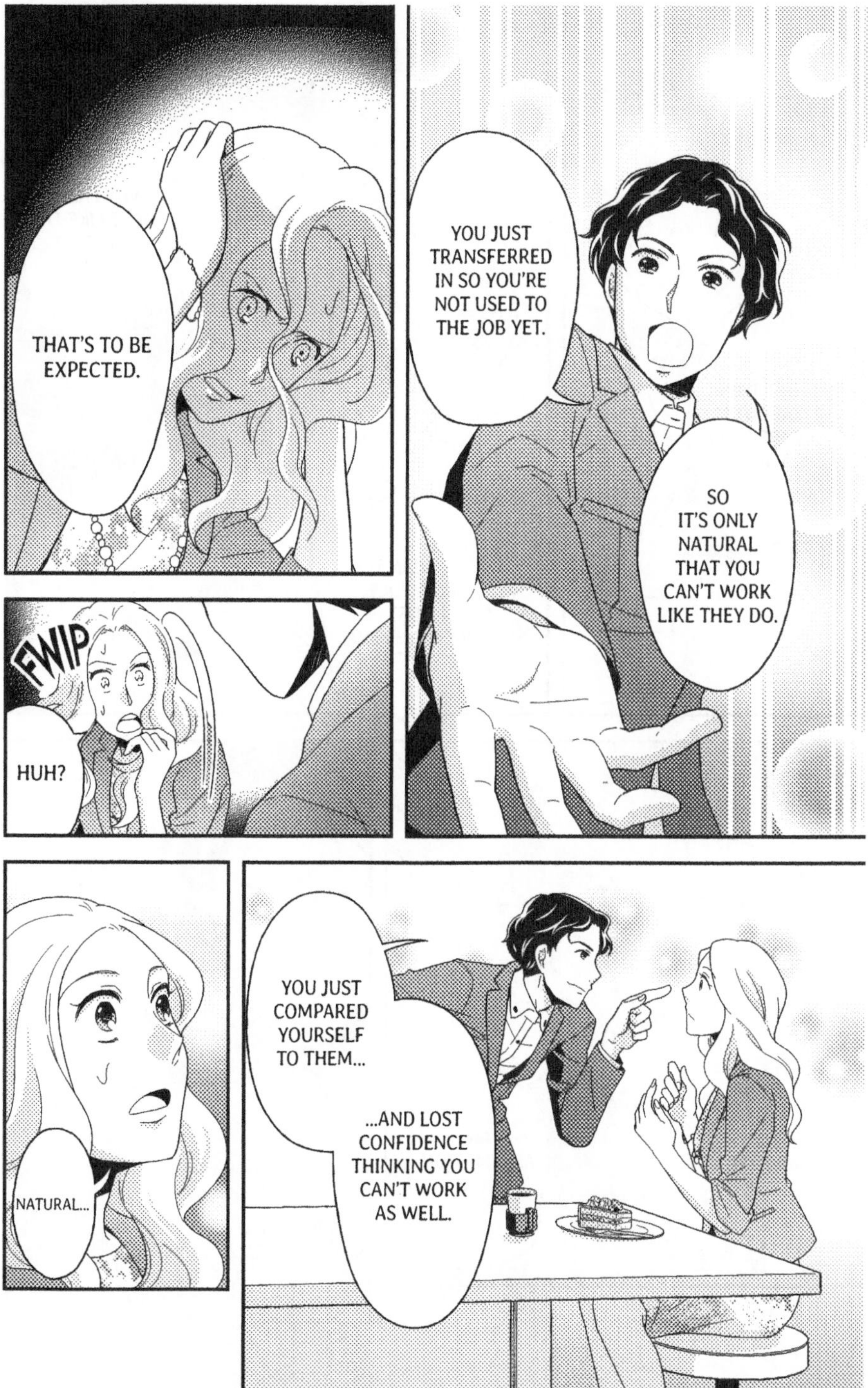
YOU JUST TRANSFERRED IN SO YOU'RE NOT USED TO THE JOB YET.
SO IT'S ONLY NATURAL THAT YOU CAN'T WORK LIKE THEY DO.
THAT'S TO BE EXPECTED.
FWIP
HUH?
YOU JUST COMPARED YOURSELF TO THEM...
...AND LOST CONFIDENCE THINKING YOU CAN'T WORK AS WELL.
NATURAL...

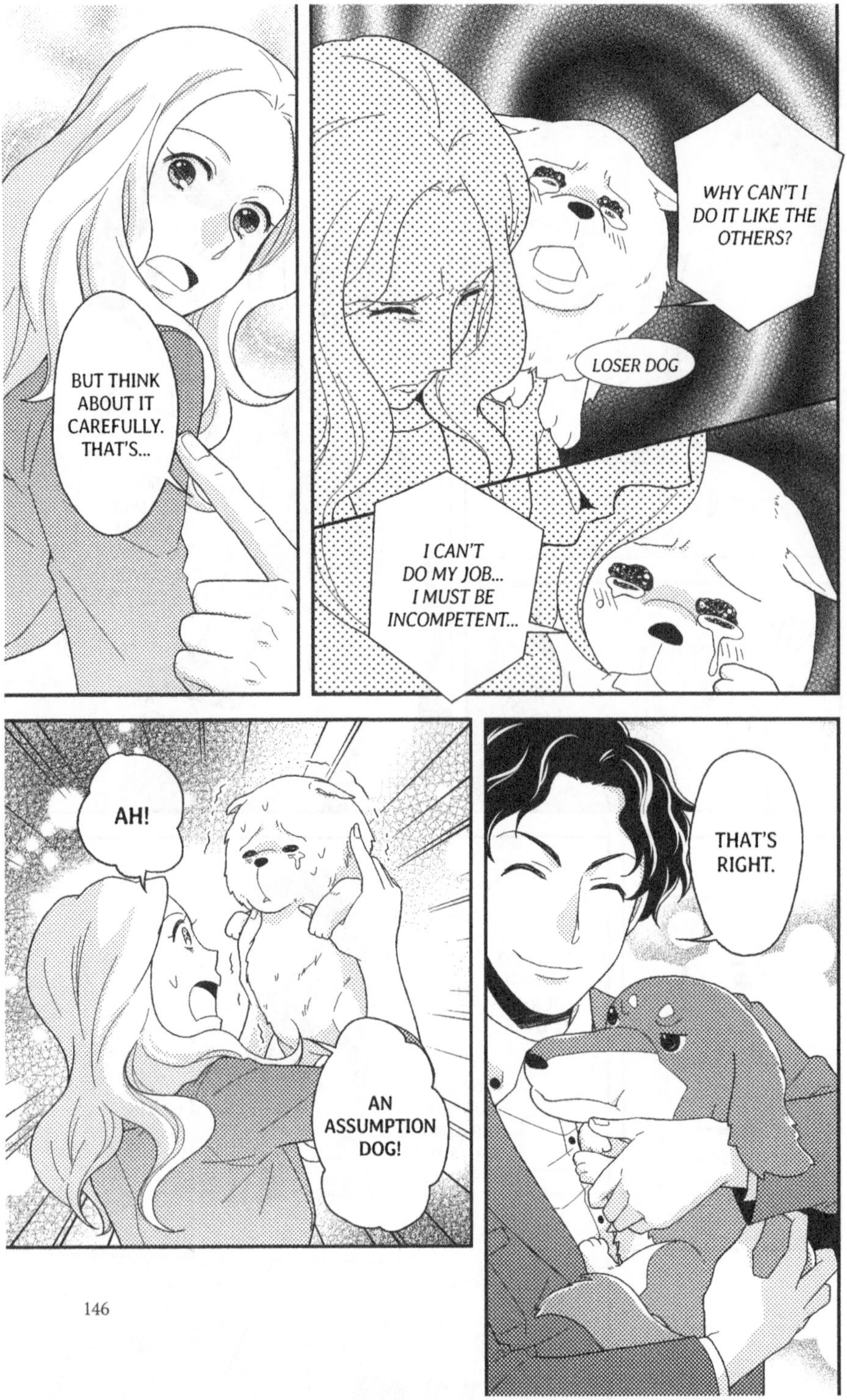
BUT THINK ABOUT IT CAREFULLY. THAT'S...
WHY CAN'T I DO IT LIKE THE OTHERS?
LOSER DOG
I CAN'T DO MY JOB... I MUST BE INCOMPETENT...
AH!
AN ASSUMPTION DOG!
THAT'S RIGHT.

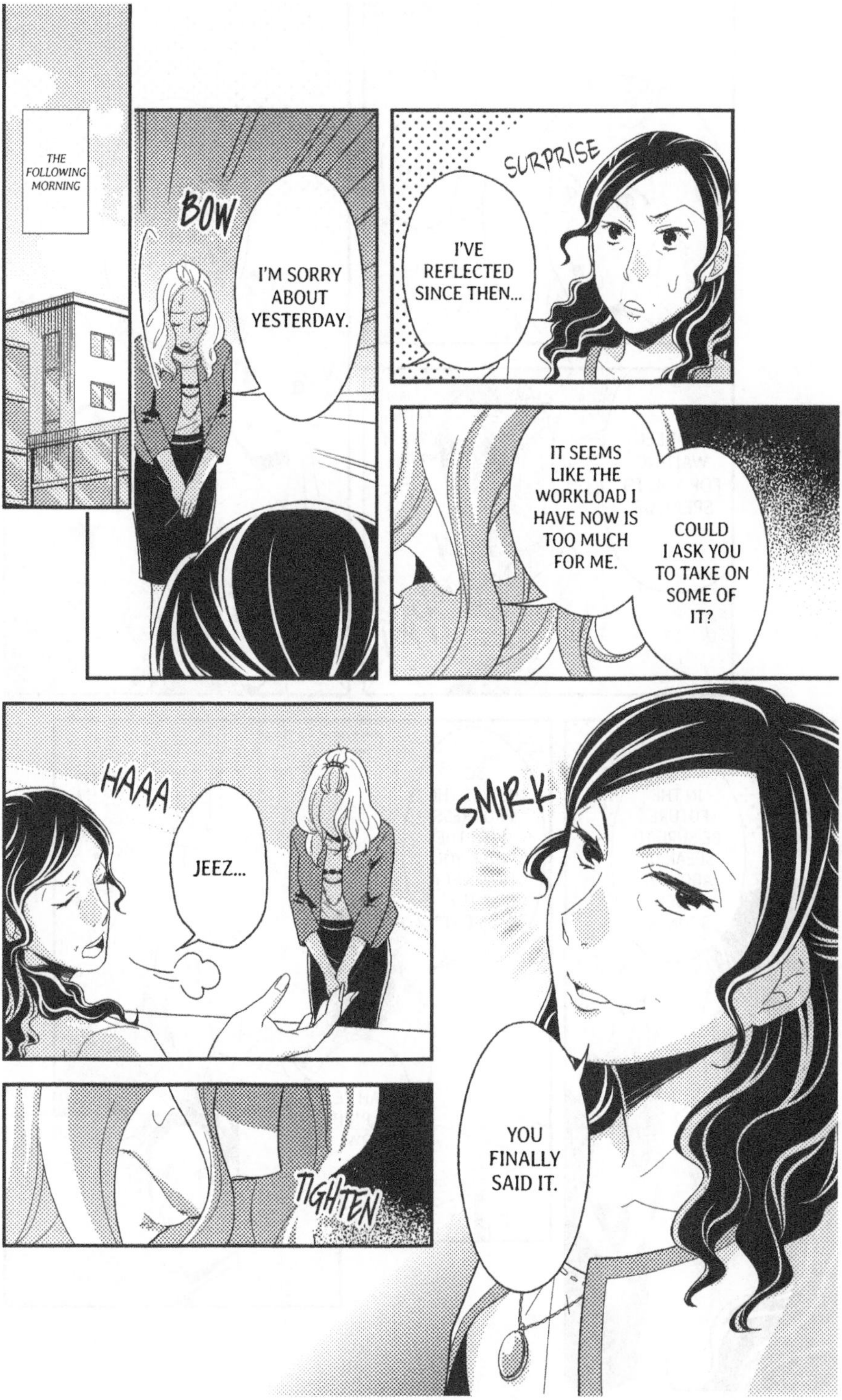
THE FOLLOWING MORNING
BOW
I'M SORRY ABOUT YESTERDAY.
SURPRISE
I'VE REFLECTED SINCE THEN...
IT SEEMS LIKE THE WORKLOAD I HAVE NOW IS TOO MUCH FOR ME.
COULD I ASK YOU TO TAKE ON SOME OF IT?
HAAA
JEEZ...
TIGHTEN
SMIRK
YOU FINALLY SAID IT.

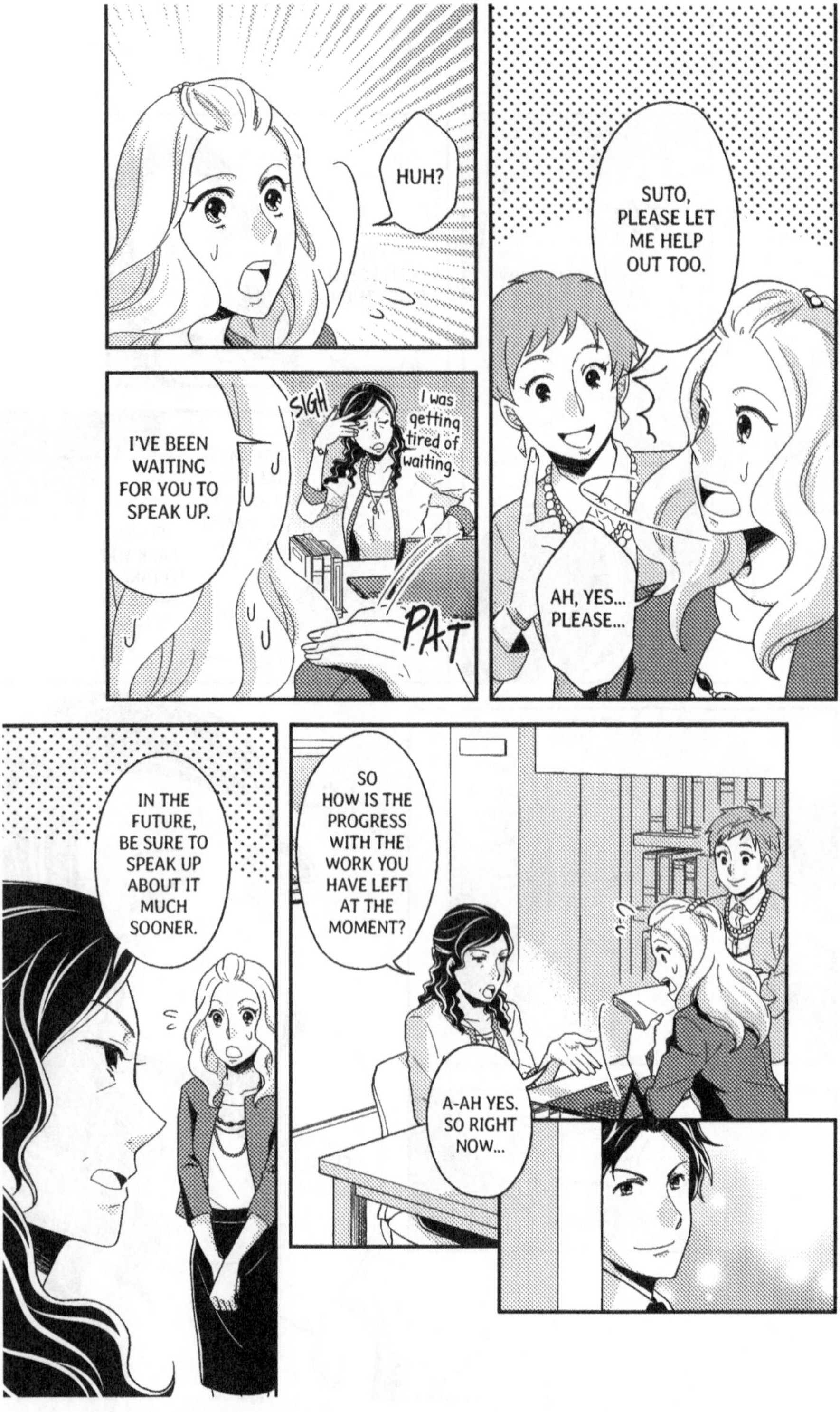
HUH?
SUTO, PLEASE LET ME HELP OUT TOO.
AH, YES... PLEASE...
SIGH
I was getting tired of waiting.
I'VE BEEN WAITING FOR YOU TO SPEAK UP.
PAT
SO HOW IS THE PROGRESS WITH THE WORK YOU HAVE LEFT AT THE MOMENT?
A-AH YES. SO RIGHT NOW...
IN THE FUTURE, BE SURE TO SPEAK UP ABOUT IT MUCH SOONER.

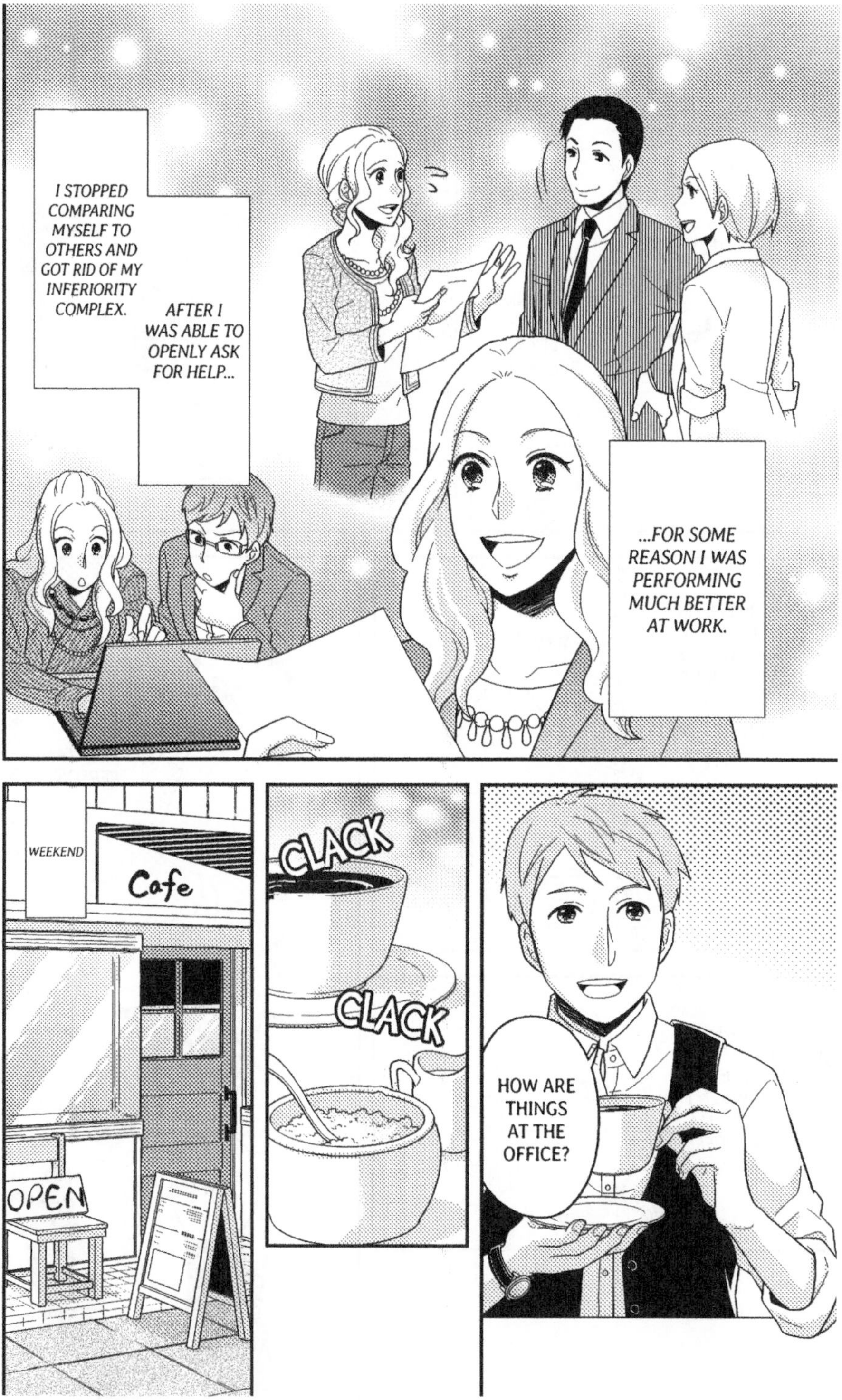
I STOPPED COMPARING MYSELF TO OTHERS AND GOT RID OF MY INFERIORITY COMPLEX.
AFTER I WAS ABLE TO OPENLY ASK FOR HELP...
...FOR SOME REASON I WAS PERFORMING MUCH BETTER AT WORK.
WEEKEND
Cafe
OPEN
CLACK
CLACK
HOW ARE THINGS AT THE OFFICE?

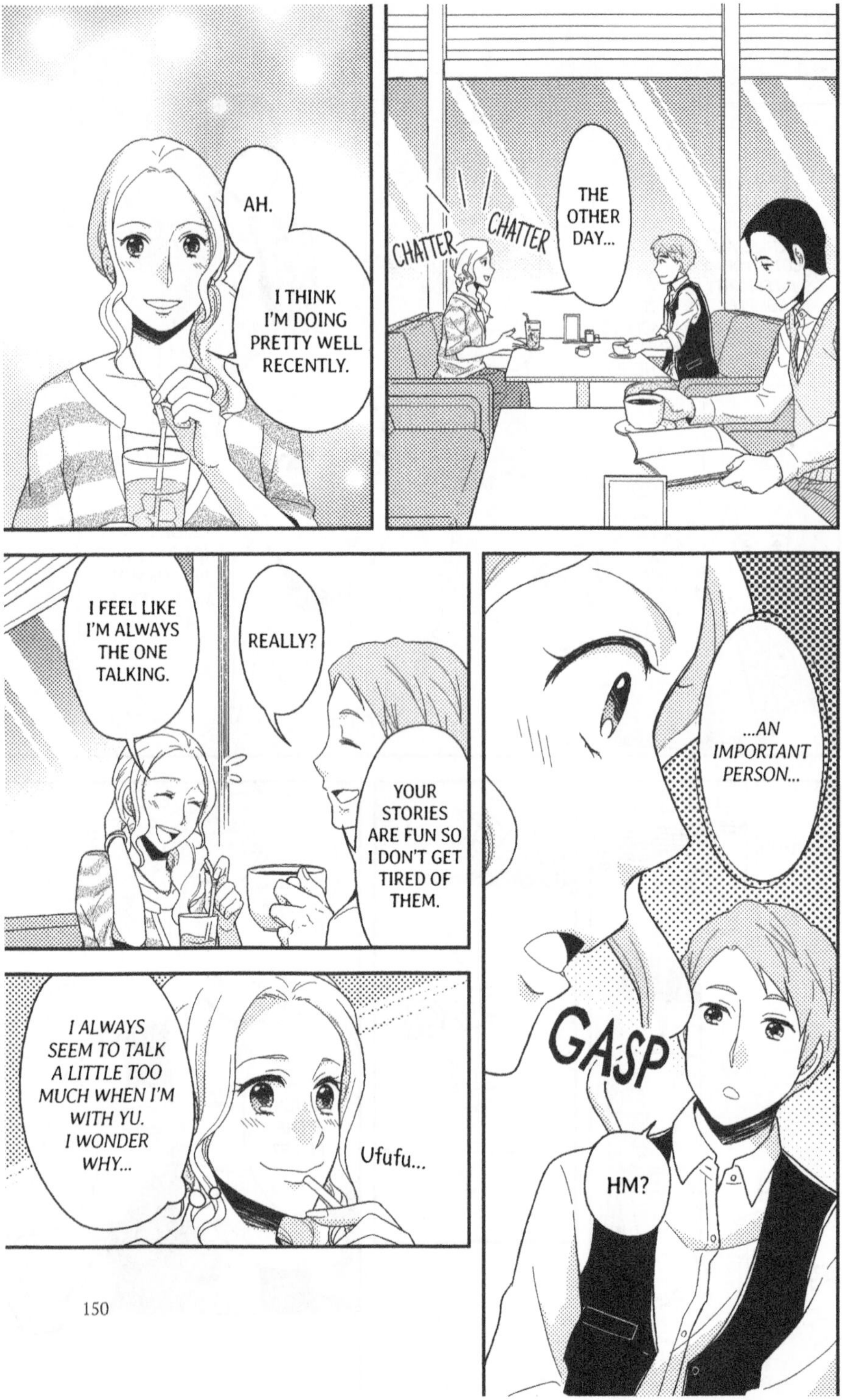
AH.
I THINK I'M DOING PRETTY WELL RECENTLY.
CHATTER
CHATTER
THE OTHER DAY...
I FEEL LIKE I'M ALWAYS THE ONE TALKING.
REALLY?
YOUR STORIES ARE FUN SO I DON'T GET TIRED OF THEM.
I ALWAYS SEEM TO TALK A LITTLE TOO MUCH WHEN I'M WITH YU. I WONDER WHY...
Ufufu...
...AN IMPORTANT PERSON...
GASP
HM?

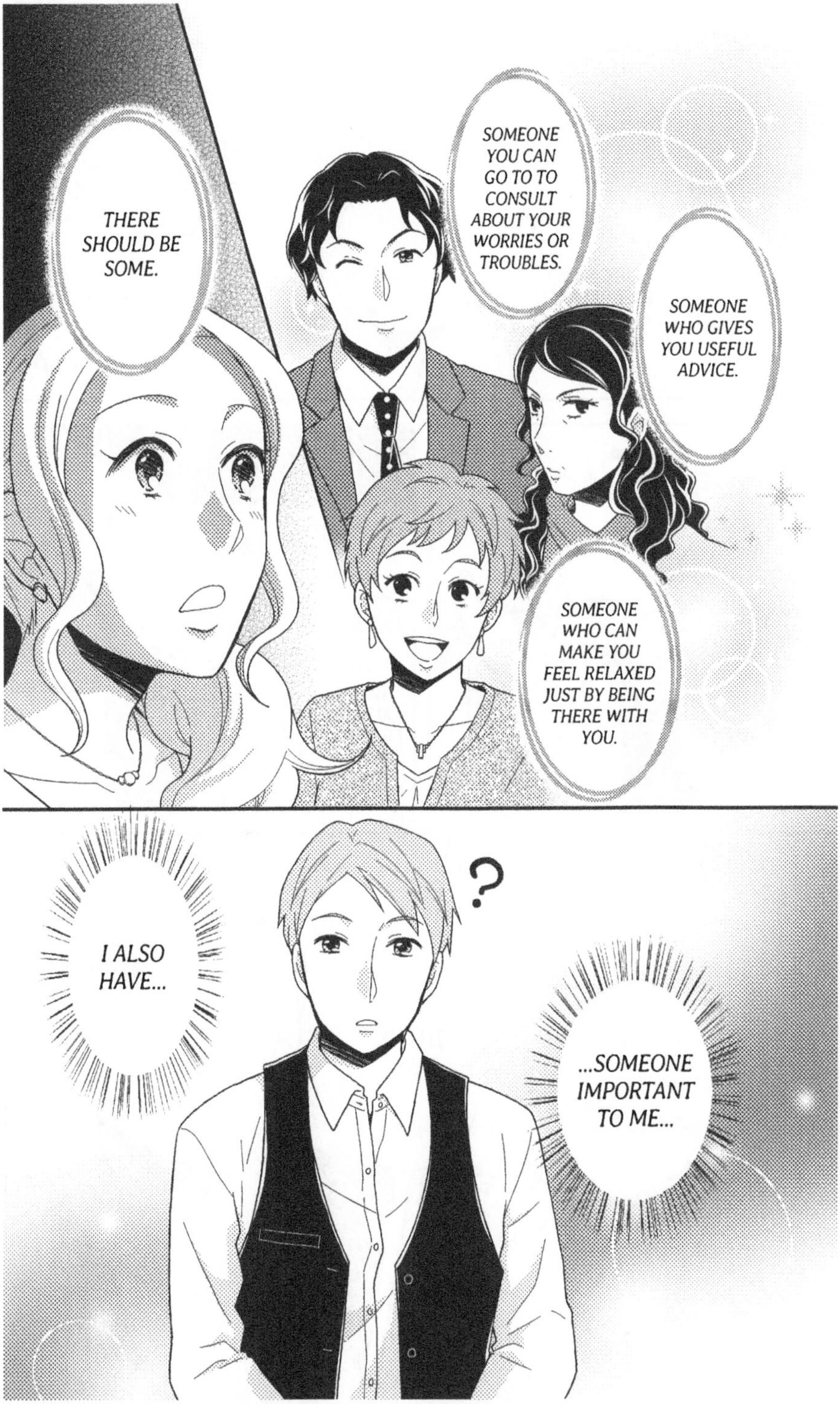
SOMEONE YOU CAN GO TO TO CONSULT ABOUT YOUR WORRIES OR TROUBLES.
THERE SHOULD BE SOME.
SOMEONE WHO GIVES YOU USEFUL ADVICE.
SOMEONE WHO CAN MAKE YOU FEEL RELAXED JUST BY BEING THERE WITH YOU.
?
...SOMEONE IMPORTANT TO ME...
I ALSO HAVE...

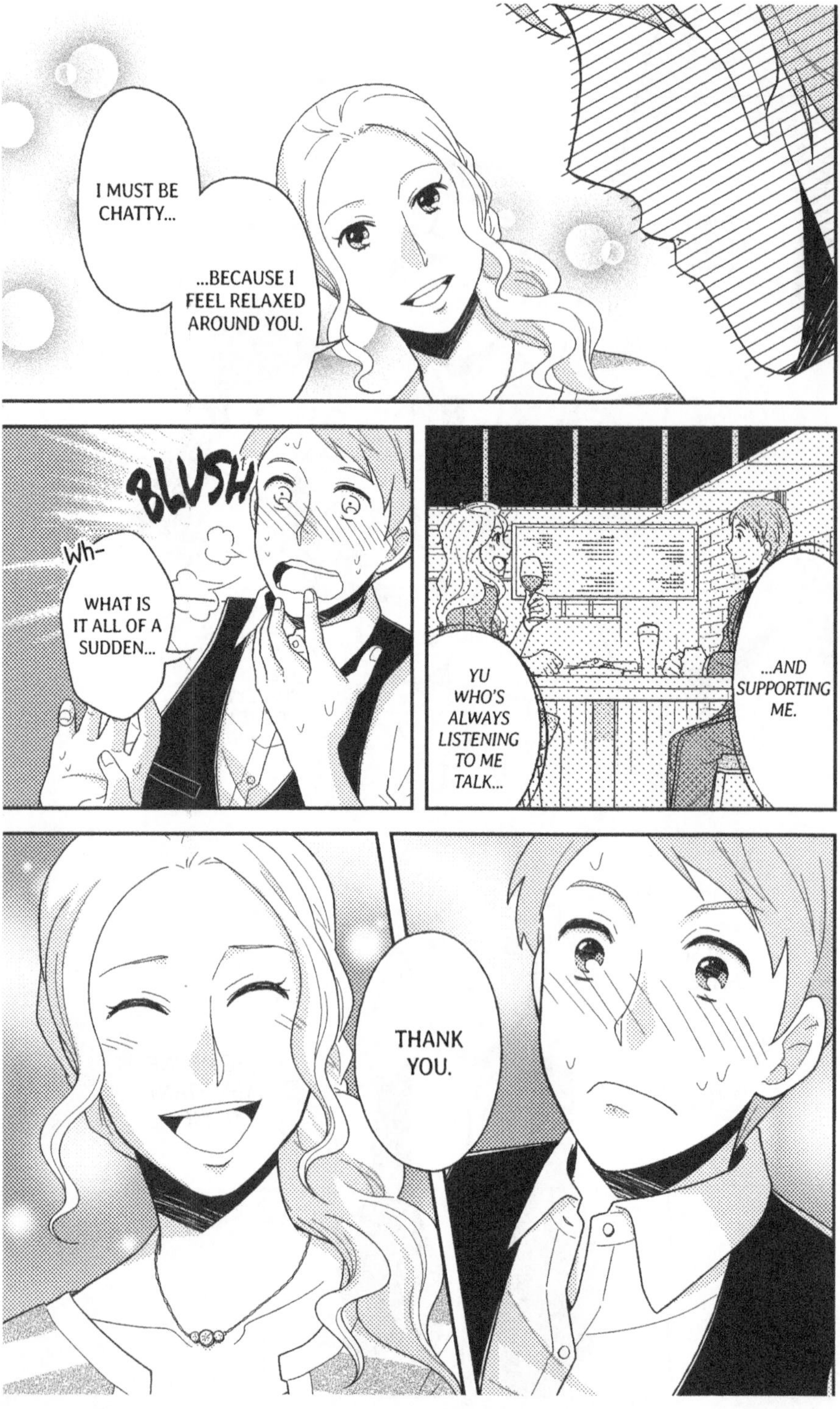
I MUST BE CHATTY...
...BECAUSE I FEEL RELAXED AROUND YOU.
BLUSH
Wh-
WHAT IS IT ALL OF A SUDDEN...
YU WHO'S ALWAYS LISTENING TO ME TALK...
...AND SUPPORTING ME.
THANK YOU.

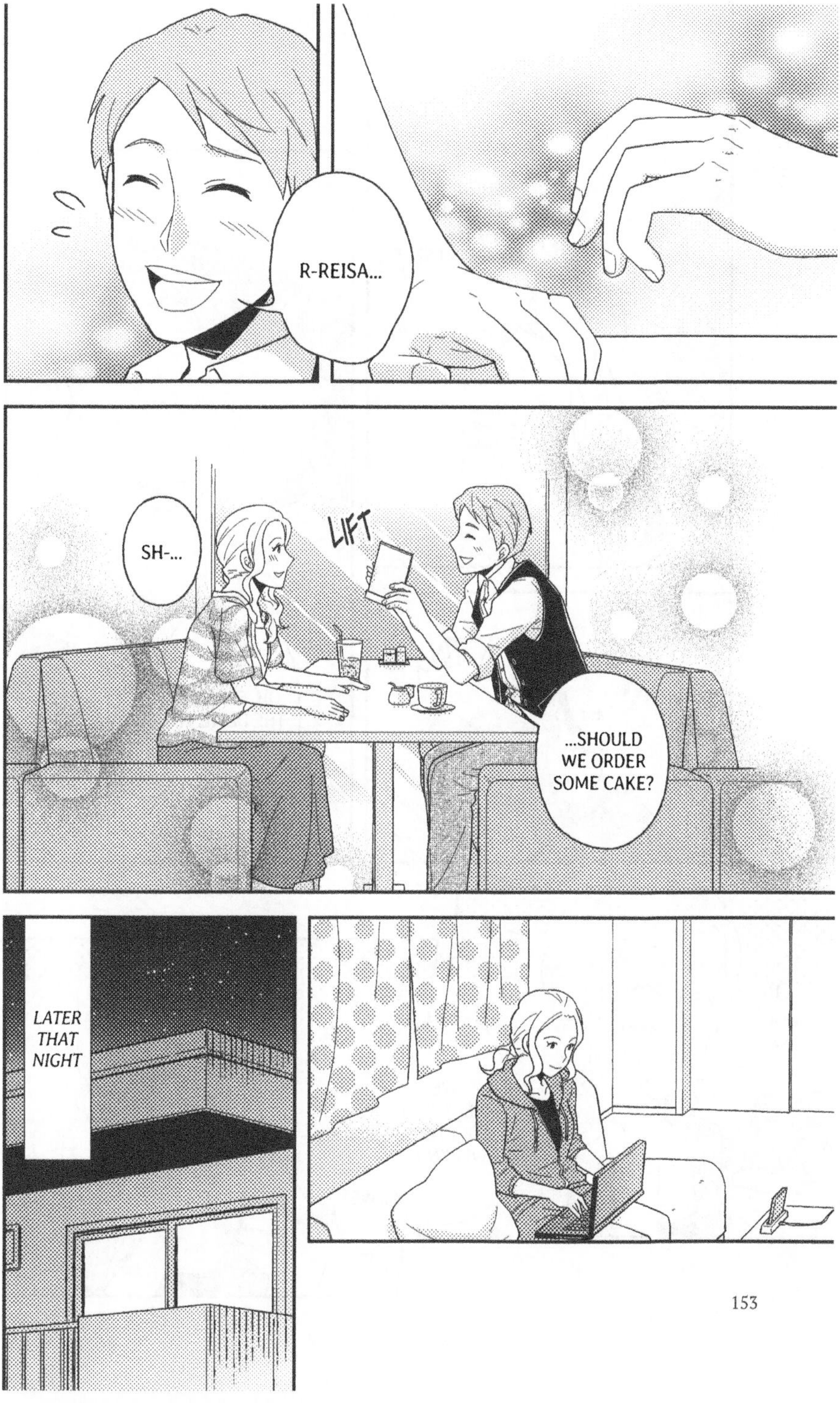
R-REISA...
SH-...
LIFT
...SHOULD WE ORDER SOME CAKE?
LATER THAT NIGHT

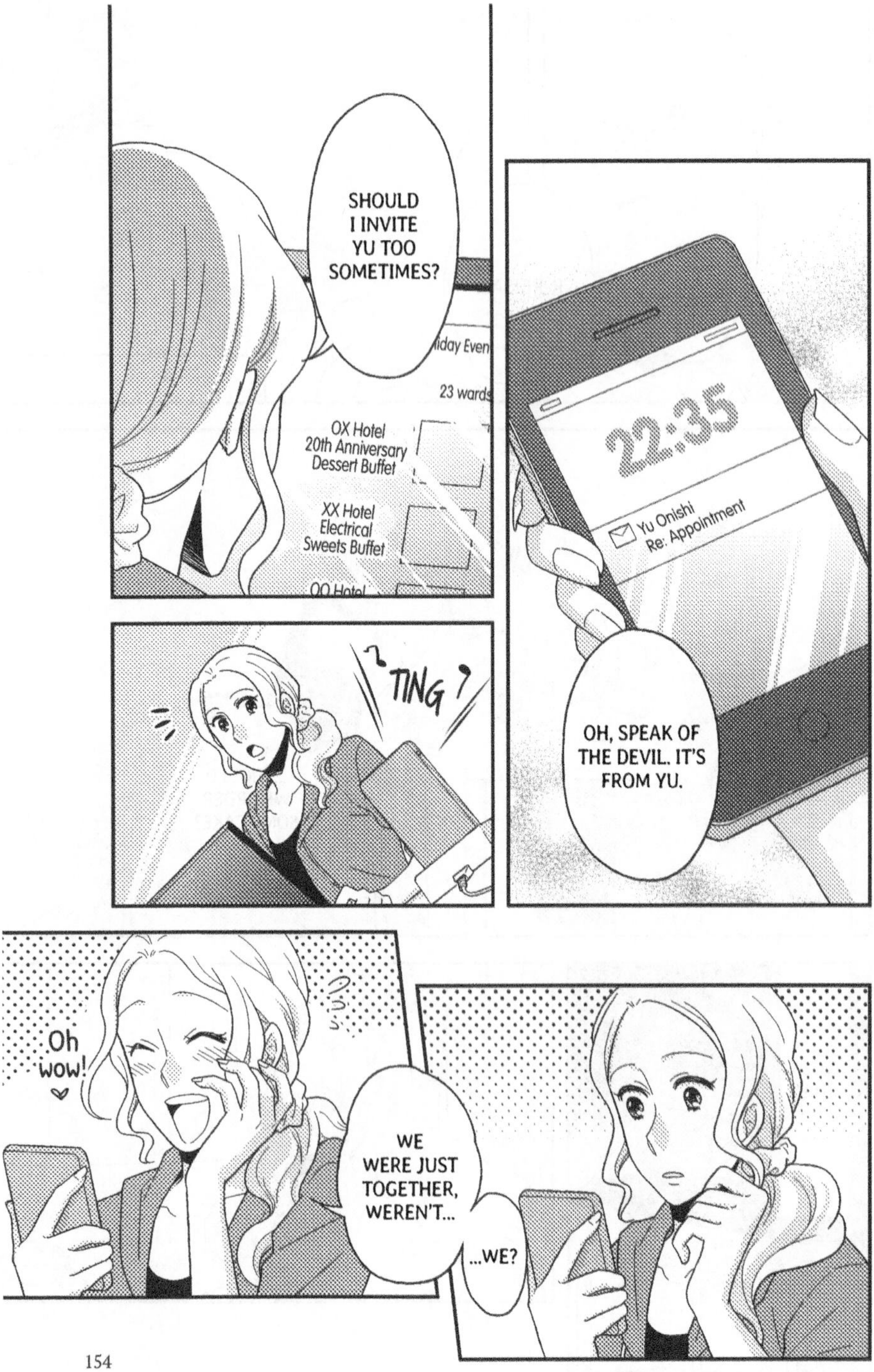
SHOULD I INVITE YU TOO SOMETIMES?
iday Even
23 wards
OX Hotel 20th Anniversary Dessert Buffet
XX Hotel Electrical Sweets Buffet
TING
22:35
Yu Onishi
Re: Appointment
OH, SPEAK OF THE DEVIL. IT'S FROM YU.
Oh wow!
WE WERE JUST TOGETHER, WEREN'T...
...WE?

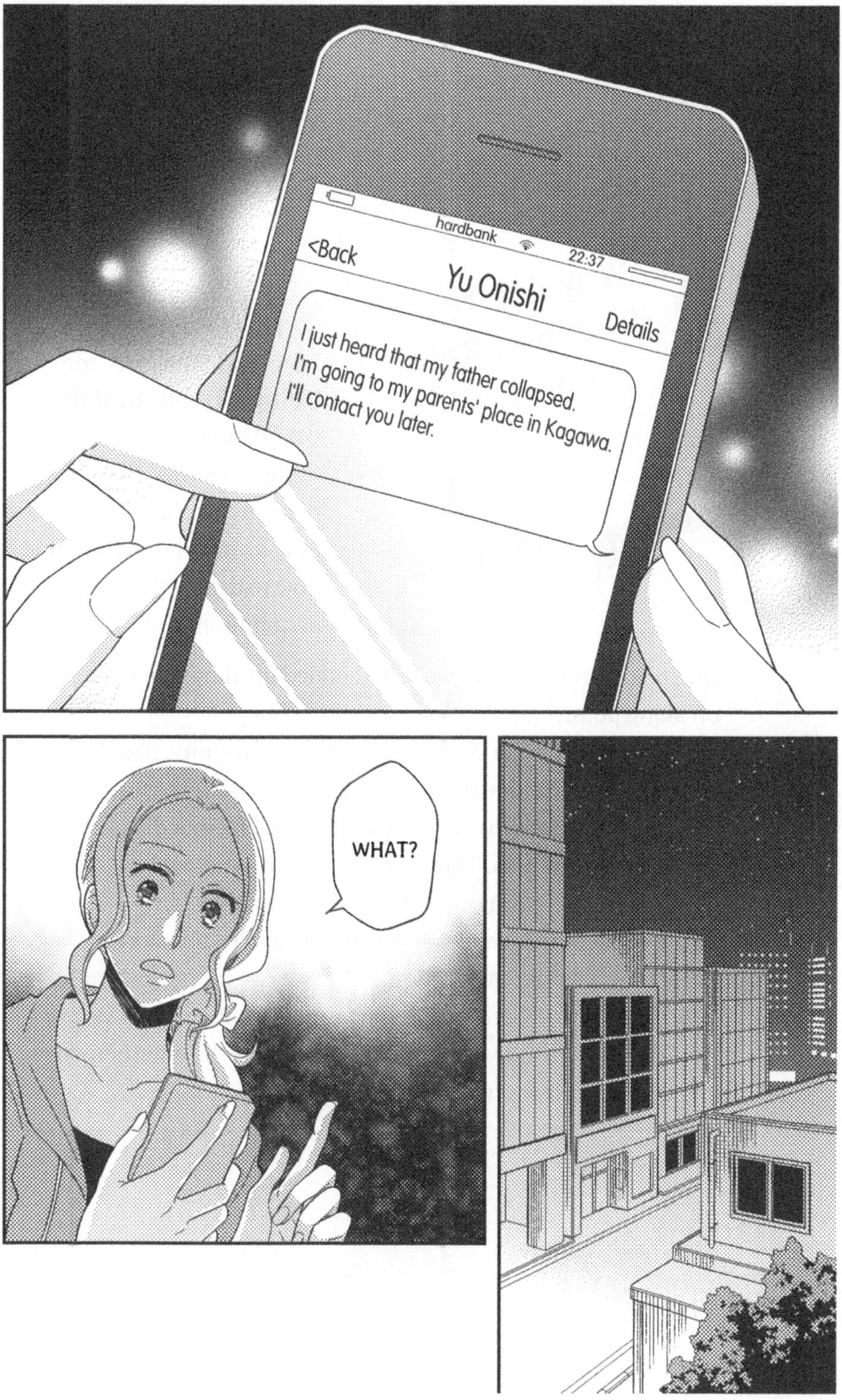
hardbank
22:37
<Back
Yu Onishi
Details
I just heard that my father collapsed.
I'm going to my parents' place in Kagawa.
I'll contact you later.
WHAT?

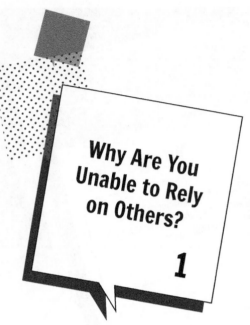

Why Are You Unable to Rely on Others?

1

⇨ **The External and Internal Reasons for Being Unable to Rely on Others**

Reisa learned the basics of resilience. She learned how to control her emotions and how to deal with negative assumptions. However, she took on too much at work and ended up almost reaching her breaking point.

People who have a strong sense of responsibility, like Reisa, tend to try too hard without asking for help from those around them. It would be a disaster if such people failed or encountered some sort of problem. They may attempt to resolve the issue themselves, increasing the amount of stress they have inside of them. The more serious the person is, the more likely they will lose motivation.

So, why is it so hard for people to rely on others? Answers to this question include external factors such as the environment and internal factors from people themselves.

⇨ The Three Features of Workplaces That Are Not Cooperative

Let's first think about external factors. Among them, even if someone is in a tough situation at work, there are others in the workplace who may be turning a blind eye or not even paying attention. The following three traits are seen in such workplaces:

• **High stress levels:** Personal relationships, especially in the workplace, are very cold. You can feel the stress aimed at others.

• **Poor ventilation:** Not only is there very little conversation, there isn't much movement going on. Employee transfers and replacements are overdue, resulting in a fixed organization.

• **Unable to see caring attitudes:** There is a lack of camaraderie within the organization. No one is interested in the work performance of other employees, and there is no mutual concern.

In a workplace where no one has concern for other employees, you will not be recognized no matter how hard you work. Employees become apathetic, and those who work hard would just be wasting their time.

As a result, the more serious someone is, the more mentally exhausted they can become, and they may burn out. The dilution that comes from the lack of connection among employees can result in a negative effect on mental health.

According to research, some features that are common in workplaces that have had an increase in mental health problems are as follows: "There's very little communication," "There has been a decrease in colleagues helping each other out," and "There has been an increase in working alone."

⇨ Assumptions Can Hinder Relationships with Others

Internal factors also play a role in the inability to ask for help when you are overwhelmed. Negative assumptions inside your heart are mostly to blame.

For example, if you are the owner of an apologetic dog who has a strong assumption called *self-accusation*, you may believe that you are responsible for every problem and not ask for help from others. Then if you fail, you may feel guilty for bothering everyone else. You may try to make up for it all by yourself.

If you have the devaluing mindset known as the loser dog, you may fear being compared to others. You may try to hide the fact that you have made a mistake in order to avoid feeling inferior when others criticize you.

Both of these issues come from low self-esteem. Instead of recognizing that anything that fails or goes wrong may be just a temporary thing that happened to occur, those with apologetic dog or loser dog assumptions believe that their abilities are the problem.

YOUR COLLEAGUES ARE GETTING THE SAME AMOUNT OF WORK DONE QUICKLY...
WHINE
LOSER DOG
YOU CAN'T COMPLAIN ABOUT SOME-THING SMALL LIKE THIS...

The reason Reisa was unable to rely on others and kept the work all to herself was because of the loser dog's assumption.

Get Social Support

2

⇨ **Build Quality Interpersonal Relationships**

In order to deal with negative assumptions as described in the previous section, you need to accept yourself and form relationships with people who are able to sympathize with your feelings.

I call them *supporters*. They will become your allies and support you, and even scold you at times.

In soccer, it's said that "there are 11 players on the field, but the cheers from the 12th player, the supporter, help the team achieve victory." In fact, teams that are playing on their home field have a higher win rate compared to when they are away.

Finding supporters and building quality interpersonal relationships on a regular basis will show their effect when you face adversity. According to research on resilience, the more people someone has around them who can provide emotional support, the faster that person recovers from mental depression.

Get Social Support

We call this *social support*. In tough times, the help of others becomes a necessity.

Supporters within a workplace are not limited to superiors and coworkers. They may include your best friend from school, your college teacher, your parents and siblings, your trusted counselor, and so on. For example, the president of a small and medium-sized enterprise I know finds his certified public accountant as an important supporter. He consults her about issues that cannot be discussed at the company.

⇨ Find Five Supporters

There may be some who wonder, "Do they think it's a pain when I ask for help?" In most cases, people feel pride in being relied on.

Many people believe that "I can handle this without asking for help from others." To tell you the truth, I was like this before. I acted very arrogantly, thinking that I would be able to solve everything by myself. At the time, I had zero supporters. I ended up facing a lot of problems that I was not able to handle and almost lost my motivation.

Because I had this painful experience, I now tell everyone: "You should have at least five people who will become your supporters."

Why five? Because one may not be enough to help you in a time of need, and more than five may be too many to handle if you are mutually helping each other out.

Supporters can be sorted into the following four categories: *assistance, information, advice,* and *intimacy.* The assistance type can help you when you're going through a tough time. The information type can provide you with knowledge when you are troubled. The advice type can give you useful suggestions or guidance when you are facing problems. The intimacy type can give you peace of mind by just being there.

You can use the following worksheet to identify five people who are important to you.

Find Five Supporters

Answer the following questions, and find a total of five supporters.

Q1. Who helps you when you're having a tough time?

Q2. Who gives you information when you're troubled?

Q3. Who gives you useful advice or guidance when you're facing problems?

Q4. Who gives you peace of mind by just being with you?

Supporter List

1. _____

2. _____

3. _____

4. _____

5. _____

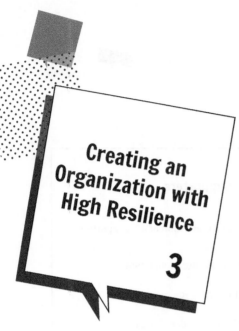

Creating an Organization with High Resilience

3

⇨ **What Are the Requirements for a Resilient Workplace?**

If an organization is connected through a relationship of mutual assistance, not only does the resilience of each employee working there increase, but the organization also becomes more resilient. If they encounter any adversity, they can bounce back in a short amount of time and overcome it.

What all resilient organizations have in common is that their employees have quality connections with one another. According to a study by Dr. Jane Dutton at the University of Michigan Business School, organizations that survive in the face of fierce global competition perform better and are worth working for because their internal connections are of a higher quality. A high-quality connection, even if the relationship is temporary, can give people energy.

Four factors are needed to form high-quality connections in both business and in private life. In the following section, we will be looking at each of these components in detail.

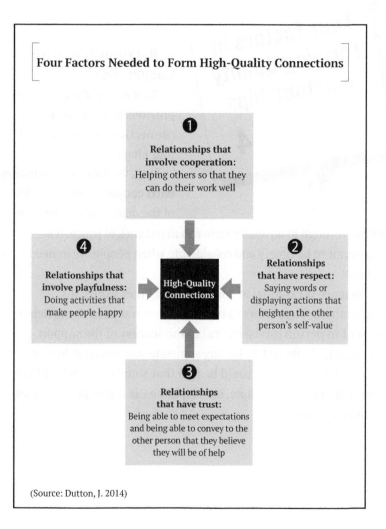

Four Factors Needed to Form High-Quality Connections

❶

Relationships that involve cooperation: Helping others so that they can do their work well

❹

Relationships that involve playfulness: Doing activities that make people happy

High-Quality Connections

❷

Relationships that have respect: Saying words or displaying actions that heighten the other person's self-value

❸

Relationships that have trust: Being able to meet expectations and being able to convey to the other person that they believe they will be of help

(Source: Dutton, J. 2014)

Four Factors in Forming Quality Relationships

4

⇨ **Relationships with Cooperation**

As was introduced on the previous page, high-quality connections are made up of four elements.

First, we have **relationships with cooperation.** The effect of the quality of connections shines through in adversity rather than in times of peace. It's important to be timely and considerate when people are in need of help.

Presence is essential at such times. In other words, it's important for supporters to be there when you need them. Being present in person can be critical to the success of the support. You may feel safe just by having someone you can trust in front of you. In that sense, it could be said that simply connecting from a far distance—for example, by telephone—is not as helpful as an in-person connection.

Get Social Support

⇨ Relationships with Respect

Next is to have relationships with respect. Whenever you interact with someone, do you act in a way that allows the other person to feel self-worth (feel respected)?

If the other person is unable to feel respected, that's because you are not paying enough attention to them. You may be disregarding their existence or ignoring them.

For example, let's say that a subordinate visits a superior's desk to make a report or ask for advice. How would the subordinate feel if the superior kept taking a glance at their phone screen. Not only will they feel uneasy, they might feel that they are not being treated as important. This is an example of a superior not respecting their subordinate.

We can also see this sort of thing in meetings. Those who look at their monitors or documents rather than at the speaker do not have enough respect for the speaker and do not have a quality connection.

The first step to showing respect to another person is to give your full attention by listening closely to them instead of listening while doing something else.

⇨ Relationships with Trust

The third factor is forming relationships with trust. When forming these relationships, you must first show sincerity. Sincerity is when the person's words match their actions. Carrying out one's words is a sign of sincerity.

Unfortunately, some people will change things up depending on whom they are talking to. They may act all high and mighty when making a declaration, but never get around to taking action. These people are all talk, no action. When this kind of behavior continues, trust with others is lost, and the quality of the connection drops.

It is also important to demonstrate trust in others through words and actions. Being sincere may not be enough. You must show that you trust others before they can trust you. Not realizing this may be a blindspot for many.

When I was working in a company, I personally felt dissatisfied and wondered, "Why doesn't my superior trust me more? They should trust me more. They should leave me in charge of this and not monitor me or nitpick." I felt irritation toward my superior who micromanaged me, just like Reisa did in our story.

However, I now believe that I was part of the problem. I never thought to convey my trust for my superior. I had a very passive attitude. If you really want to form a relationship based on trust, it is important to show your trust first.

⇨ Relationships with Playfulness

The final factor is relationships with playfulness. To form high-quality connections, it's helpful to take part in events together and work as a team toward a common goal in a game-like manner. Through play, you are able to create a psychological sense of ease that blows away any worries you may have. Games provide an opportunity to develop a deeper understanding of your teammates, leading to improved teamwork at the end of the day.

Ina Food Industry, a top-ranking company located in Ina City, Nagano Prefecture in Japan, is famous as a company that emphasizes the happiness of its employees. One of their big events is their annual employee trip. The destination is decided about a half a year in advance, and all the employees are divided into multiple groups to create a plan. On the first night of the event, a large banquet is held. The cost of hosting the banquet is large, but they continue to hold it because it increases the quality of connections between employees and provides an opportunity where employees can match the names and faces of others.

In addition, IT-related venture companies, which are said to be highly rewarding to work for, hold athletic meets and club activities with their employees the way large companies did in the Showa era.* Such activities exhibit playfulness and create quality connections. This contributes to raising the retention rate of excellent employees by making them feel pride in being a member of the company. In this way, doing fun and playful things together can go a long way in building quality relationships.

*Note: In Japan, the Showa era was from 1926 to 1989.

Part 4

Restoring Your Self-Confidence

HEARING THAT GIVES ME CONFIDENCE.
THANK YOU.
...AND GO...
BAM
...TO HIM!
AND CAKE-CHAN...
...MAYBE YOU COULD THINK ABOUT WHAT YOU REALLY WANT, TOO.

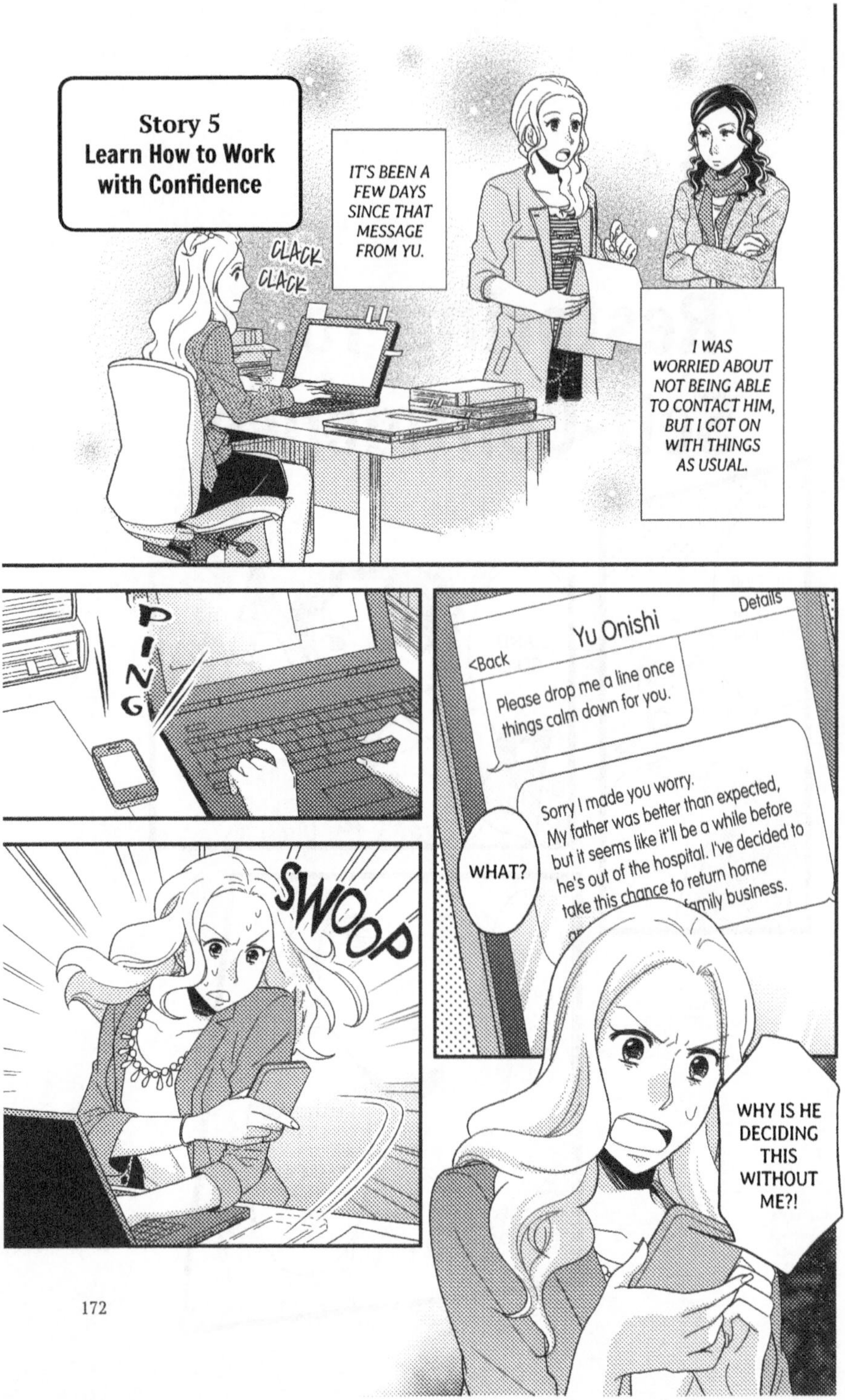
Story 5
Learn How to Work with Confidence
IT'S BEEN A FEW DAYS SINCE THAT MESSAGE FROM YU.
CLACK CLACK
I WAS WORRIED ABOUT NOT BEING ABLE TO CONTACT HIM, BUT I GOT ON WITH THINGS AS USUAL.
PING
Yu Onishi
Details
<Back
Please drop me a line once things calm down for you.
Sorry I made you worry.
My father was better than expected,
but it seems like it'll be a while before
he's out of the hospital. I've decided to
take this chance to return home
family business.
WHAT?
SWOOP
WHY IS HE DECIDING THIS WITHOUT ME?!

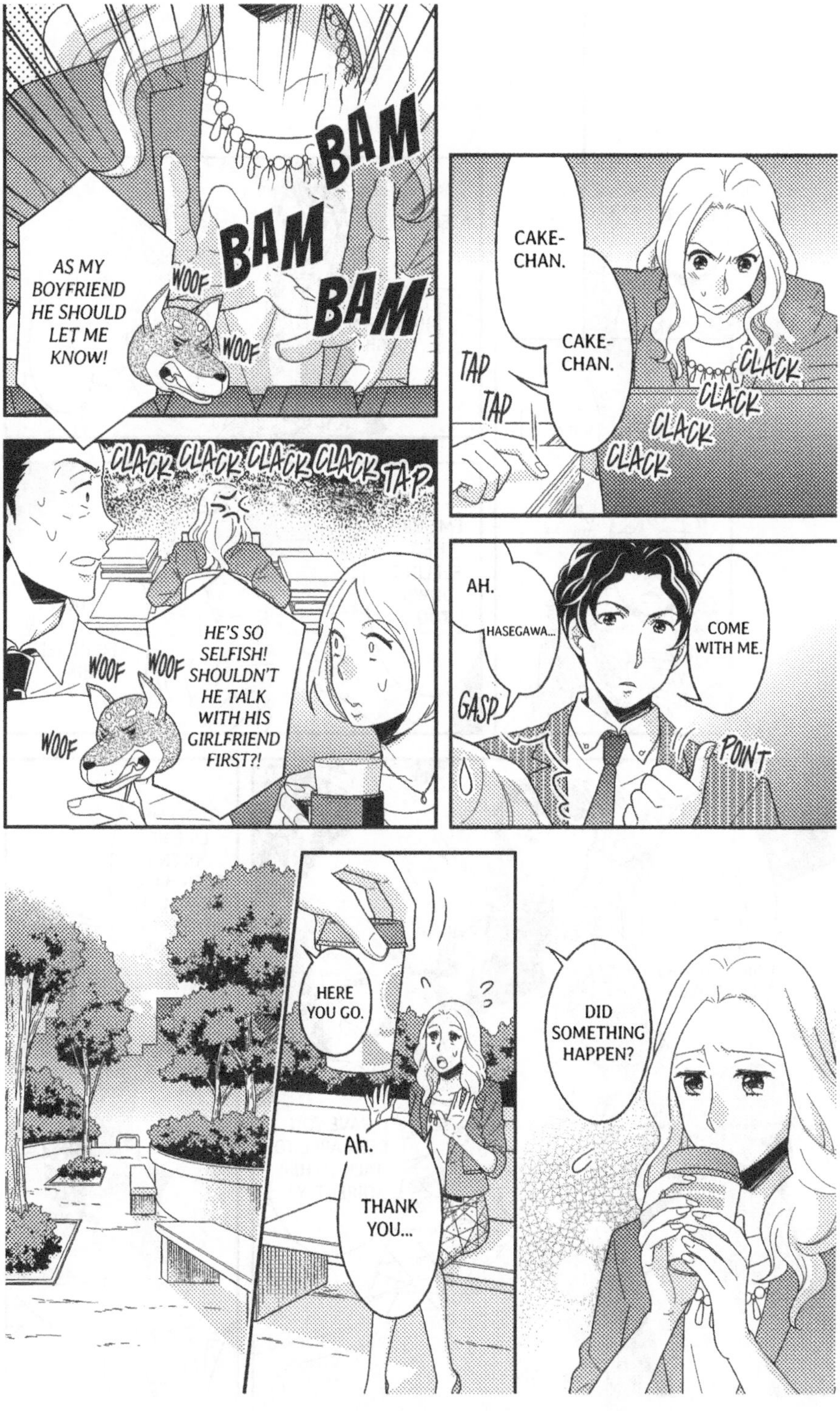
BAM
BAM
BAM
WOOF
WOOF
AS MY BOYFRIEND HE SHOULD LET ME KNOW!
CAKE-CHAN.
CAKE-CHAN.
TAP
TAP
CLACK
CLACK
CLACK
CLACK
CLACK CLACK CLACK CLACK TAP
HE'S SO SELFISH! SHOULDN'T HE TALK WITH HIS GIRLFRIEND FIRST?!
WOOF
WOOF
WOOF
COME WITH ME.
AH.
HASEGAWA...
GASP
POINT
HERE YOU GO.
Ah.
THANK YOU...
DID SOMETHING HAPPEN?

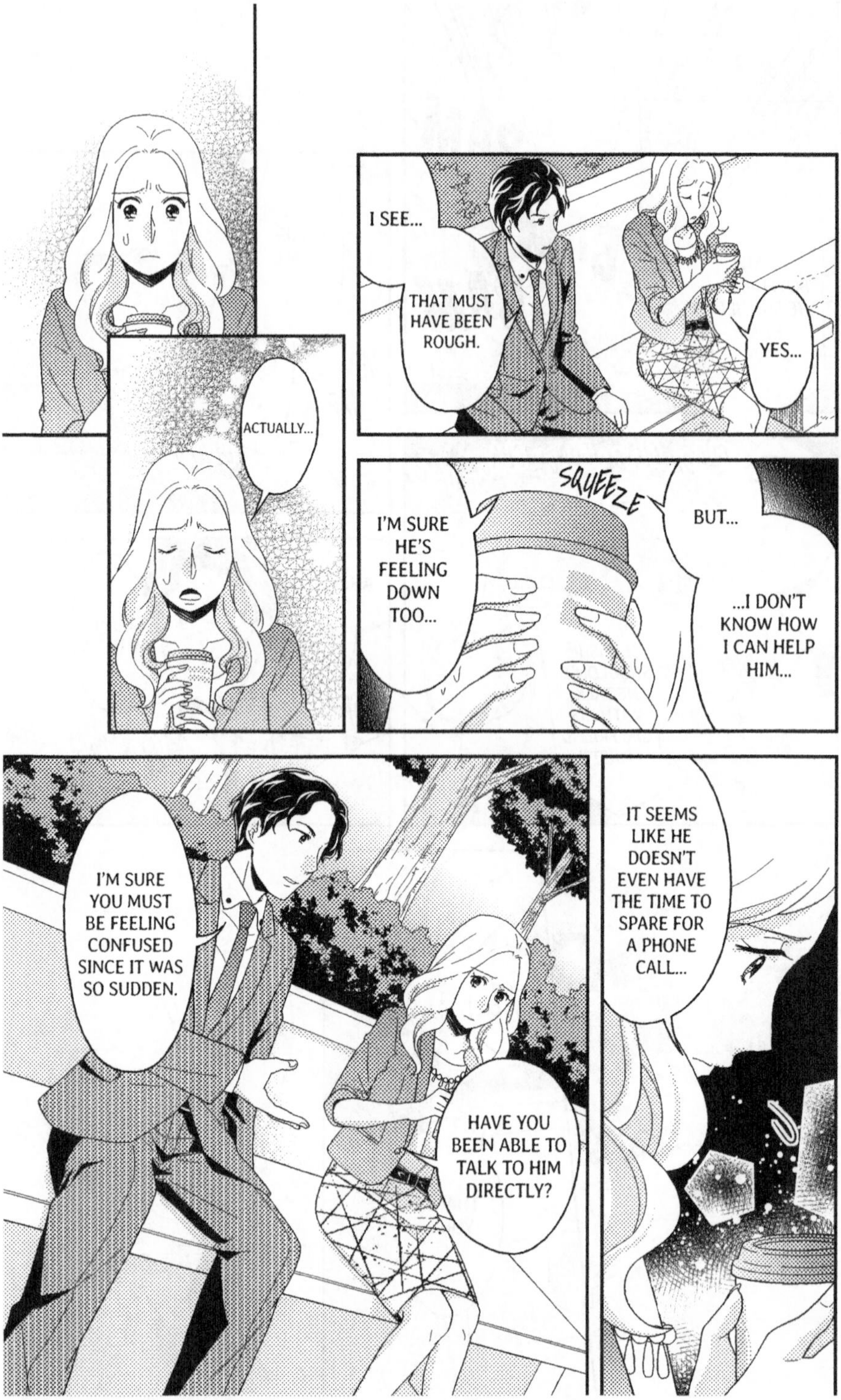
I SEE...
THAT MUST HAVE BEEN ROUGH.
YES...
ACTUALLY...
I'M SURE HE'S FEELING DOWN TOO...
SQUEEZE
BUT...
...I DON'T KNOW HOW I CAN HELP HIM...
HAVE YOU BEEN ABLE TO TALK TO HIM DIRECTLY?
IT SEEMS LIKE HE DOESN'T EVEN HAVE THE TIME TO SPARE FOR A PHONE CALL...
I'M SURE YOU MUST BE FEELING CONFUSED SINCE IT WAS SO SUDDEN.

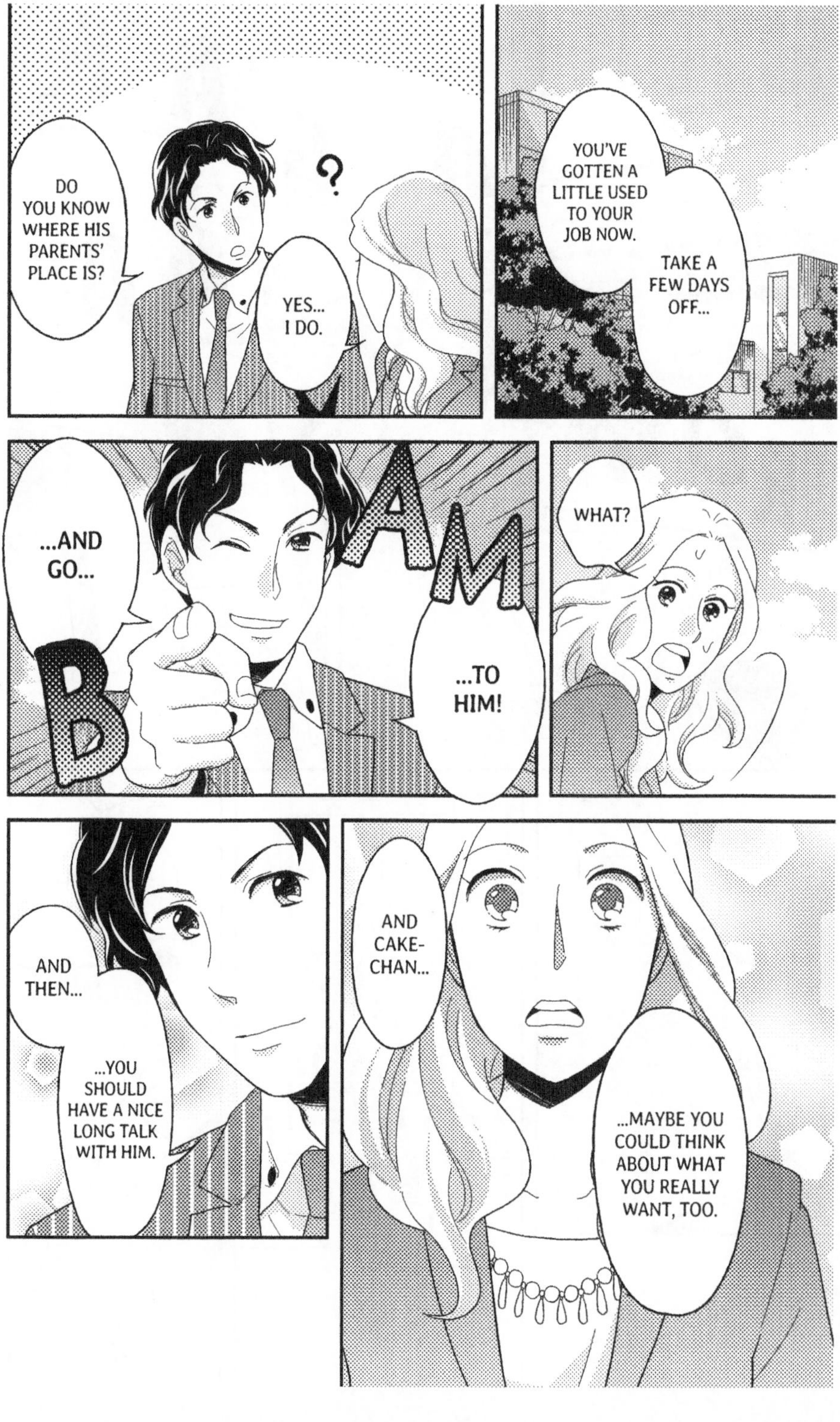
DO YOU KNOW WHERE HIS PARENTS' PLACE IS?
?
YES... I DO.
YOU'VE GOTTEN A LITTLE USED TO YOUR JOB NOW.
TAKE A FEW DAYS OFF...
...AND GO...
BAM
...TO HIM!
WHAT?
AND THEN...
...YOU SHOULD HAVE A NICE LONG TALK WITH HIM.
AND CAKE-CHAN...
...MAYBE YOU COULD THINK ABOUT WHAT YOU REALLY WANT, TOO.

15 Takamatsu 533

I'll fly down
tomorrow morning.

Huh?

I'll pick you up at
the airport so tell me
when you'll arrive.

Estimated arrival
is 10:50 AM at
Takamatsu Airport.

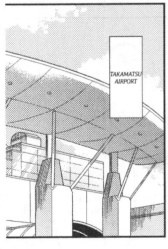

TAKAMATSU
AIRPORT

REISA!

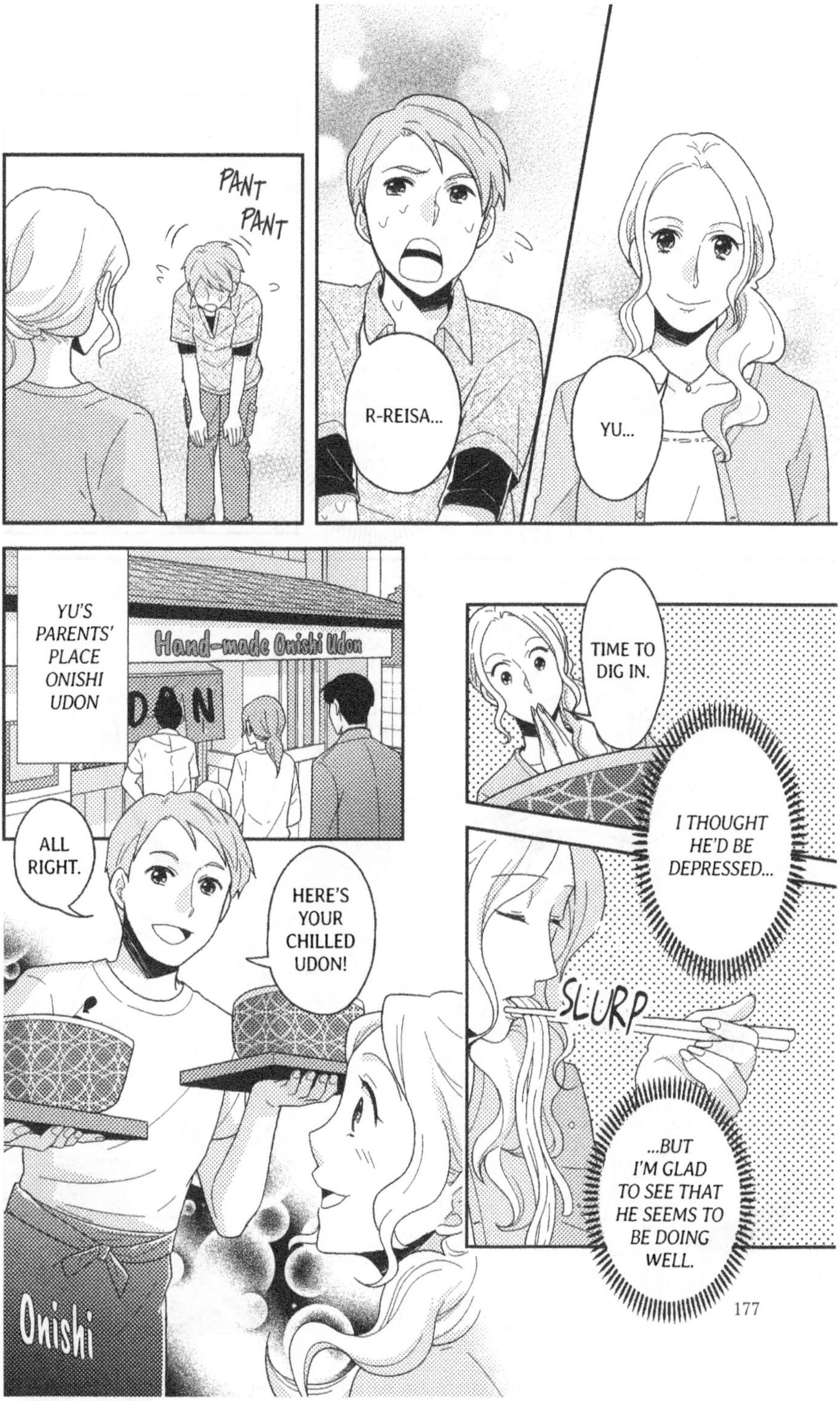
PANT PANT
R-REISA...
YU...
YU'S PARENTS' PLACE ONISHI UDON
Hand-made Onishi Udon
DON
ALL RIGHT.
HERE'S YOUR CHILLED UDON!
Onishi
TIME TO DIG IN.
I THOUGHT HE'D BE DEPRESSED...
SLURP
...BUT I'M GLAD TO SEE THAT HE SEEMS TO BE DOING WELL.

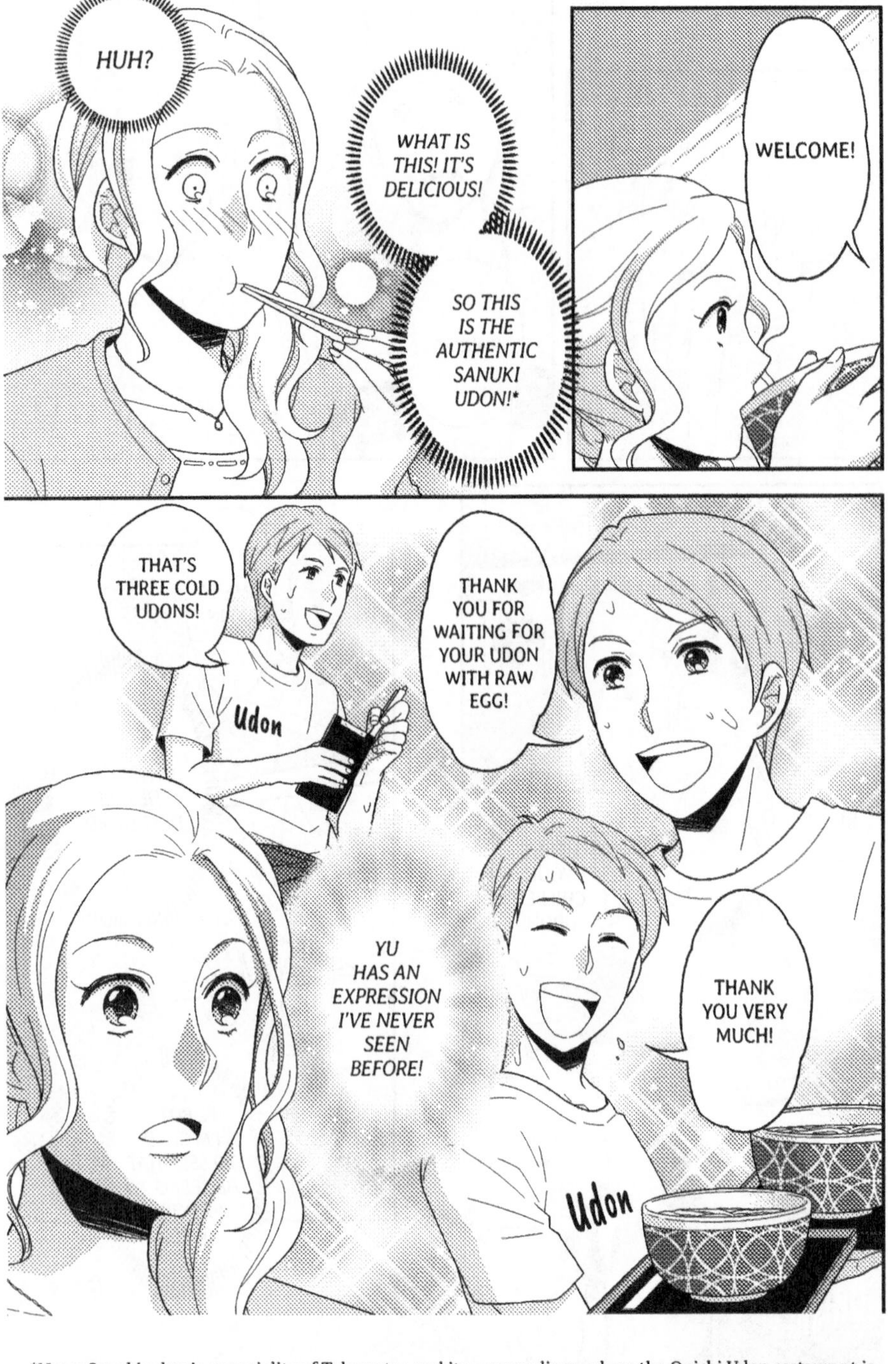
WELCOME!
HUH?
WHAT IS THIS! IT'S DELICIOUS!
SO THIS IS THE AUTHENTIC SANUKI UDON!*
THANK YOU FOR WAITING FOR YOUR UDON WITH RAW EGG!
THAT'S THREE COLD UDONS!
Udon
THANK YOU VERY MUCH!
YU HAS AN EXPRESSION I'VE NEVER SEEN BEFORE!
Udon

*Note: Sanuki udon is a speciality of Takamatsu and its surroundings, where the Onishi Udon restaurant is.

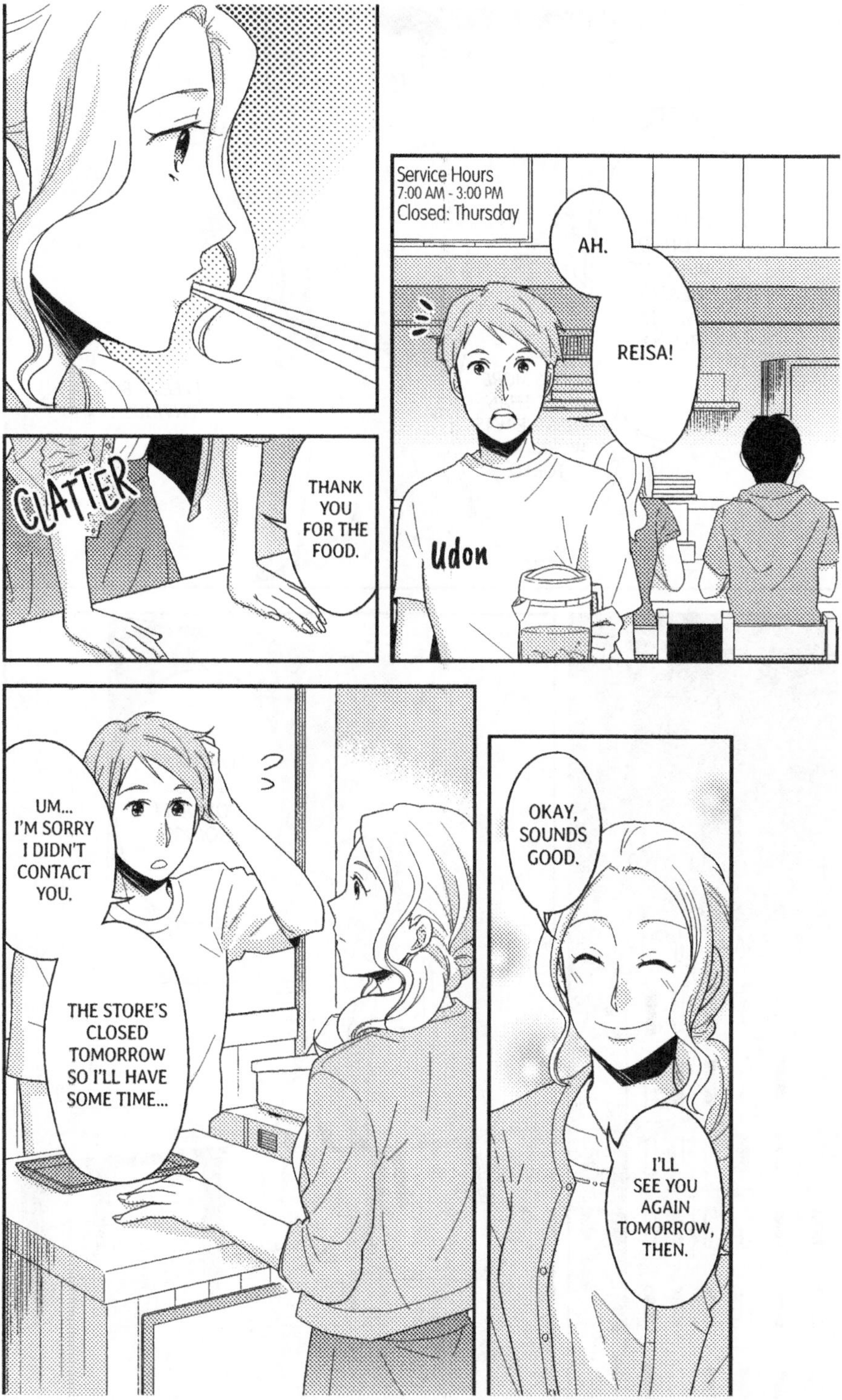
Service Hours
7:00 AM - 3:00 PM
Closed: Thursday
AH.
REISA!
Udon
CLATTER
THANK YOU FOR THE FOOD.
UM... I'M SORRY I DIDN'T CONTACT YOU.
THE STORE'S CLOSED TOMORROW SO I'LL HAVE SOME TIME...
OKAY, SOUNDS GOOD.
I'LL SEE YOU AGAIN TOMORROW, THEN.

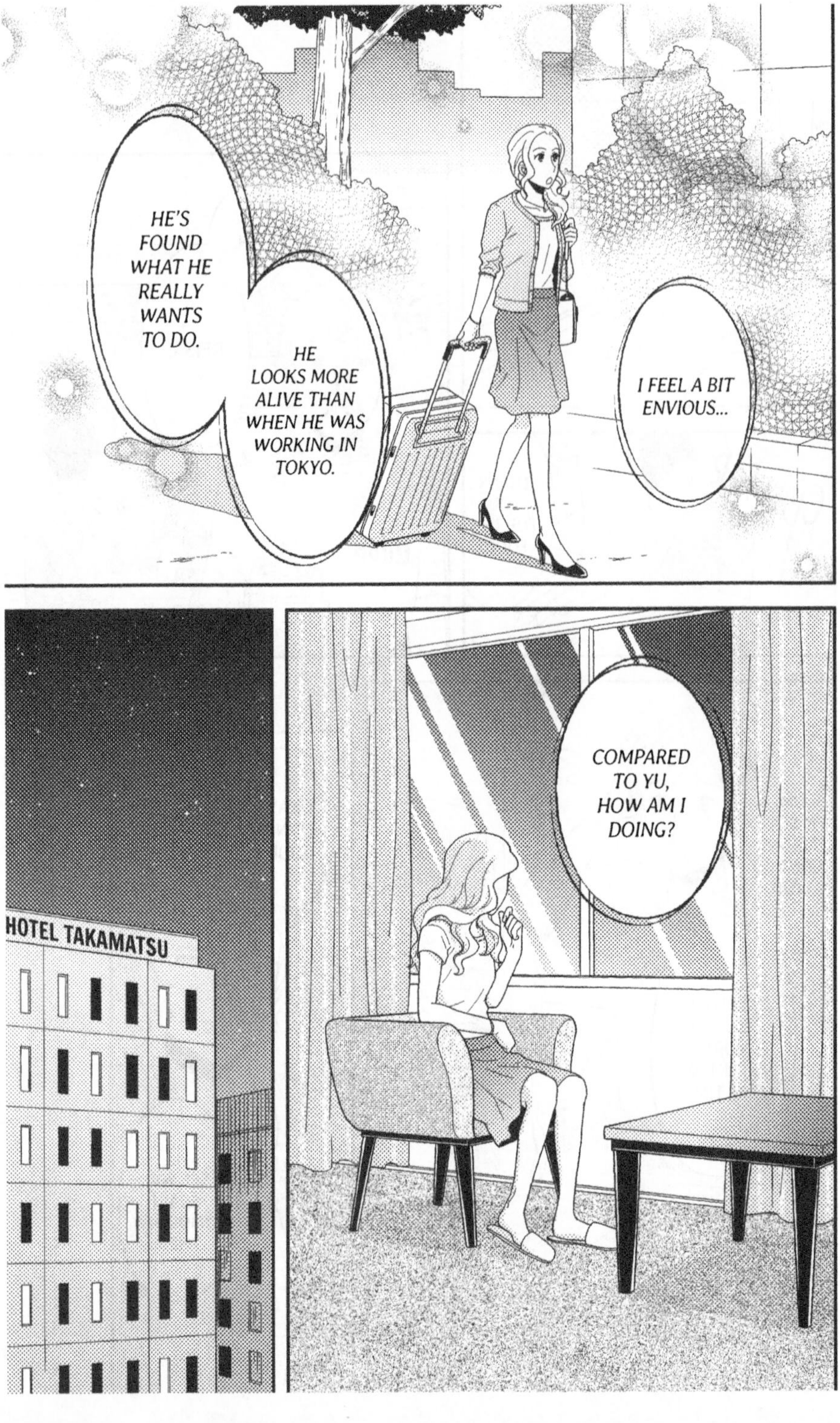
HE'S FOUND WHAT HE REALLY WANTS TO DO.
HE LOOKS MORE ALIVE THAN WHEN HE WAS WORKING IN TOKYO.
I FEEL A BIT ENVIOUS...
HOTEL TAKAMATSU
COMPARED TO YU, HOW AM I DOING?

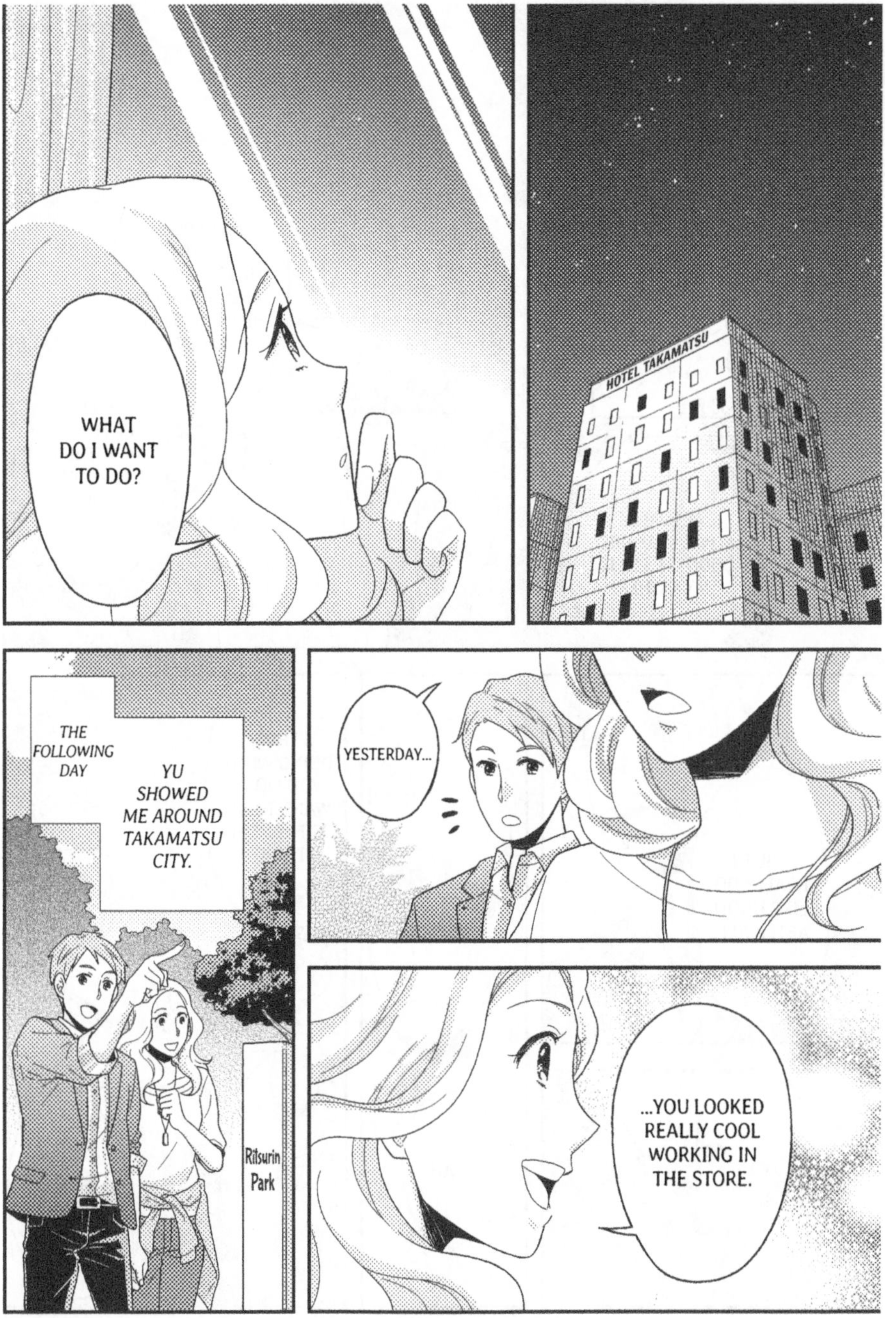
WHAT DO I WANT TO DO?
HOTEL TAKAMATSU
THE FOLLOWING DAY
YU SHOWED ME AROUND TAKAMATSU CITY.
Ritsurin Park
YESTERDAY...
...YOU LOOKED REALLY COOL WORKING IN THE STORE.

R-REALLY?

BUT I WAS TOLD IT'S A HARSH WORLD AND IT WOULD BE IMPOSSIBLE FOR ME.

SO I GAVE UP BACK THEN AND FOUND A JOB...

...ACTUALLY, I ALWAYS ADMIRED UDON CHEFS LIKE MY FATHER.

...BUT I REALLY DO LIKE UDON AFTER ALL.

YEAH...

I THINK DOING WHAT YOU MOST WANT TO DO IS THE BEST THING.

Y-YOU THINK?

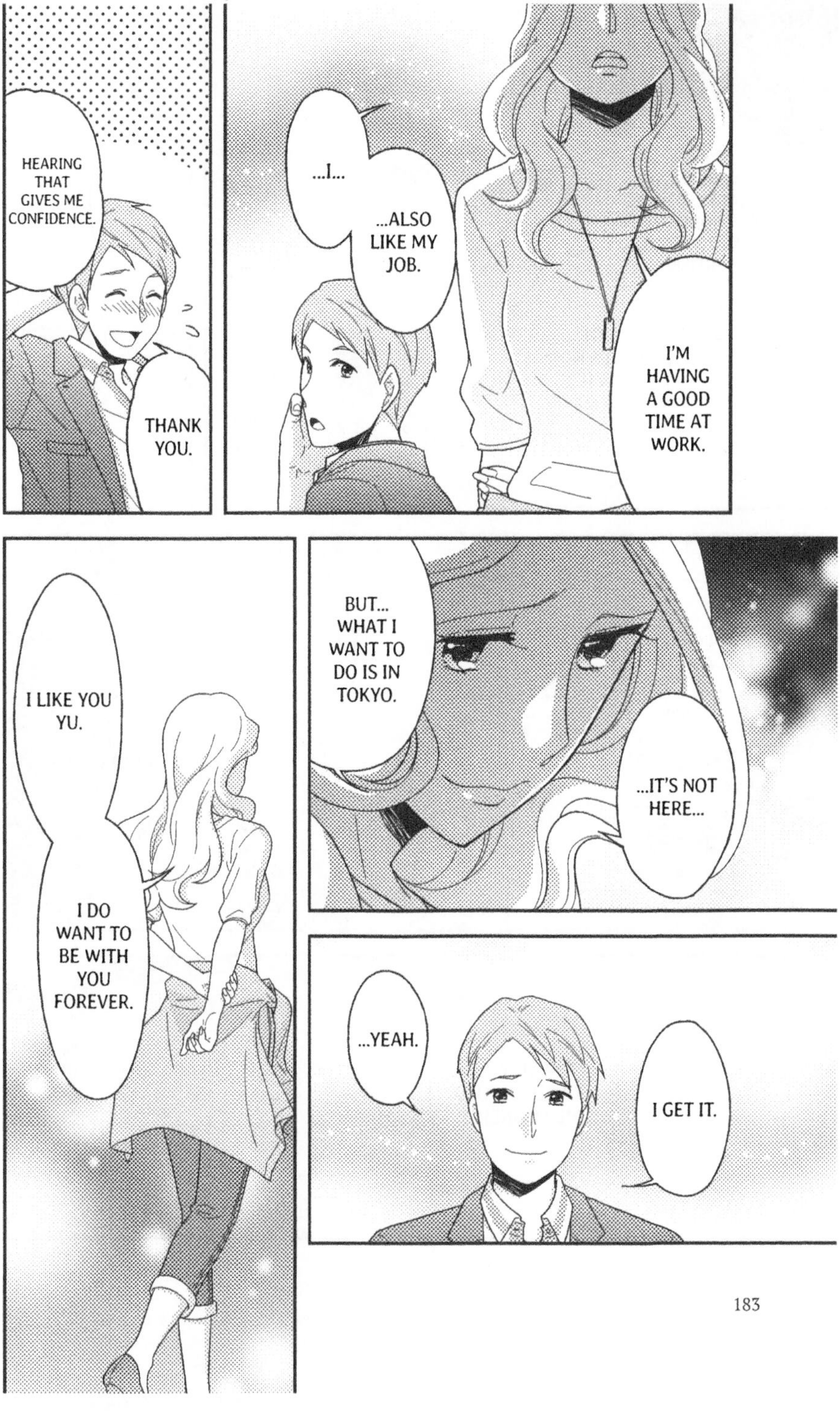
...I...
...ALSO LIKE MY JOB.
I'M HAVING A GOOD TIME AT WORK.
THANK YOU.
HEARING THAT GIVES ME CONFIDENCE.
BUT... WHAT I WANT TO DO IS IN TOKYO.
...IT'S NOT HERE...
...YEAH.
I GET IT.
I LIKE YOU YU.
I DO WANT TO BE WITH YOU FOREVER.

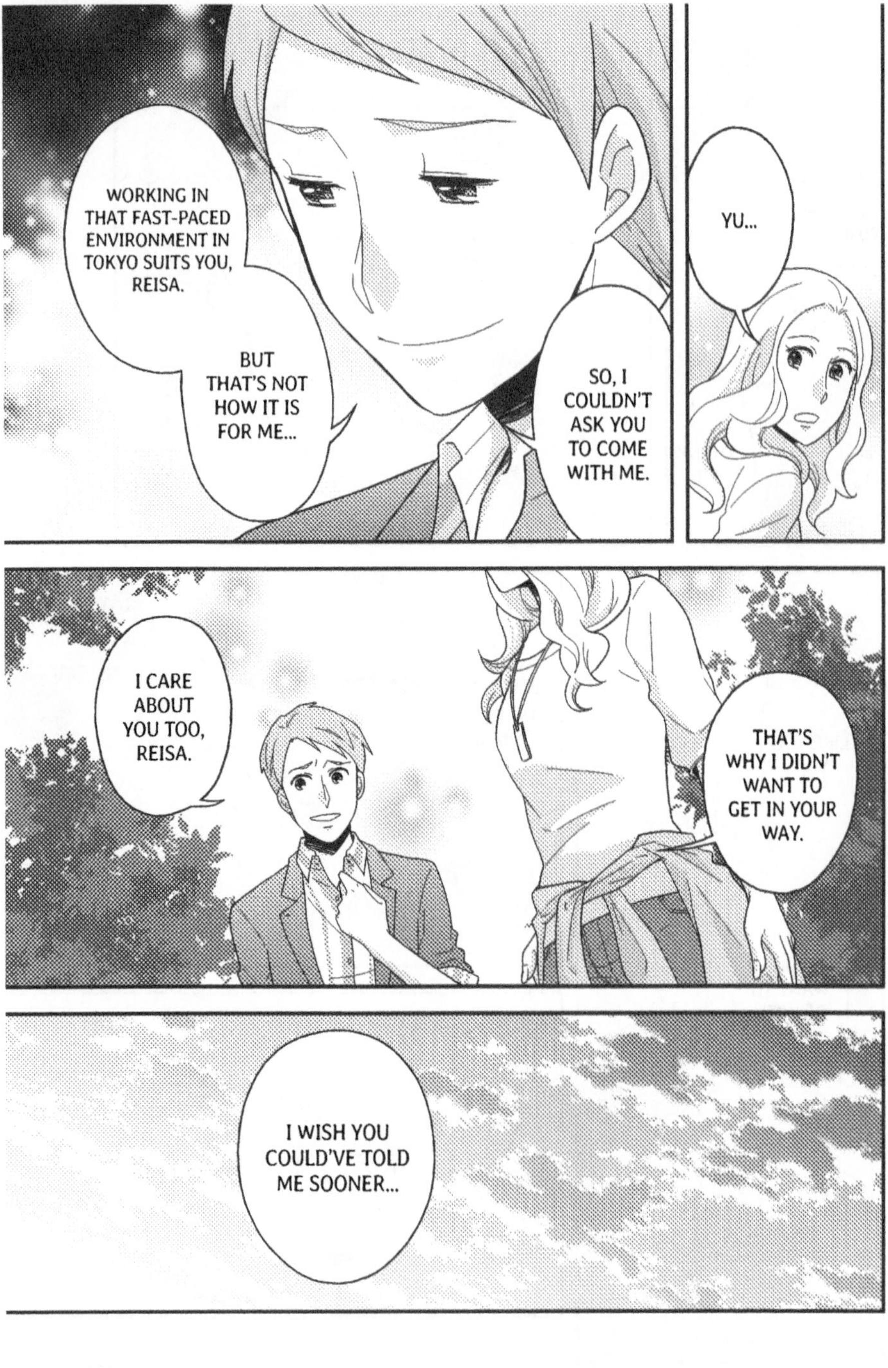
YU...
WORKING IN THAT FAST-PACED ENVIRONMENT IN TOKYO SUITS YOU, REISA.
BUT THAT'S NOT HOW IT IS FOR ME...
SO, I COULDN'T ASK YOU TO COME WITH ME.
THAT'S WHY I DIDN'T WANT TO GET IN YOUR WAY.
I CARE ABOUT YOU TOO, REISA.
I WISH YOU COULD'VE TOLD ME SOONER...

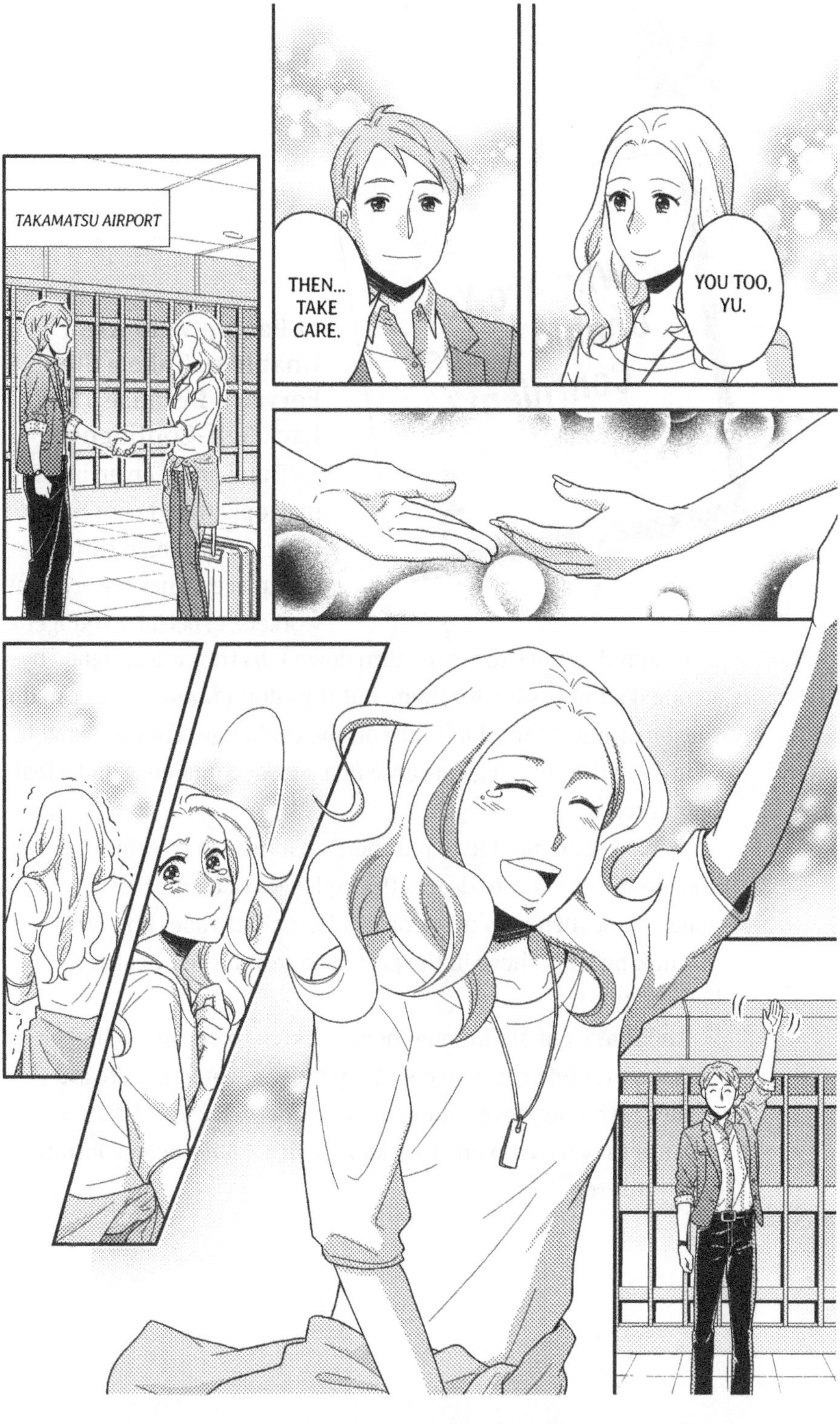

TAKAMATSU AIRPORT
THEN... TAKE CARE.
YOU TOO, YU.

Why Are You Unable to Feel Confident?

1

⇨ **People Who Are Unable to Take a Step Forward Because They Lack Self-Confidence**

There has been an increase in people who do not have self-confidence. In various workplaces, I have heard that workers, especially younger ones, stand out because they turn down jobs they are assigned by saying it's impossible for them. But they don't know if they can do the job or not if they don't take on the challenge. They are unable to take on the challenge because of a lack of confidence and a fear of failure.

Managers are unable to put their trust in such "newbies" and are unsure how to deal with employees of a different generation. Such employees have different attitudes and ways of thinking from those in the past. As a result, their hearts become tired.

And that's not all. Among those selected to engage in higher ranks to promote the active participation of women, there are some who do not have confidence as leaders. They feel distressed because they have no one to ask for advice. I have been consulted about this too.

There has been an increase in the number of middle-aged employees who have no confidence in their careers. Once they reach the turning point of their career, somewhere between 40 and 45 years of age, their valuation within the company will become set in stone.

Some people come to realize that continuing in the same job does not open up future prospects. However, fear of the risks prevents them from taking new steps like changing jobs. And while they sit still, they pass the age where they are suitable to change jobs, and their future prospects are blocked.

Some leaders are also unable to feel confident, because in the present age where change has become the norm, it's not possible for them to make use of the rules of thumb from the past. It's not easy to make decisions in uncertain times. Procrastinating or being unable to decide on anything may also be a sign of lack of confidence.

⇨ What Happens When You Are Unable to Have Self-Confidence?

Lack of self-confidence can keep you from progressing in your work and career and can lead to psychological stagnation. It also poses a risk to your mental health, making it easier to lose heart when faced with adversity. The weaker someone's resilience becomes, the more they lose confidence in themselves. Even if a good opportunity shows up for them, out of their fear of failure, they may choose to maintain the status quo to protect themselves.

They end up facing their backs to the opportunities life gives to them. If they keep at this, they won't be successful at work and won't be able to improve themselves.

⇨ The Reason You Lose Self-Confidence

Why are there so many people who lack confidence in themselves? Indeed, why do people lose confidence?

Negative emotions are behind the loss of self-confidence. When our palms get sweaty and our hearts start to beat quickly, negative emotions are born inside of us. That emotion holds us behind and prevents us from taking a step forward. Four negative emotions contribute to our loss of confidence: worry, fear, depressed feelings, and helplessness. If you can learn to control these feelings, you will be able to build self-confidence.

• **Worry:** Worry is anxiety or concern caused by negative predictions of future events or uncertainty about the future.

Typical Negative Accounts That Hinder Self-Confidence

Worry	• Cause: Negative predictions about the future • Concerns about the uncertain future • Avoid taking action

Fear	• Cause: A threat beyond your control • Includes the fear of failure • Can increase the risk of cardiovascular illnesses

Depressed Feelings	• Cause: Prediction of losing something important • Lowers self-esteem • Encourages withdrawal-type behavior

Helplessness	• Cause: Lack of self-determination • Believing that you are unable to change anything • Decrease in the energy to take action

• **Fear:** Fear is an emotion born from the thought that something is beyond your control. It includes the fear of failure.

• **Depressed Feelings:** Self-deprecating thoughts such as "Is it possible that I'm useless to this company?" create melancholy and depressed feelings. You lose self-esteem and feel down.

• **Helplessness:** Helplessness is an emotion that is born from the prediction that you are unable to change anything in the future when encountering a problem out of your control. This emotion is often seen in employees who appear to be expressionless, have soulless eyes, and are apathetic.

The Psychological Resources to Heighten Self-Confidence

2

⇨ Increasing Self-Efficacy

Many books have been written that address motivation and confidence, but they often differ in their definitions of what confidence is. What is clear, however, is psychological research regarding the connection between self-efficacy and self-confidence. Practical methods to improve self-efficacy have been well-established, and what is certain is that *increasing self-efficacy is the shortcut to greater self-confidence.*

⇨ What Is Self-Efficacy?

Self-efficacy was first advocated in 1977 by Alfred Bandura, a professor of psychology at Stanford University. He defined *self-efficacy* as "the belief in yourself that you can work toward a worthy goal." In a nutshell, it's the strong conviction that you can accomplish your goals if you try, along with the confidence that you can produce expected results when faced with a difficult task.

The feeling that you can do it on your own encourages positive actions. It goes without saying that a high sense of self-efficacy is important for success in life and work.

⇨ Self-Efficacy and Resilience

People who have high self-efficacy have the following traits:

- They show high performance at work.
- They are able to perform effectively in stressful situations.

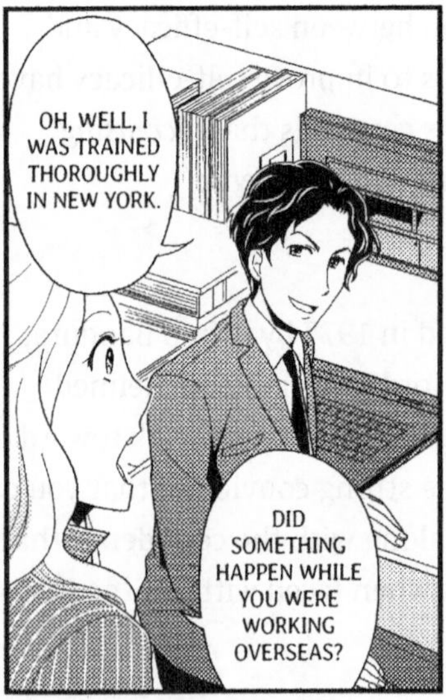
OH, WELL, I WAS TRAINED THOROUGHLY IN NEW YORK.
DID SOMETHING HAPPEN WHILE YOU WERE WORKING OVERSEAS?

The experience of overcoming adversity while working abroad increased Hasegawa's self-efficacy and strengthened his resilience.

• They maintain their physical health.
• They keep good personal relationships.
• They are able to achieve success in both
academics and sports.

People with a sense of self-efficacy tend to be more resilient. They are tolerant of stress, able to handle hardships, and have a robust spirit to overcome adversity.

When people with a high sense of self-efficacy come together, a sense of organizational efficacy is born. The highly motivated teams that result are able to achieve their goals. In both business and sports, teams that are highly effective are more likely to become winners.

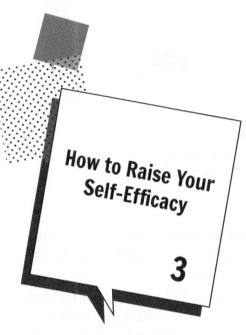

How to Raise Your Self-Efficacy

3

⇨ **Four Sources of Efficacy Beliefs**

So how do you raise self-efficacy, the foundation for your confidence? Professor Albert Bandura believed that the following four sources of efficacy beliefs could be used to increase self-efficacy:

1. Mastery experiences
2. Vicarious experiences
3. Verbal persuasion
4. Psychological and emotional states

Among these, the most effective is mastery experiences. Taking on challenges yourself and accumulating experiences of accomplishment and success are highly effective in increasing self-efficacy. But challenges that do not go well may result in feelings of failure with a loss of confidence. Therefore, the other three sources need to be employed to balance out the weaknesses of any one alone.

By combining the four sources together, we can steadily increase our confidence. In the next part, we will look at various approaches and ways of thinking to increase self-efficacy based on these four sources.

⇨ **What You Need to Tie Accomplishments to Self-Efficacy**

As mentioned above, mastery experiences involve going through the actual experience. The experience of achieving a goal you set for yourself strengthens your outlook—that you can do it, even if the next challenge is difficult. In particular, the experience of persevering and overcoming adversity establishes a stronger sense of self-efficacy.

Four Sources of Self-Efficacy Beliefs

Mastery Experiences	Vicarious Experiences
Self-Efficacy	
Verbal Persuasion	Physiological and Affective States

(Source: Bandura, 1997)

However, this doesn't mean you should blindly gather experience. The important point is how you perceive your experience because people who are confident and those who are not have different ways of perceiving the same event.

For example, when things go well, people who can interpret that their efforts have paid off can increase their self-efficacy even more, since they feel that they can do it the next time too. People who are unable to interpret success this way will instead attribute their accomplishment to good luck, to being in a good environment, or to the help of their peers. People who have this sort of thinking tend to be unable to raise their self-efficacy because they think that the reason things went well was due to an external force.

Such humility is considered a virtue for Japanese people. However, if it becomes excessive, it can lead to a biased view. It's unrealistic to think that you are not contributing to the success of something when it is actually the result of careful preparation, hard work, and perseverance. While having selfish thoughts, such as "This was all thanks to my strength alone. It was all because of me," can be a problem, underestimating your own abilities is also a barrier to building self-confidence.

⇨ How to Handle Failure

How you perceive your experiences with failure is also important in building confidence. When you make a mistake, if you make a broad interpretation that "the problem will continue," you will lose more and more confidence. This is characteristic of people with low self-efficacy.

On the other hand, people with high self-efficacy don't immediately conclude that something is a failure when things don't go their way. By thinking, "I just haven't figured out a solution yet," or "I'll get through this problem in the end," it stops them from viewing the event as a failure. As a result of working hard on it, you might accomplish your goal. In other words, those who can trust their own abilities will never experience a drop in their self-efficacy even if they experience failure.

People who do not believe in their own abilities do not increase their self-efficacy even when successful. On top of that, their self-efficacy decreases with each failure. Can you see the importance in the way we perceive experience?

⇨ Build Up Small Achievements

An effective approach to increasing self-efficacy is to accumulate small achievements rather than aiming for one large achievement. If you set a goal that's too high, you may lose confidence from failing to achieve it.

In the business world, it's recommended that you create a goal that is far out of your reach. I believe, however, that this method is rather risky for someone who has low confidence. Instead, setting up a step-by-step approach to goals and achieving them one step at a time is a safer and a more consistent way to increase self-efficacy.

Let me introduce a story of my own. When I was just starting out in the working world, I needed to quickly gain confidence in speaking business English. English was the official language in the company, so I wouldn't have been able to work without the ability to speak it. I had to improve my English in a short period of time.

English proficiency is becoming an essential skill for many business people. However, for some, even if they go to an English conversation school, they may not be able to improve their English. I believe that the cause is not in the amount of memorization of English words or skills, but rather in the psychological aspects of learning a new language. Many people believe that they are not good at English because their self-efficacy in English communication is low. In my case, I was given the opportunity to go to the United States immediately after joining the company and was given four months of business English training at a consulting company. Looking back, there was a mechanism to improve self-efficacy regarding English proficiency.

First, instead of aiming to be able to speak fluently with native speakers right away, the approach was to develop the skills necessary for business English step by step. In order to gradually improve 10 categories necessary for business English, each week, we set a goal. At the end of the week, we would check in with the teacher in charge about our progress and come up with a plan for the following week. We built on this slow but steady progress. In addition, rather than classroom lectures, frequent communication with instructors and people living in the area was prioritized to increase the number of "sessions." By accumulating these small successes step by step, my self-confidence increased and my English proficiency improved.

⇨ Examples Increase Confidence

Vicarious experiences, or learning by example, will increase self-efficacy. By observing the behavior of others, it's possible for you to believe, "I can do that too," even if you haven't actually experienced it. We call this *observational learning.*

Observational learning occurs best with role models. Neuroscience research confirms the importance of role models. Motor neurons in our brains "resonate" with what we see as if it were our own; we call these neurons *mirror neurons.* You can put yourself in someone else's shoes and experience their behavior as if you were doing it, without actually doing it yourself.

To increase self-efficacy, you should first experience things yourself, first-hand, but at the same time, you should find role models who have already achieved the goals you want to achieve or who have the skills you want to learn.

The key is to find someone who is close to you in age or social standing to be your role model, because it will be easier for you to believe that you can do it. They will be more effective as a role model. If you follow a guru or a professional who is far different from you, you may give up and say, "No, I can't be like that person." They are great as an object of admiration, but not as a role model for building self-confidence.

Looking back on my intensive training in business English, the seven people who studied English with me became my role models. At the start, all seven students lacked confidence in their English. However, there were individual differences in the speed at which they learned the language. When I saw my fellow students confidently conversing with native speakers, I felt an irrational confidence that I should be able to speak in the same way. In that sense, if you have friends who will work hard with you, you will gain the advantage that your sense of self-efficacy will increase more quickly.

There's a saying, "If you want to walk far, walk with someone." If you aim for a high goal, it will be easier to achieve it as a team rather than alone.

⇨ Encouragement Becomes the Source of Self-Confidence

Verbal persuasion, or encouragement, can also increase self-efficacy. This is when someone points out your ability and repeatedly encourages you by saying, "You can do it." Confidence improves faster when you have someone encouraging you.

In my case, an essential part of the process in building confidence in business English was my American teacher, Doug. He was a quiet gentleman, but he was a master at finding and telling people their strengths.

Meeting with Doug became a custom once a week. I later realized that the weekly meetings were a time to be recognized and encouraged in what I was able to do, what I had learned, and how I had improved. "You're really enthusiastic about improving your English listening skills." "I admire your patience." These were some of the words he said to me in encouragement. Those words reminded me of my strengths, passion, and perseverance, which I had taken for granted and hadn't paid much attention to.

By recognizing their own strengths, people can improve their self-efficacy. Self-affirmation is a theme that has been researched in psychology for many years. People with a sense of high self-esteem are characterized by feeling value in themselves and not excessively denying themselves even when they make mistakes. In other words, being recognized for your strengths creates new confidence.

There are important points to consider when praising and encouraging people. Process-focused compliments create a more growth-oriented mindset than results-focused communication. My English teacher, Doug, also made a conscious effort to acknowledge my efforts to learn English, including my efforts to have many conversations with people I met at the local sports club as an extracurricular study. Receiving compliments of the process motivated me to think, "If I keep doing this, I can improve further." This made me work harder, and as a result, my English skills improved.

⇨ Positive Attitudes Stimulate Self-Confidence

Good physical and mental health and a positive mood boost self-confidence. We call these states of being *physiological* and *affective* states.

In particular, positive emotions and positive moods have the effect of increasing self-efficacy. If the workplace where you spend most of your time has a positive atmosphere, the organization itself will become filled with confidence. During the English training I went through, parties were held at the teacher's home on the weekends. Occasionally, we would enjoy a barbecue at a house with a garden in a sunny neighborhood near San Francisco. We practiced our basic English conversation skills there.

Your confidence increases in a place that makes you feel safe and happy. I myself was able to interact more actively with the people around me than in the usual classroom. The mood of the location has a positive effect psychologically.

⇨ "Places" Where You Can Feel Positive

In our story, Reisa's boyfriend was worried about not being confident at work. Even in front of Reisa, he would show his lack of self-confidence and this irritated her. After he went back to his parents' home, he surprised Reisa by showing a confident attitude, as if he had become a different person. Working at his family's udon restaurant gave him confidence.

He must have experienced the joy of working when he saw customers tasting and enjoying the udon noodles he made. Words of encouragement from local customers, such as "Yu's udon is delicious," must have boosted his confidence too.

Again, being able to find a job that makes you feel happy and fulfills your heart has a positive effect on building your self-confidence. To regain self-confidence, it is necessary to find a place where your feelings can be positive. It may even be necessary to take a bold step in changing the place.

THANK YOU FOR WAITING FOR YOUR UDON WITH RAW EGG!
THAT'S THREE COLD UDONS!
Udon
THANK YOU VERY MUCH!
YU-SAN HAS AN EXPRESSION I'VE NEVER SEEN BEFORE!
Udon

⇨ Self-Efficacy Can Help

So far, we've talked about how to develop a sense of self-efficacy that boosts confidence. Confidence is needed when overcoming obstacles and difficulties.

The decisive factor in rebuilding self-confidence after failing is whether or not you have a sense of self-efficacy. I recommend that you improve your self-efficacy in your daily life, since the heart's muscle is necessary for resilience. It will become the mental power to help you in an emergency.

Part 5

Putting Your Strengths to Good Use at Work

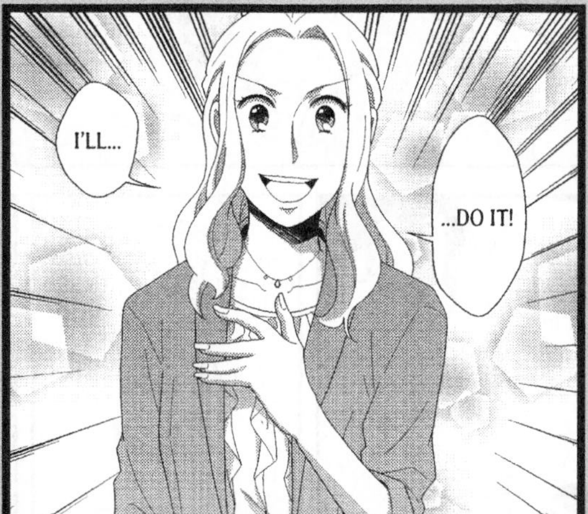
I'LL...
...DO IT!

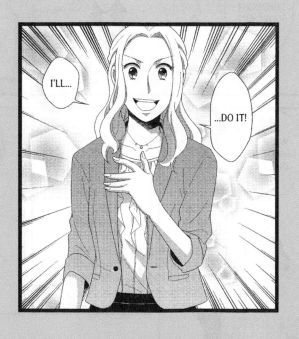

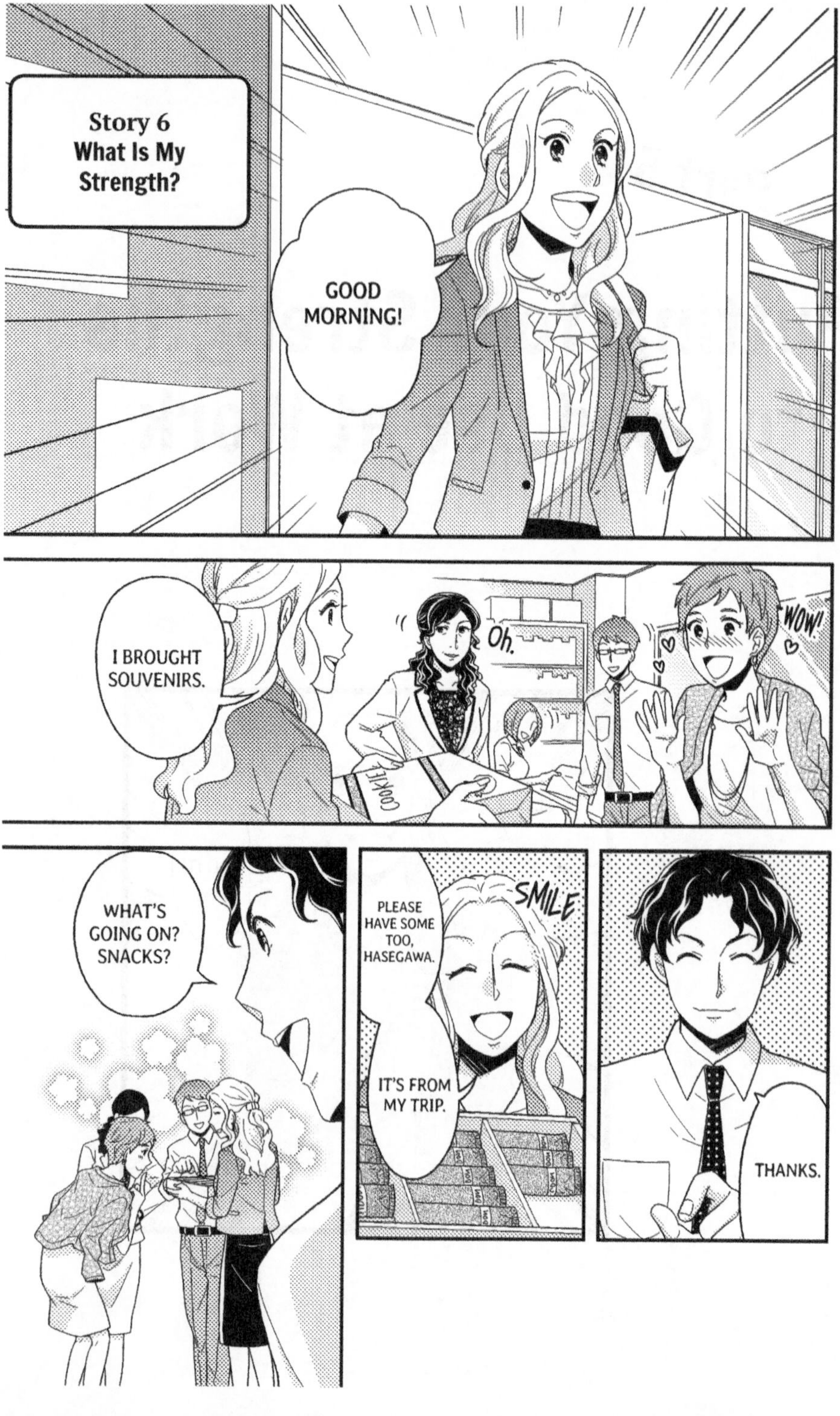
Story 6
What Is My Strength?
GOOD MORNING!
I BROUGHT SOUVENIRS.
Oh.
WOW!
COOKIE
WHAT'S GOING ON? SNACKS?
PLEASE HAVE SOME TOO, HASEGAWA.
SMILE
IT'S FROM MY TRIP.
THANKS.

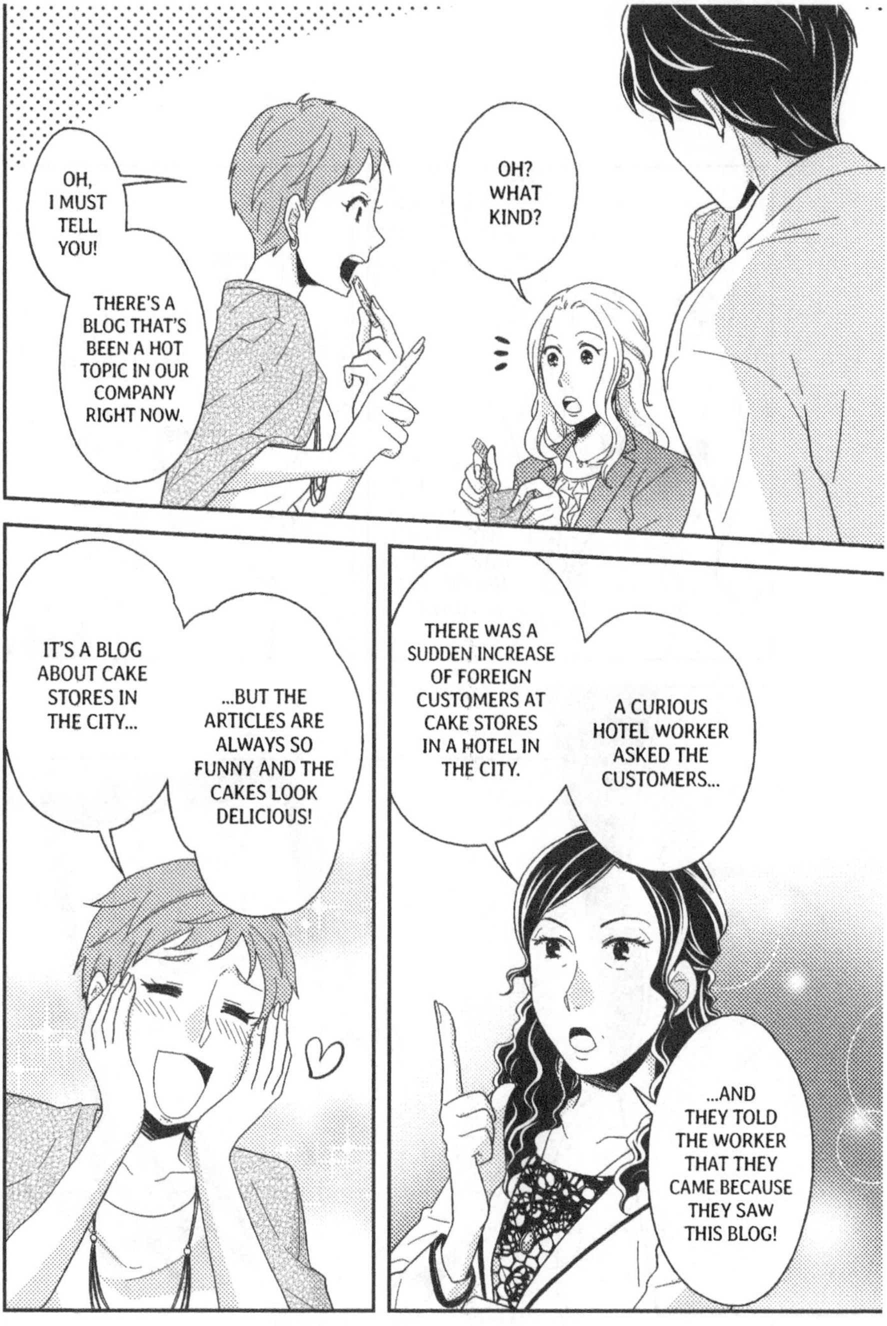
OH, I MUST TELL YOU!
THERE'S A BLOG THAT'S BEEN A HOT TOPIC IN OUR COMPANY RIGHT NOW.
OH? WHAT KIND?
IT'S A BLOG ABOUT CAKE STORES IN THE CITY...
...BUT THE ARTICLES ARE ALWAYS SO FUNNY AND THE CAKES LOOK DELICIOUS!
THERE WAS A SUDDEN INCREASE OF FOREIGN CUSTOMERS AT CAKE STORES IN A HOTEL IN THE CITY.
A CURIOUS HOTEL WORKER ASKED THE CUSTOMERS...
...AND THEY TOLD THE WORKER THAT THEY CAME BECAUSE THEY SAW THIS BLOG!

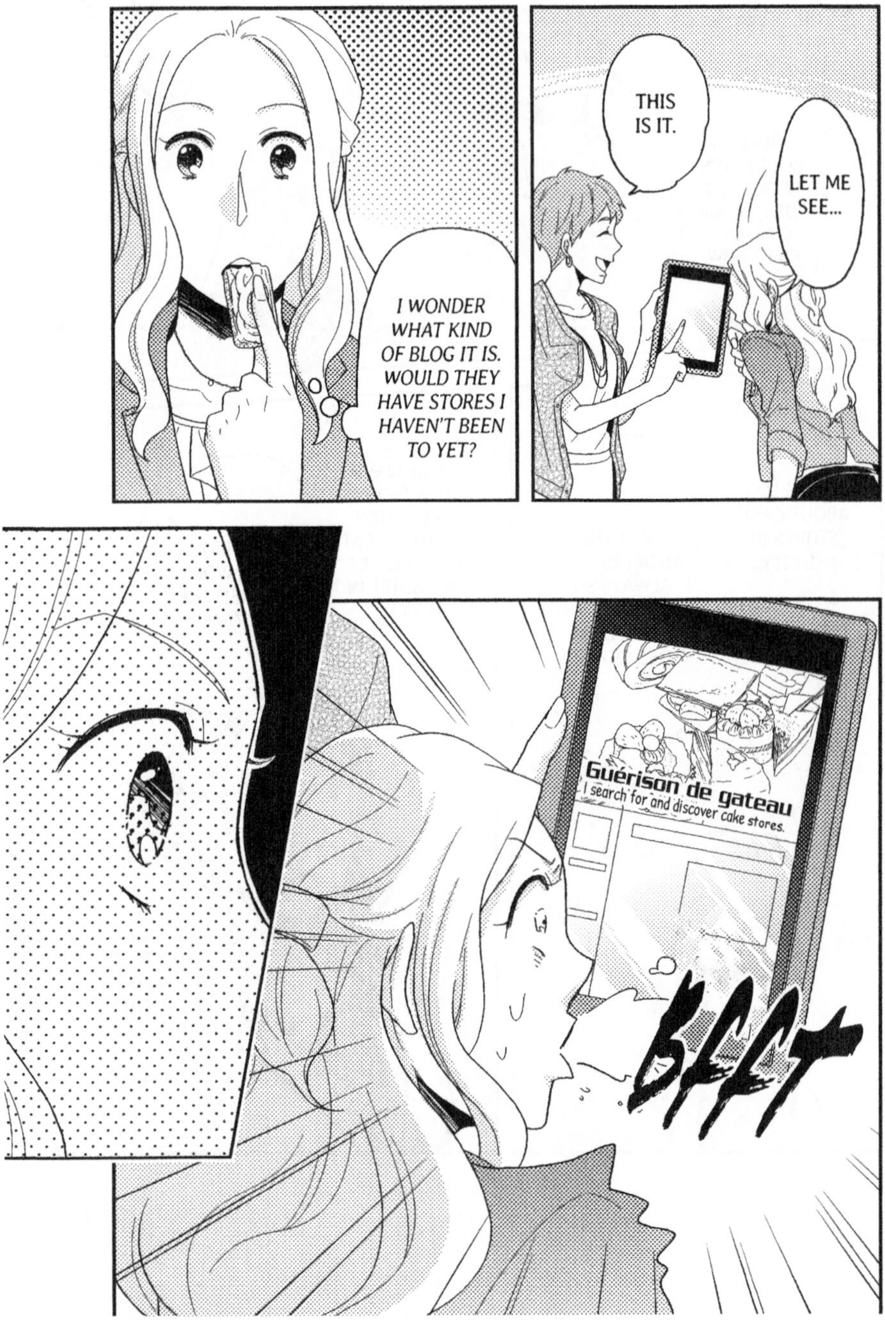
THIS IS IT.
LET ME SEE...
I WONDER WHAT KIND OF BLOG IT IS. WOULD THEY HAVE STORES I HAVEN'T BEEN TO YET?
Guérison de gateau
I search for and discover cake stores.
BFFT

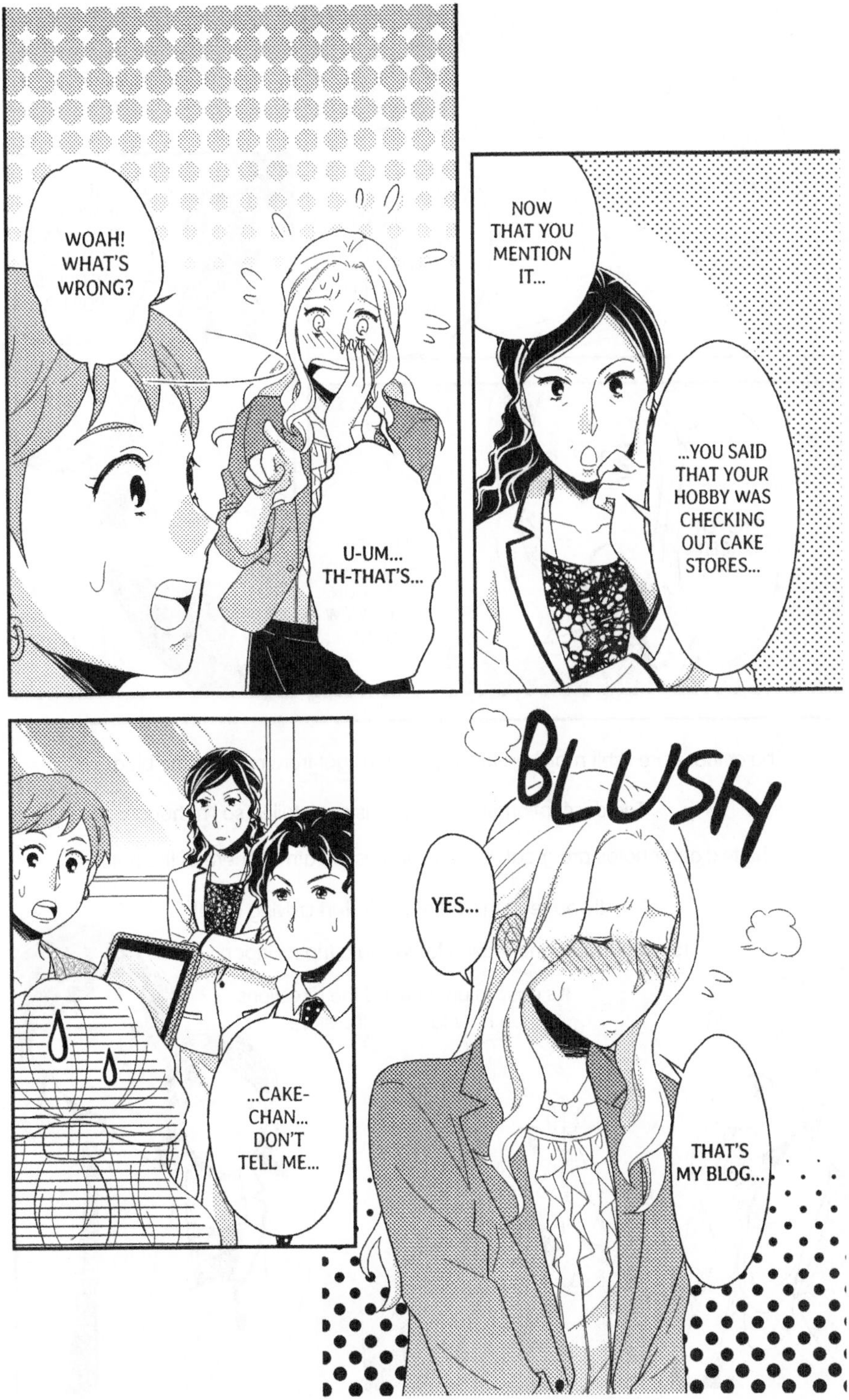
WOAH! WHAT'S WRONG?
U-UM... TH-THAT'S...
NOW THAT YOU MENTION IT...
...YOU SAID THAT YOUR HOBBY WAS CHECKING OUT CAKE STORES...
...CAKE-CHAN... DON'T TELL ME...
BLUSH
YES...
THAT'S MY BLOG...

Access History

JP		
UK		
KO		
TA		
UK		
UE		
US		
JP		

IT'S TRUE... THERE'S BEEN AN INCREASE IN OVERSEAS VIEWERS IN THE PAST FEW MONTHS.

IF YOU SEARCH THE BLOG NAME, A LOT OF ARTICLES POP UP.

HUH? IS THAT TRUE?

I NEVER NOTICED...

I NEVER REALLY PAID ATTENTION TO THE VIEW COUNT.

The actual store itself matched the impression I got from reading the blog!

The description of the cake was so detailed so I'm hungry now.

The text and photos are great! It even conveys the atmosphere of the hotel.

If you read this blog, you'll start craving cake!

It's my number one reason for taking a trip to Japan.

It's easy to understand the directions on how to get to the store.

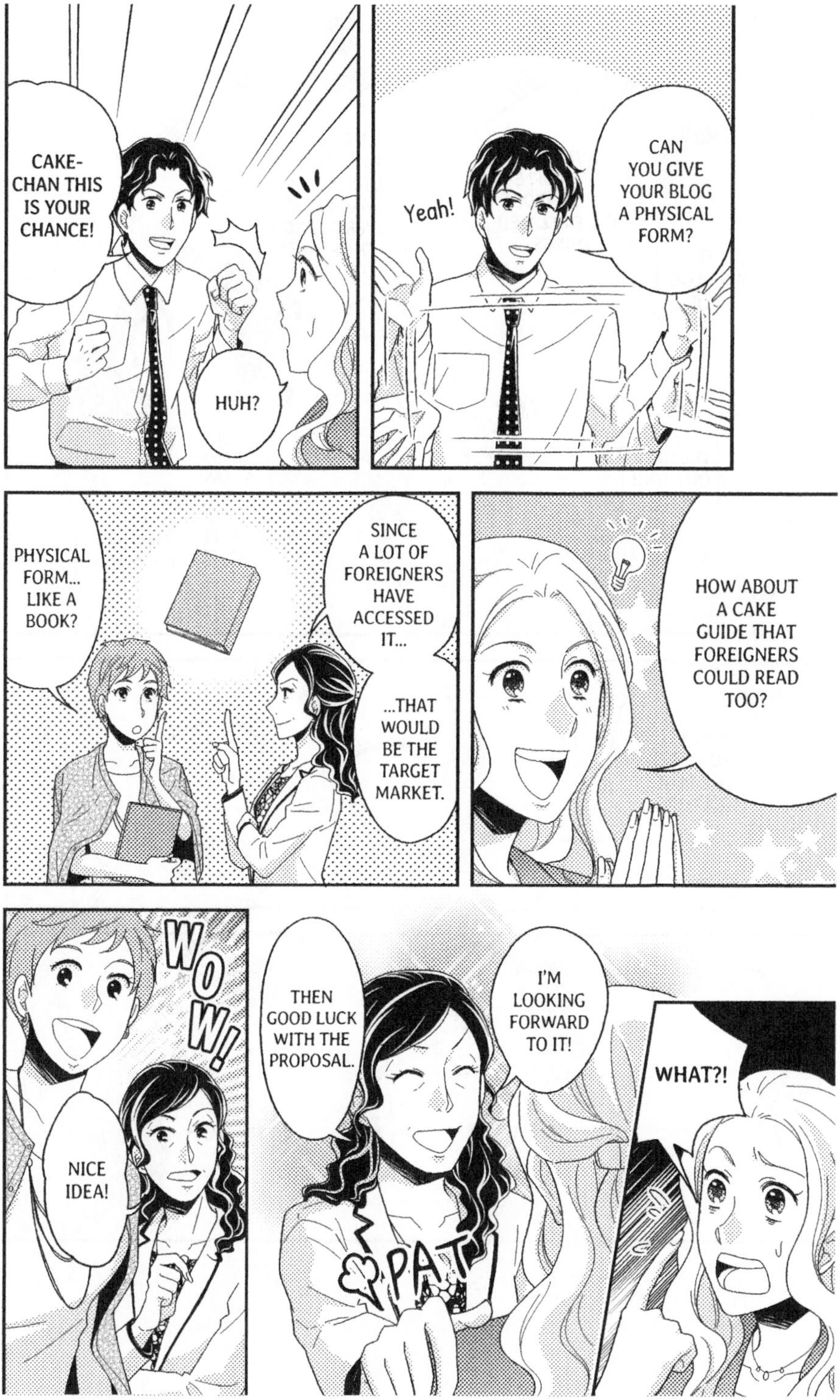
CAKE-CHAN THIS IS YOUR CHANCE!
HUH?
CAN YOU GIVE YOUR BLOG A PHYSICAL FORM?
Yeah!
PHYSICAL FORM... LIKE A BOOK?
SINCE A LOT OF FOREIGNERS HAVE ACCESSED IT...
...THAT WOULD BE THE TARGET MARKET.
HOW ABOUT A CAKE GUIDE THAT FOREIGNERS COULD READ TOO?
WOW!
NICE IDEA!
THEN GOOD LUCK WITH THE PROPOSAL.
PAT
I'M LOOKING FORWARD TO IT!
WHAT?!

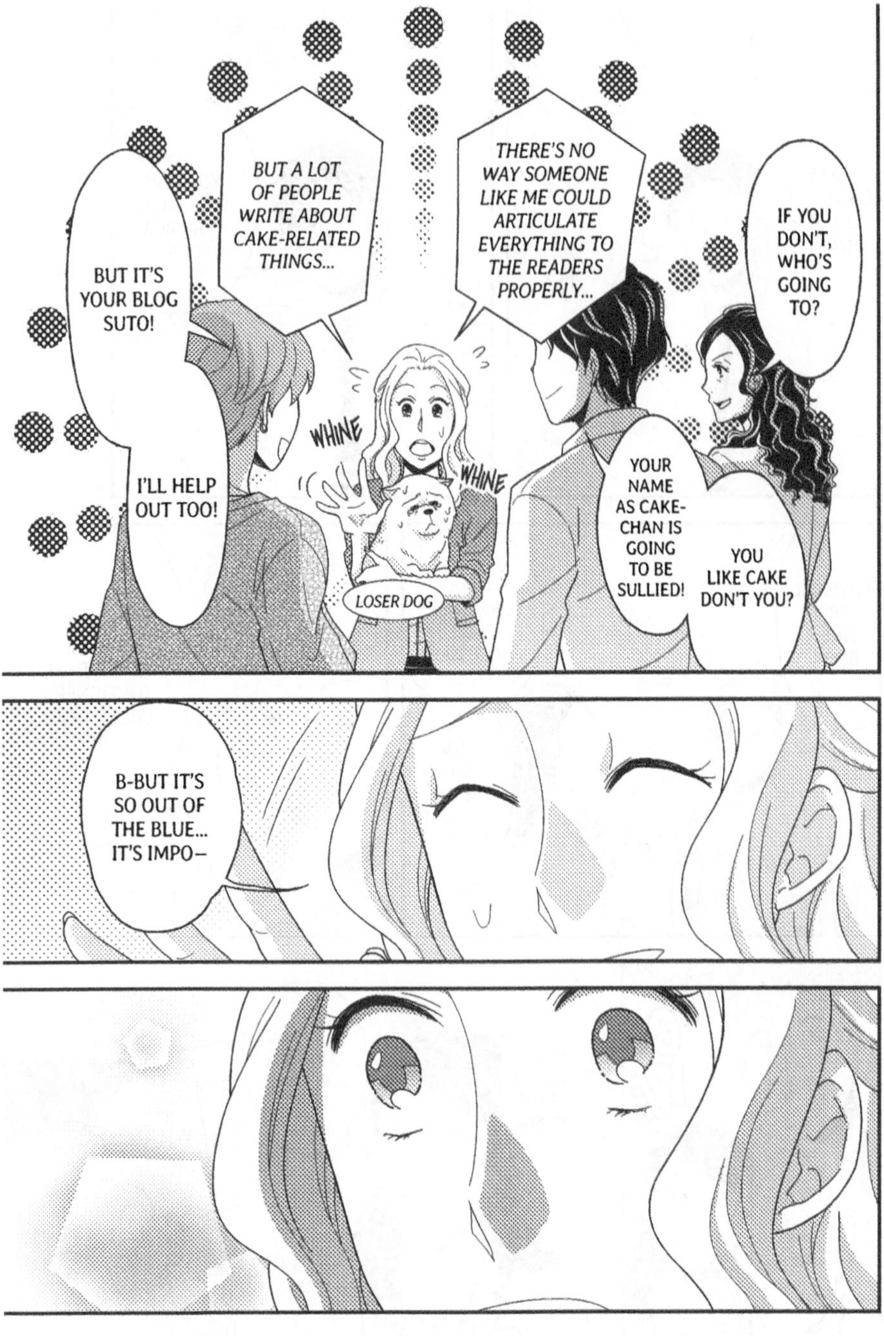
IF YOU DON'T, WHO'S GOING TO?
THERE'S NO WAY SOMEONE LIKE ME COULD ARTICULATE EVERYTHING TO THE READERS PROPERLY...
BUT A LOT OF PEOPLE WRITE ABOUT CAKE-RELATED THINGS...
BUT IT'S YOUR BLOG SUTO!
YOU LIKE CAKE DON'T YOU?
YOUR NAME AS CAKE-CHAN IS GOING TO BE SULLIED!
WHINE
WHINE
I'LL HELP OUT TOO!
LOSER DOG
B-BUT IT'S SO OUT OF THE BLUE... IT'S IMPO—

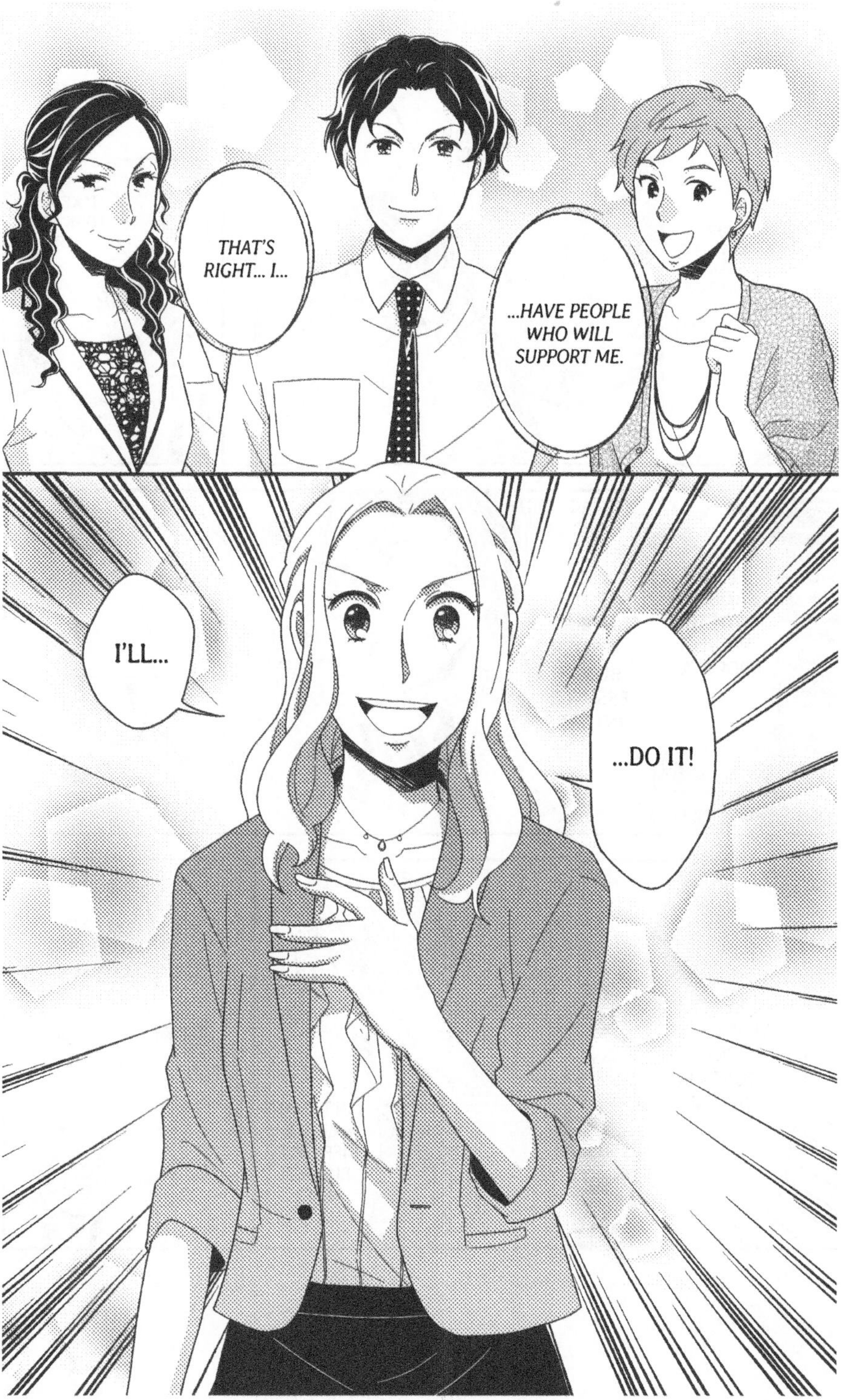
THAT'S RIGHT... I...
...HAVE PEOPLE WHO WILL SUPPORT ME.
I'LL...
...DO IT!

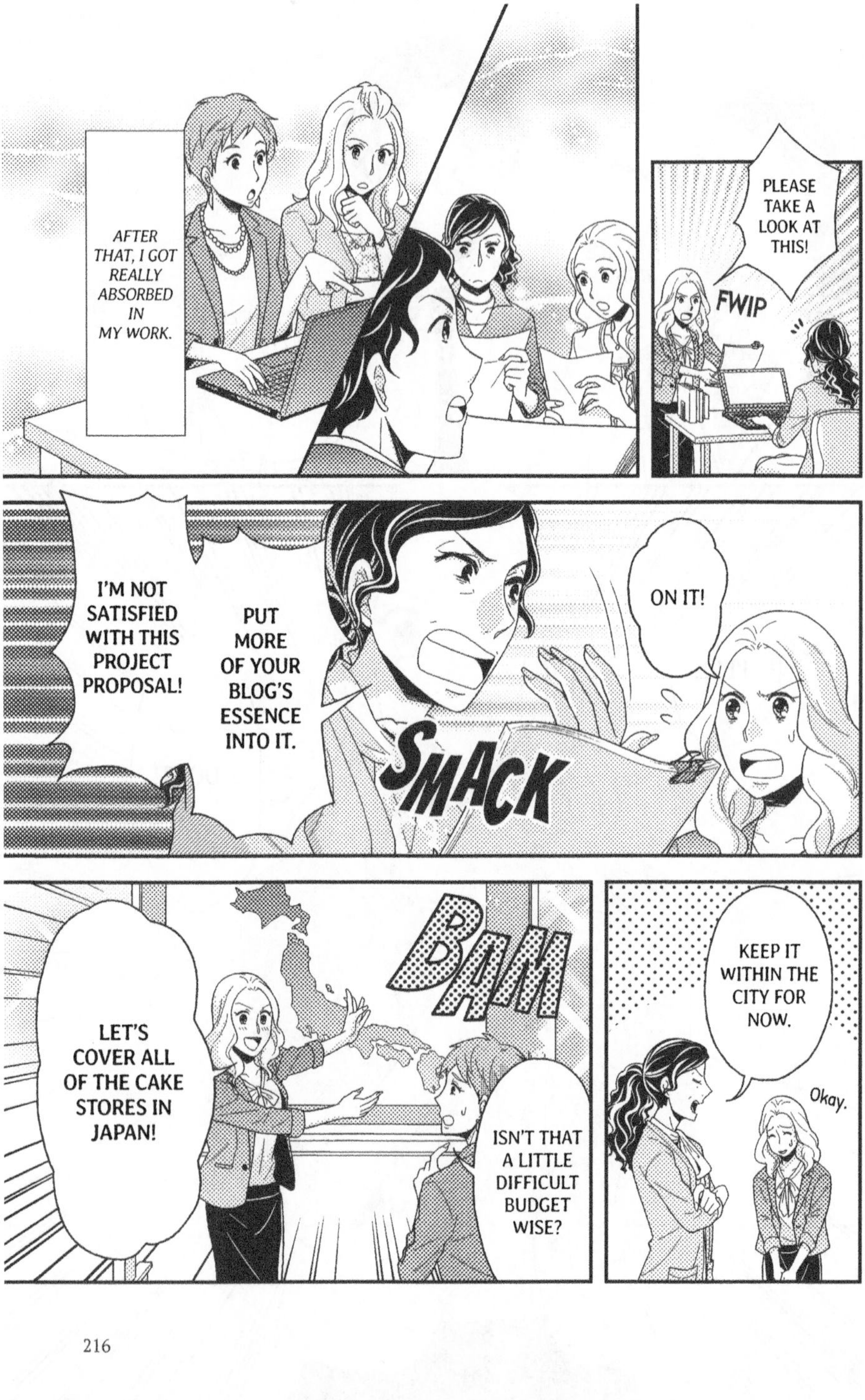
AFTER THAT, I GOT REALLY ABSORBED IN MY WORK.
PLEASE TAKE A LOOK AT THIS!
FWIP
I'M NOT SATISFIED WITH THIS PROJECT PROPOSAL!
PUT MORE OF YOUR BLOG'S ESSENCE INTO IT.
ON IT!
SMACK
LET'S COVER ALL OF THE CAKE STORES IN JAPAN!
BAM
ISN'T THAT A LITTLE DIFFICULT BUDGET WISE?
KEEP IT WITHIN THE CITY FOR NOW.
Okay.

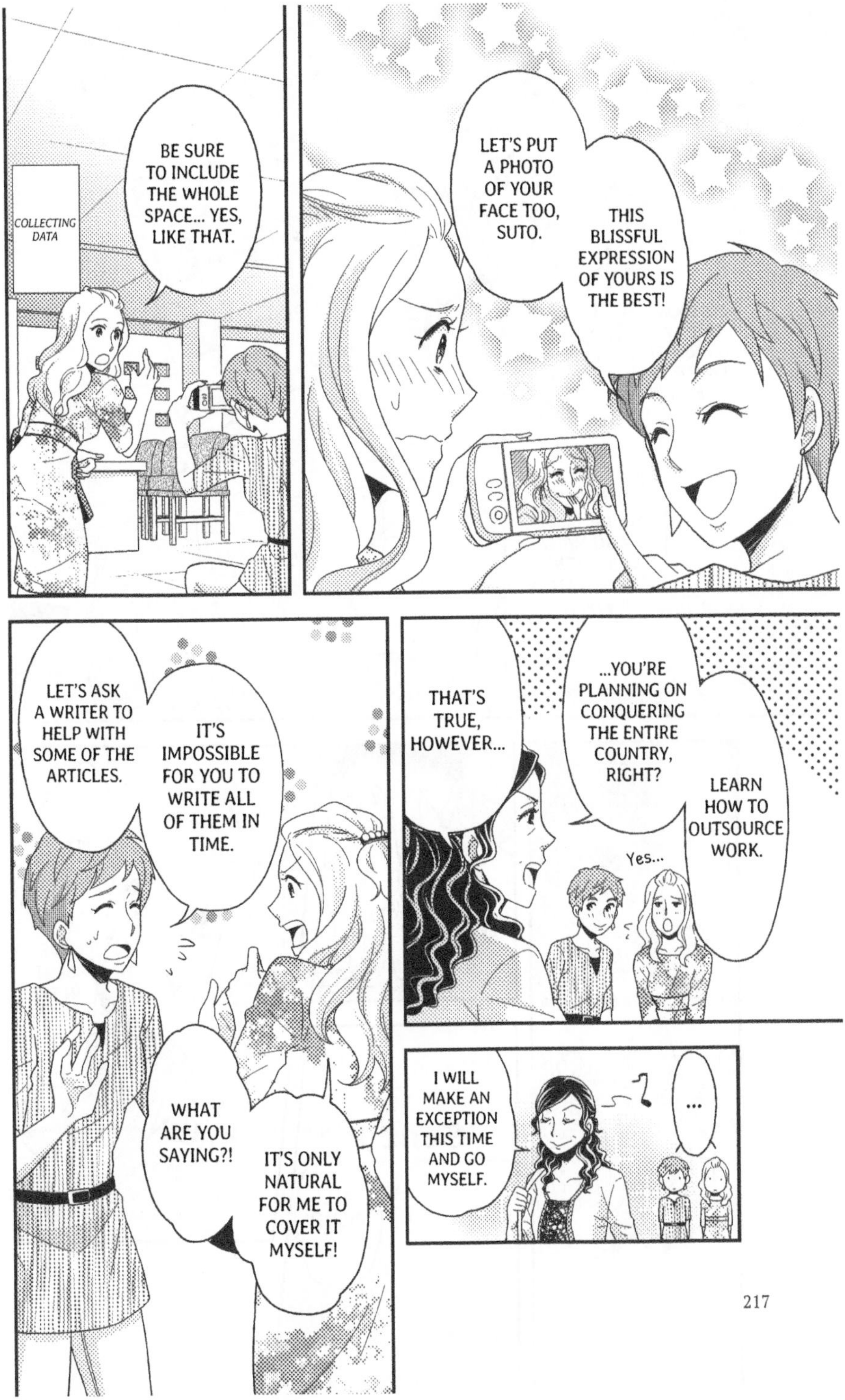
COLLECTING DATA
BE SURE TO INCLUDE THE WHOLE SPACE... YES, LIKE THAT.
LET'S PUT A PHOTO OF YOUR FACE TOO, SUTO.
THIS BLISSFUL EXPRESSION OF YOURS IS THE BEST!
LET'S ASK A WRITER TO HELP WITH SOME OF THE ARTICLES.
IT'S IMPOSSIBLE FOR YOU TO WRITE ALL OF THEM IN TIME.
WHAT ARE YOU SAYING?!
IT'S ONLY NATURAL FOR ME TO COVER IT MYSELF!
THAT'S TRUE, HOWEVER...
...YOU'RE PLANNING ON CONQUERING THE ENTIRE COUNTRY, RIGHT?
LEARN HOW TO OUTSOURCE WORK.
Yes...
I WILL MAKE AN EXCEPTION THIS TIME AND GO MYSELF.
...

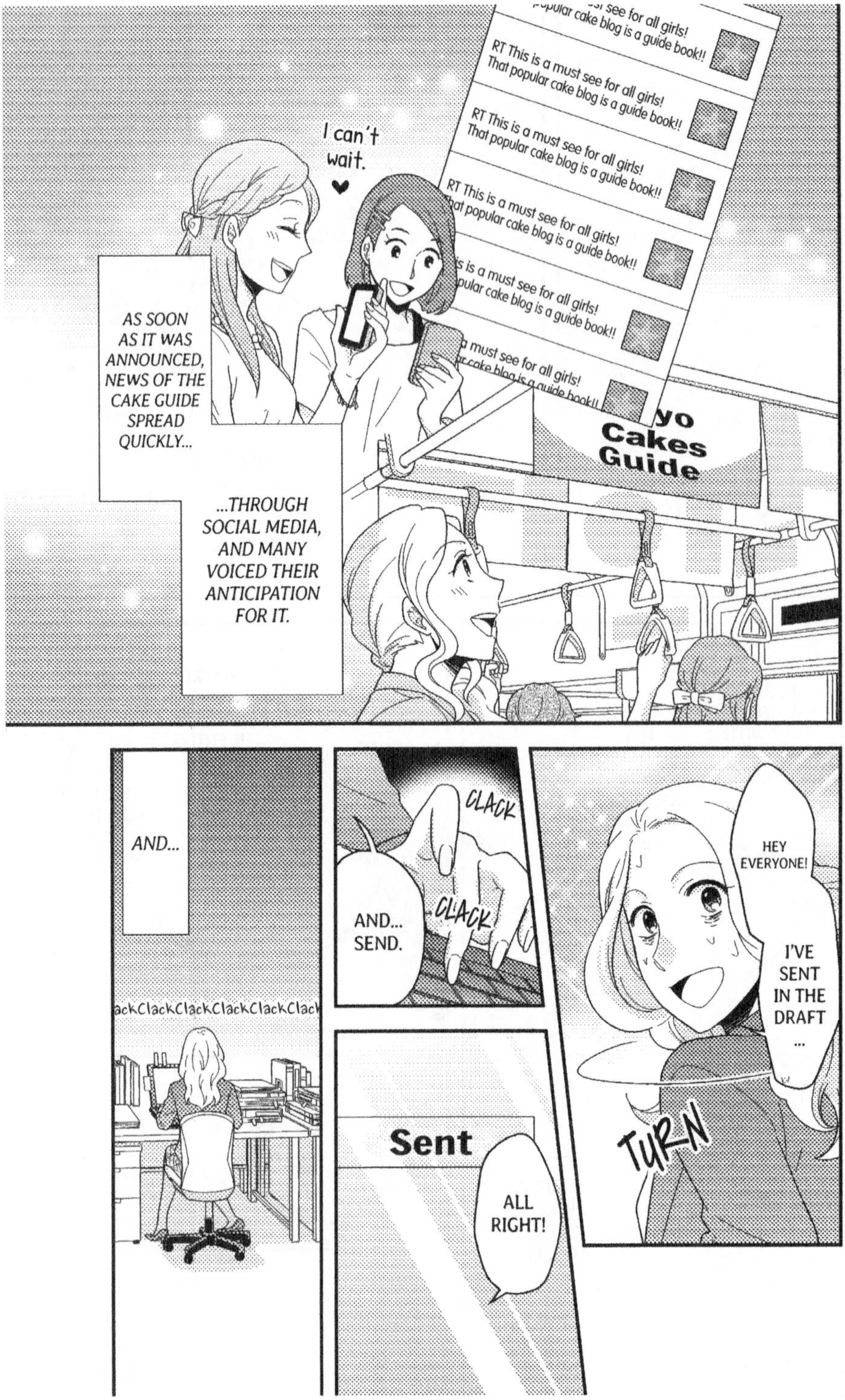

RT This is a must see for all girls! That popular cake blog is a guide book!!
RT This is a must see for all girls! That popular cake blog is a guide book!!
RT This is a must see for all girls! That popular cake blog is a guide book!!
I can't wait.
AS SOON AS IT WAS ANNOUNCED, NEWS OF THE CAKE GUIDE SPREAD QUICKLY...
...THROUGH SOCIAL MEDIA, AND MANY VOICED THEIR ANTICIPATION FOR IT.
Cakes Guide
AND...
ClackClackClackClackClack
CLACK
CLACK
AND... SEND.
Sent
ALL RIGHT!
HEY EVERYONE!
I'VE SENT IN THE DRAFT...
TURN

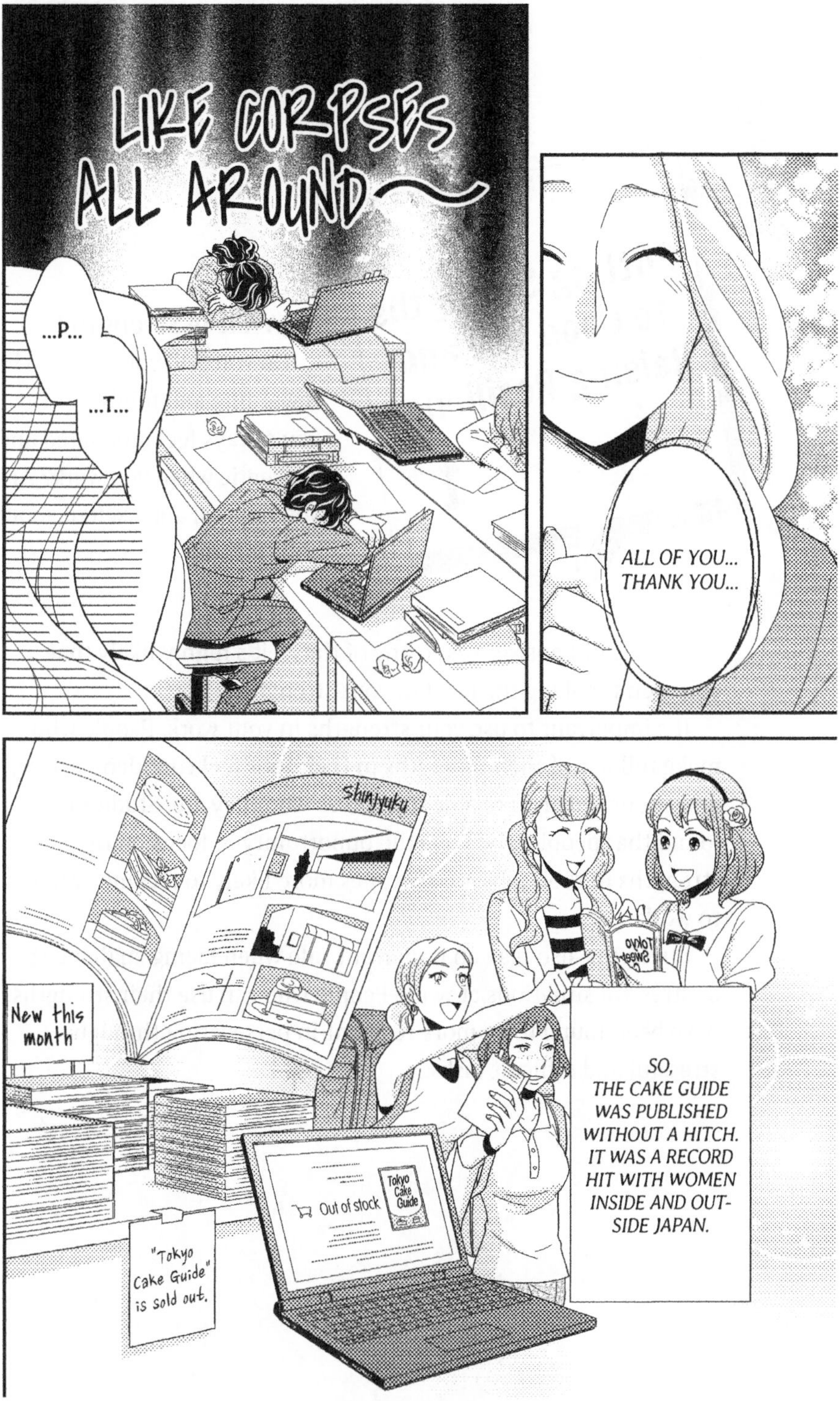

LIKE CORPSES ALL AROUND~
...P...
...T...
ALL OF YOU... THANK YOU...
Shinjyuku
New this month
Tokyo Sweets
Tokyo Cake Guide
Out of stock
"Tokyo Cake Guide" is sold out.
SO, THE CAKE GUIDE WAS PUBLISHED WITHOUT A HITCH. IT WAS A RECORD HIT WITH WOMEN INSIDE AND OUT-SIDE JAPAN.

Putting Strengths to Good Use and Raising Resilience

1

⇨ What Is Strength?

Do you find your work to be rewarding and fulfilling? Do you always feel motivated and energetic when you work? Are you hopeful and excited about your future?

If you can't answer yes to any of these, it's highly likely that you aren't making the most of your strengths.

It's important to use your strengths in your work. People who make full use of their strengths in their jobs feel confident, active, and energized and are able to express who they are. Studies have found that people who have the opportunity to focus on their strengths in their jobs are six times more likely to feel motivated to work.

Strengths also play an important role when facing challenges or stressful situations at work. People who can use their strengths have been found to be more resilient in persevering through stressful and difficult tasks.

⇨ Look for Strengths Rather Than Weak Points

Many people do not realize their own strengths. They are well aware of their shortcomings and weaknesses but either don't know their strengths or take them for granted and don't recognize them as strengths. As a result, they're unable to choose a job that allows them to make full use of their strengths and are unable to make the most of their strengths at work.

It is true that we are more aware of our weaknesses than we are of our strengths. We are naturally motivated to try to prevent failures and mistakes, but if you want to grow, you will need to look at things differently. You will be able to exceed expectations only when you focus on your strengths and put them to good use.

⇨ Three Ways to Figure Out Your Strengths

How can you understand what your strengths are? You can implement three strategies to identify them:

1. Ask yourself some questions.
2. Ask people around you.
3. Use a strength diagnostic tool.

First, ask yourself these questions:

"What am I good at?"
"What am I doing that inspires me?"
"When do I get excited?"

Next, ask the people you know around you the same questions about you. Ask them what kinds of characteristics or tendencies you show or what kinds of strengths you are making use of when you are doing well at work, demonstrating your full abilities, or producing results that exceed expectations.

We're blind when it comes to our own strengths because we just think they're normal. However, even if you don't realize your own strengths, you can see them through someone else's eyes.

The last method is to use diagnostic tools. As an example, I have used the diagnostic tool provided by VIA Laboratories in the United States. After answering an online questionnaire, the user is given a report that ranks 24 types of personality strengths. Out of these, the top five will be the ones that are the user's. See the next page for an illustration of this tool. Other diagnostic tools are available to you.

Once you've found your strengths by combining these methods, think next about how to apply those strengths at work. We feel happy when our strengths are used in new ways.

VIA's 6 Virtues and 24 Personality Strengths

Wisdom

- Creativity
- Curiosity
- Passion for knowledge
- Judgment
- Broad perspective

Courage

- Honesty
- Bravery
- Perseverence
- Enthusiasm

Human Nature

- Kindness
- Love
- Social awareness

Justice

- Fairness
- Leadership
- Teamwork

Abstinence

- Tolerance / Mercy
- Modesty / Humility
- Thoughtfulness
- Self-regulation

Transcendency

- Sense of beauty
- Thankfulness
- Hope
- Humor
- Spirituality

(Source: Peterson, C., & Seligman, M. E. P. (2004). *Character strengths and virtues: A handbook and classification.* New York: Oxford University Press and Washington, DC: American Psychological Association. www.viacharacter.org)

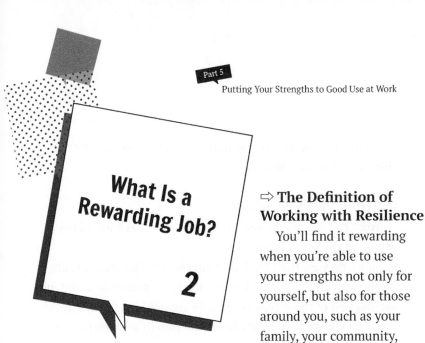

What Is a Rewarding Job?

2

⇨ **The Definition of Working with Resilience**

You'll find it rewarding when you're able to use your strengths not only for yourself, but also for those around you, such as your family, your community, and for society.

People who find meaning in their work have solid resilience. Having a high sense of purpose gives them the strength to overcome difficulties and predicaments.

However, according to a 2015 survey of men and women aged 18 to 29 by the Dentsu Institute, many found their work to be unfulfilling. Only about 10% stated that their reason for working was "to gain a purpose in life," while about 30% answered that "they don't want to work if possible." The most common response at 69% was "for a stable income." And when asked about how they choose jobs, "I want to work at a company that is as stable as possible," at 37%, outnumbered "I want to choose a job/company where I can earn as much money as possible," at 24%.

From a psychological research perspective, we can see that this view of work is biased.

⇨ Three Views on Work

Work can be categorized in three ways: (1) as a job, (2) as a career, or (3) as a calling.

People who view their work as a job see it as "working to earn money and for daily life." The productivity, motivation, and job satisfaction of these types of people are not high. Such individuals tend to look for sources of life satisfaction in activities outside of work.

People who view their work as a career view work as income, but also as avenues for promotion, salary increases, honor, and power. As a result, they are passionate about their work.

Finally, there are people who view their work as a calling. Originally, this word, in the religious sense, referred to "a role bestowed from heaven." In psychology, it's come to be defined as "oriented to feel meaning and significance in one's work." People with this sense of work are positive and satisfied with their job and life.

Three Views on Work

Job	• Work is a financial reward and a duty. • External motivation • Seeks fulfillment in life outside of work

Career	• Work is a means to gain higher status and responsibility. • External motivation • Happiness after achieving the goal does not last long.

Calling	• Work is fulfilling and socially meaningful. • Internal motivation • High job satisfaction and happiness

(Source: Wrzesniewski, 1997)

⇨ Start with Putting Your Strengths to Good Use

There's a large difference between the job, career, and calling types of workers. For the first two, the work rewards are external, such as money from the company, compliments from their superiors, promotions, raises, and commendations.

On the other hand, the calling type of worker has an internal motivation. They use the sense of meaning inside them as the motivation for their work. In addition, the calling type also feels fulfillment in the process as well. Their goal is to be immersed in the work itself. The result is merely secondary.

People who have this calling view have been found to be more satisfied with their work and lives. They tend to have better physical and mental health and are more likely to succeed in both personal and public life. As previously mentioned, approaching work with a sense of purpose helps improve resilience.

The important thing to remember is that you should not work with a feeling of being forced to do it; you should work proactively because you find the work rewarding. Even in psychology, people are found to be more motivated and productive when their three basic needs are met: "I want to do what I chose to do," "I want to demonstrate my abilities," and "I want to connect with people."

In our story, Reisa's boyfriend found a job he found rewarding. Reisa herself also developed her hobby into a full-blown project at work.

I consider Reisa's strengths to be curiosity and enthusiasm. The hobby that made use of those strengths was her cake store blog. Once she jumped at the chance to become an author and developed her sense of purpose in helping others, she started to feel satisfaction with her work.

Let's start by using your strengths at work. Not only will it increase your resilience, but it will also become a shortcut to a happy and fulfilling life.

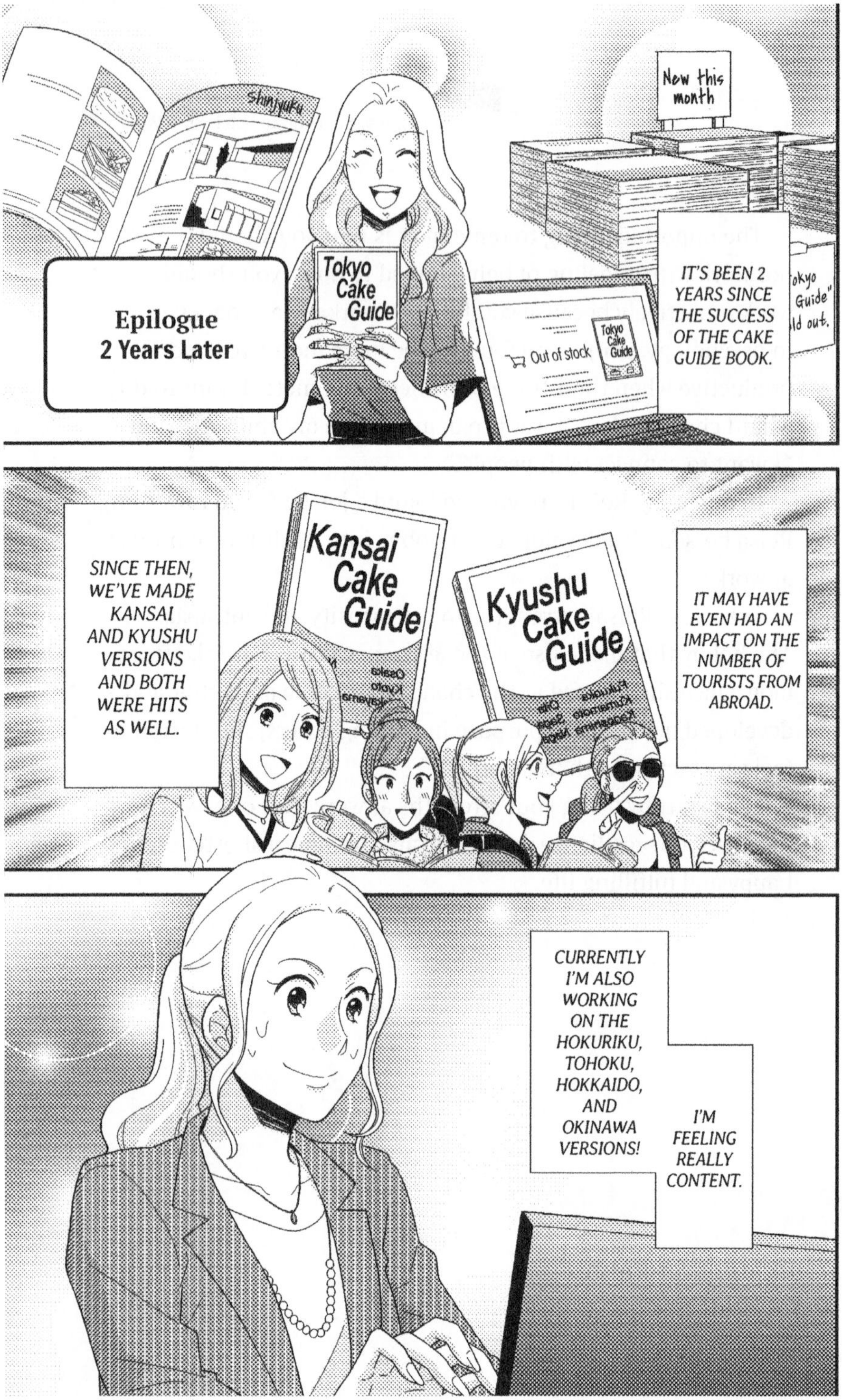
Shinjuku
Tokyo Cake Guide
Epilogue
2 Years Later
New this month
Out of stock
Tokyo Cake Guide
IT'S BEEN 2 YEARS SINCE THE SUCCESS OF THE CAKE GUIDE BOOK.
SINCE THEN, WE'VE MADE KANSAI AND KYUSHU VERSIONS AND BOTH WERE HITS AS WELL.
Kansai Cake Guide
Kyushu Cake Guide
IT MAY HAVE EVEN HAD AN IMPACT ON THE NUMBER OF TOURISTS FROM ABROAD.
CURRENTLY I'M ALSO WORKING ON THE HOKURIKU, TOHOKU, HOKKAIDO, AND OKINAWA VERSIONS!
I'M FEELING REALLY CONTENT.

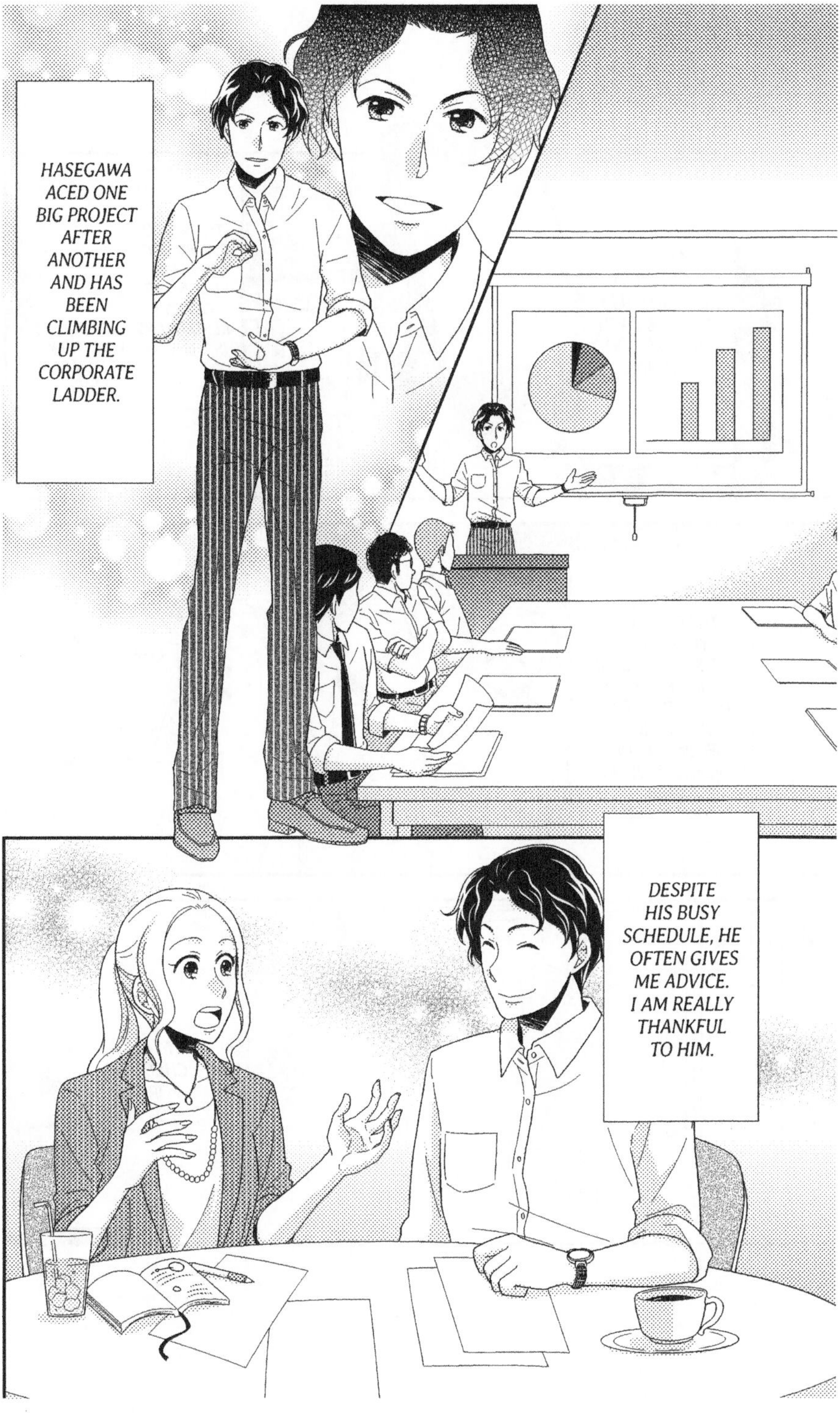
HASEGAWA ACED ONE BIG PROJECT AFTER ANOTHER AND HAS BEEN CLIMBING UP THE CORPORATE LADDER.
DESPITE HIS BUSY SCHEDULE, HE OFTEN GIVES ME ADVICE. I AM REALLY THANKFUL TO HIM.

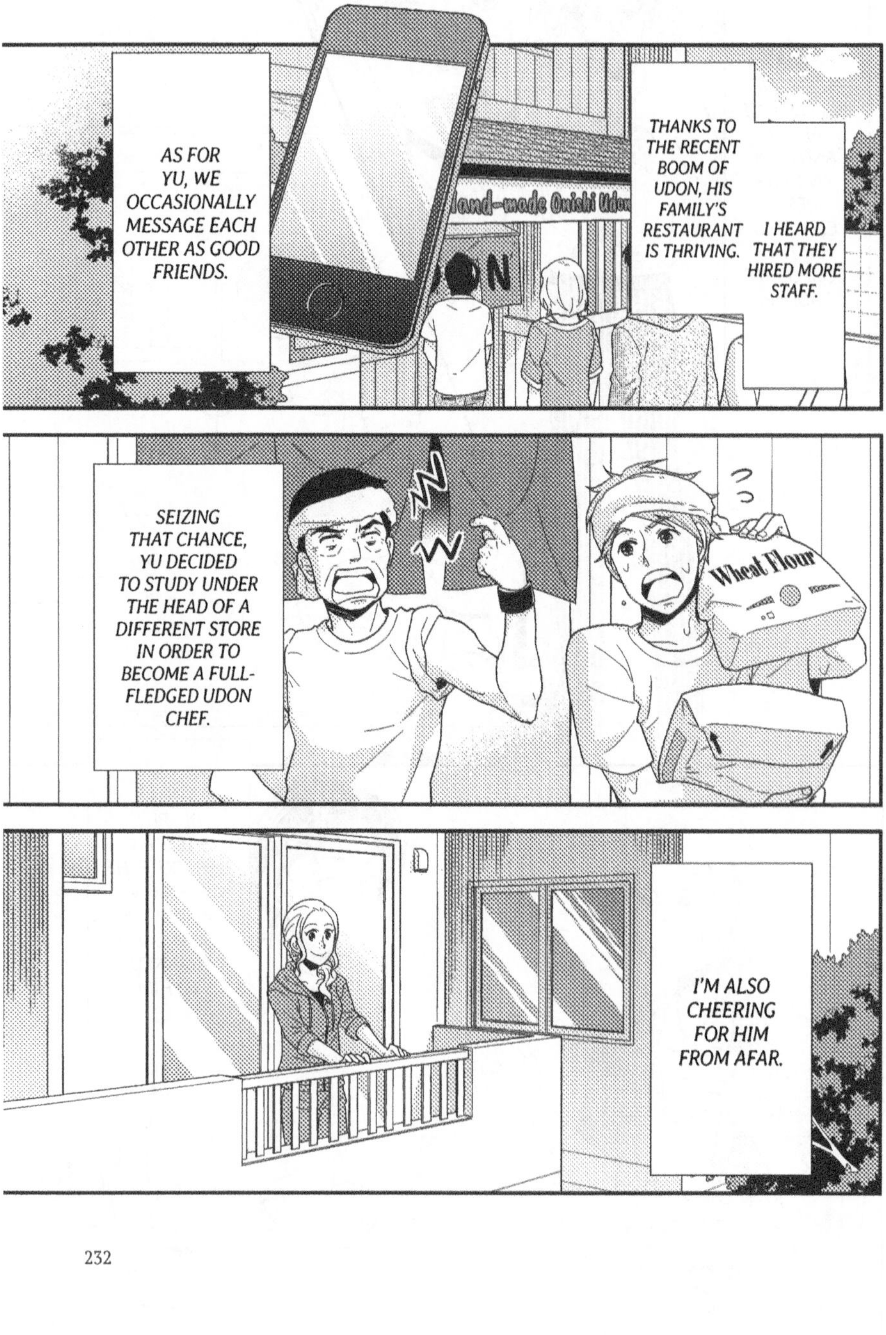
AS FOR YU, WE OCCASIONALLY MESSAGE EACH OTHER AS GOOD FRIENDS.
THANKS TO THE RECENT BOOM OF UDON, HIS FAMILY'S RESTAURANT IS THRIVING.
I HEARD THAT THEY HIRED MORE STAFF.
SEIZING THAT CHANCE, YU DECIDED TO STUDY UNDER THE HEAD OF A DIFFERENT STORE IN ORDER TO BECOME A FULL-FLEDGED UDON CHEF.
Wheat Flour
I'M ALSO CHEERING FOR HIM FROM AFAR.

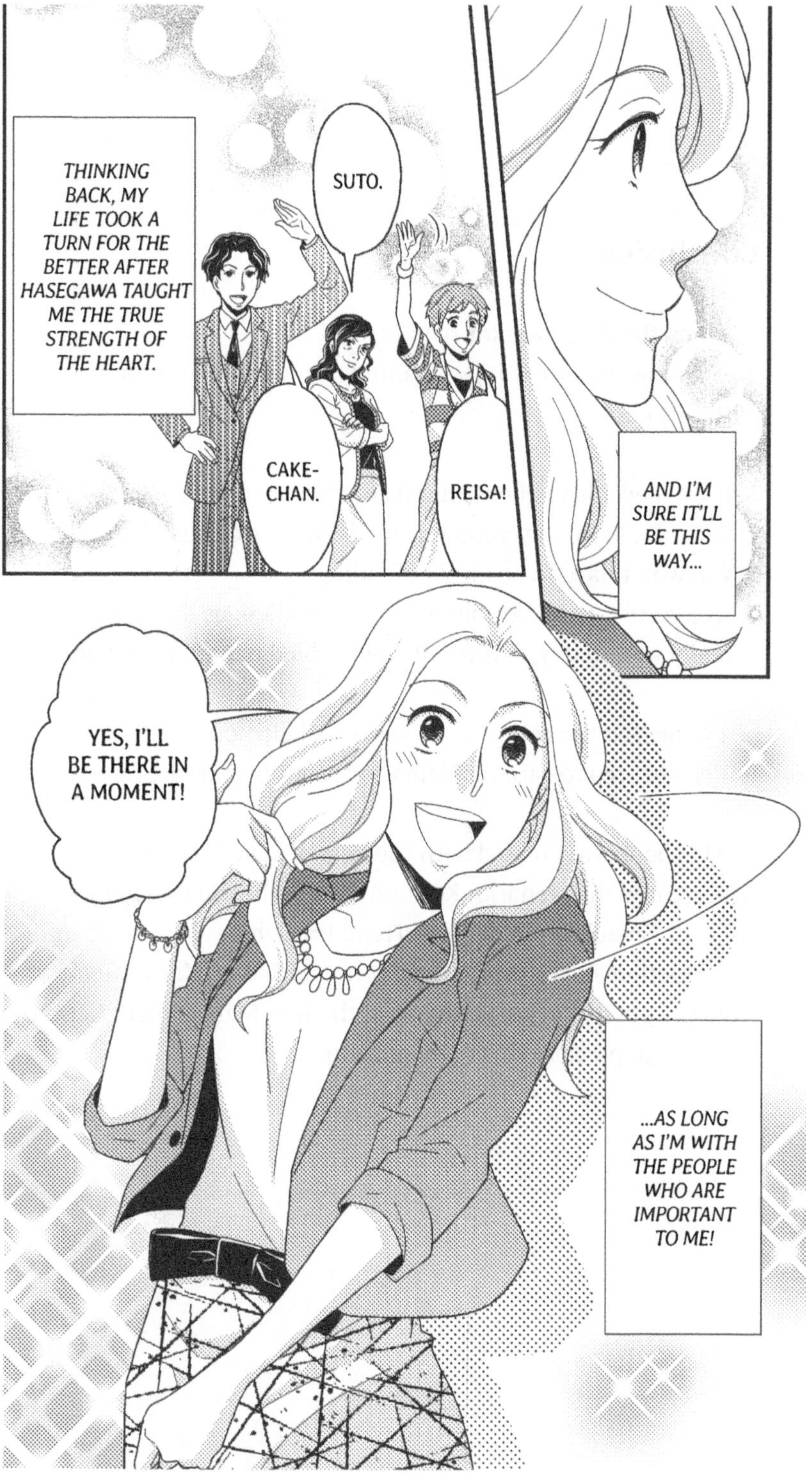
THINKING BACK, MY LIFE TOOK A TURN FOR THE BETTER AFTER HASEGAWA TAUGHT ME THE TRUE STRENGTH OF THE HEART.
SUTO.
CAKE-CHAN.
REISA!
AND I'M SURE IT'LL BE THIS WAY...
YES, I'LL BE THERE IN A MOMENT!
...AS LONG AS I'M WITH THE PEOPLE WHO ARE IMPORTANT TO ME!

Conclusion

Many thanks to you for reading this.

There were three things I wanted to convey to everyone with this book:

1. If you become resilient, you'll stop feeling discouraged.
2. Once you have the confidence to bounce back quickly, you won't have to be afraid of failing.
3. As a result, you'll be able to take on challenges that you really want to try, and you'll feel fulfilled in both work and life.

I hope that the contents of this book help you take that important step toward resiliency for your life and career.

This book was created with the help of Yoko Matsuo, who created the scenario; Koromo Asato, who did the manga artwork; Shizuka Fukuda from Trend Pro, who was in charge of the direction and manga production; and Satomi Kashiwabara from the publishing department of the JMA Management Center.

I truly appreciate this team of people.

I'd also like to thank all the certified instructors who teach resilience alongside me, my mentor Dr. Ilona Boniwell, and my family for their support.

October 2015
Representative of The School of Positive Psychology
Koji Kuze

References

• 2012 Health Survey of Workers (Ministry of Health, Labor and Welfare)

• Handbook of Post-traumatic Growth by Kanako Taku (IGAKU-SHOIN Ltd.)

• SPARK Resilience Training by Ilona Boniwell & Lucy Ryan (Positran)

• The World's Elites Value This More Than IQ & Educational Background! How to Train "Resilience" by Koji Kuze (Jitsugyo no Nihon Sha, Ltd.)

• Supporting "Subordinates with Good Prospects" by Tomohiko Taniguchi (PRESIDENT Inc.)

• Positive Psychology in a Nutshell by Ilona Boniwell, Mayumi Naruse (Translation Supervisor), translated by Sayuri Nagashima and co. (Kokusho Kankokai)

• Baumeister, R. F., Bratslavsky, E., Finkenauer, C., & Vohs, K. D. (2001). Bad is stronger than good. Review of General Psychology, 5(4), 323.

• Rainy Brain, Sunny Brain: The New Science of Optimism and Pessimism by Elaine Fox, translated by Kaoru Moriuchi (Bungeishunju Ltd.)

• Emotional Vampires: Dealing with People Who Drain You Dry by Albert Bernstein (McGraw-Hill)

• Practicing Positive Leadership by Kim Cameron
(Berrett-Koehler Publisher)
• Full Catastrophe Living by Jon Kabat-Zinn, translated by
Haruki Yutaka (Kitaooji Shobo Publishing Ltd.)
• How to Be a Positive Leader. Small Actions, Big Impact by
Jane Dutton (Berrett-Koehler Publisher)
• Let's Make a Good Company by Hiroshi Tsukakoshi (Bunya)
• Self-Efficacy in Changing Societies by Albert Bandura, Hiroshi
Motoaki, and Kyoko Noguchi (Translation Supervisor),
translated by Hiroshi Motoaki and co. (Kaneko Shobo)
• Self-Efficacy: The Exercise of Control Albert Bandura (Worth
Publishers)
• Peterson, C., & Seligman, M. E. P. (2004). Character Strengths
and Virtues: A Handbook and Classification. New York: Oxford
University Press and Washington, DC: American Psychological
Association. www.viacharacter.org
• Martin Seligman: The New Era of Positive Psychology
(TED Talk)
• Young People x Work Survey (Dentsu Institute)
• Wrzesniewski, A., McCauley, C., Rozin, P., & Schwartz, B.(1997).
Jobs, Careers, and Callings: People's Relations to Their Work.
Journal of Research in Personality, 31(1), 21–33.

BOOKS IN THE **MANGA FOR SUCCESS** SERIES

TAKASHI YASUDA

MANGA FOR SUCCESS

MARKETING

THE FUN WAY TO LEARN
THE BASICS OF MARKETING!

ALL THE IMPORTANT
CONCEPTS YOU NEED TO KNOW,
INCLUDING:

- THE 4 "P'S" OF MARKETING
- THE CUSTOMER JOURNEY
- ANALYZING YOUR COMPETITOR'S
  STRENGTHS & WEAKNESSES

AND MORE

KOJI KUZE

MANGA FOR SUCCESS

RESILIENCE, CONFIDENCE, & POSITIVE THINKING

CREATE A STRESS-RESISTANT, STRONG MIND & HEART

MANAGE NEGATIVE EMOTIONS
AND DISAPPOINTMENTS

GET THE SOCIAL SUPPORT YOU NEED

RESTORE YOUR SELF-CONFIDENCE
AND USE YOUR STRENGTH!

MANGA FOR SUCCESS

THE PSYCHOLOGY OF PERSONAL GROWTH & BETTER RELATIONSHIPS

- CHANGE YOUR PERSPECTIVE,
  AND YOUR LIFE WILL BE EASIER!
- FIND THE COURAGE TO HAVE
  DIFFICULT, BUT IMPORTANT,
  CONVERSATIONS
- GET THE SUPPORT YOU NEED
  FROM OTHERS

BASED ON THE GLOBALLY
INFLUENTIAL WORK OF
PSYCHOLOGIST ALFRED ADLER

KAZUHIKO NAKAMURA

MANGA FOR SUCCESS

MANAGING CHANGE

LEARN POWERFUL TECHNIQUES FOR OVERCOMING
OLD MINDSETS AND RESISTANCE TO CHANGE

THE SCIENCE OF ORGANIZATION
DEVELOPMENT CAN MAKE IT EASIER

BECOME A CHANGE AGENT, AND
CREATE A CORE TEAM FOR CHANGE!

TAKAYUKI KITO
KEISUKE YAMABE

MANGA FOR SUCCESS

BUSINESS PROBLEM-SOLVING & STRATEGY

USE "SWOT ANALYSIS," "5 FORCES" AND OTHER
TOOLS TO UNDERSTAND YOUR MAJOR CHALLENGES

DEVELOP A STRATEGY FOR ANY BUSINESS SITUATION

MAKE AN ACTION PLAN AND
EXECUTE SUCCESSFULLY!

MASUMI TANI

MANGA FOR SUCCESS

LEADING MEETINGS & TEAMS

LEARN BASIC FACILITATION SKILLS
TO IMPROVE GROUP PERFORMANCE

GET FULL PARTICIPATION, HIGHER ENERGY, AND
STRONGER BUY-IN FROM ALL TEAM MEMBERS

ASK GREAT QUESTIONS THAT WILL
DRAW OUT EVERYONE'S OPINION

AVAILABLE WHEREVER BOOKS ARE SOLD

WILEY

Printed and bound by CPI Group (UK) Ltd, Croydon, CR0 4YY

24/04/2023

03212940-0001